Vocabulary

Isabel L. Beck, Ph.D., and
Margaret G. McKeown, Ph.D.

Teacher's Guide

Harcourt Achieve
Rigby • Steck-Vaughn

www.HarcourtAchieve.com
1.800.531.5015

Acknowledgments

Editorial Director	Stephanie Muller
Lead Editor	Terra Tarango
Design Team	Cynthia Ellis, Cynthia Hannon, Joan Cunningham
Media Researcher	Nicole Mlakar
Production Team	Mychael Ferris-Pacheco, Paula Schumann, Ted Krause, Alan Klemp, Donna Brawley, Greg Gaspard
Editorial, Design, and Production Development	The Quarasan Group, Inc.

Illustrations

Annette Cable T5; Renee Graef 169, 176; Reggie Holladay T4; Yuri Salzman T3; Jason Wolff T5

Photo Acknowledgements

pp. T11, T12, T13, T21, T23b ©Dennis Fagan; p. T23a ©Jim Craigmyle/Masterfile.com; p. T29 ©LWA-Dann Tardif/CORBIS; pp. T30,T32 ©Rob Lewine/ CORBIS; p.T36 ©LWA-Dann Tardif/CORBIS; p.T38 ©Tom & Dee Anne McCarthy/CORBIS; p.T39 ©LWA-Sharie Kennedy/CORBIS; p. T40 ©Steve Dunwell/Getty Images.

Additional photography by BrandX/Getty Royalty Free and PhotoDisc/Getty Royalty Free.

ALEXANDER AND THE TERRIBLE, HORRIBLE, NO GOOD, VERY BAD DAY by Judith Viorst, illustrated by Ray Cruz. Text copyright © 1997 Judith Viorst. Illustration copyright © 1997 by Ray Cruz. Published by Atheneum Books for Young Readers, Simon & Schuster Children's Publishing Division.

ISBN 0-7398-8458-1

Printed in China

6 7 8 9 10 985 08

Contents

Vocabulary Lessons

Welcome to Vocabulary

from the Authors

We both admit to a fascination with words, and can recall learning certain words that we found particularly interesting. Learning the word *earnest,* for example, and finding that everyone seemed to be using that word all the time! Or figuring out that *infatuate* was a fancy way of saying you had a crush on someone. Our attachment to words and their meanings has fueled a desire to impart that same word consciousness to today's children. In our years as both teachers and researchers, we have engaged in studies of all the major aspects of reading: decoding, vocabulary, and comprehension. But vocabulary remains our favorite!

By *vocabulary* we mean adding new words to a child's store of word meanings (in contrast to teaching children to read words whose meanings they already know). As we analyzed traditional vocabulary instruction, we concluded that it wasn't rich enough, interesting enough, or extensive enough to have a strong impact. So we developed vocabulary instruction that provided thoughtful, interactive encounters with words and frequent practice with word meanings and their uses, and also prompted children to take the words they learned beyond the classroom.

> *"... a rich vocabulary is the hallmark of a proficient reader."*

It is this method of instruction that we are presenting in *Steck-Vaughn Elements of Reading: Vocabulary.* The words introduced in this program are likely not to be picked up from children's everyday conversations— words like *amble, predicament, linger, pursue, collide, hesitate, splendid,* and *shrewd.* Of course, these kinds of descriptive words are not the common ways for young children to express themselves. But these are the kinds of words that are active parts of good readers' and writers' vocabulary repertoires. After all, a rich vocabulary is the hallmark of a proficient reader.

How can sophisticated words become part of children's "mental dictionaries?" Since young children's oral competence develops in advance of their literacy competence—they can think and talk about much more sophisticated ideas than they are able to read on their own—we can take advantage of their listening and speaking abilities to enhance their vocabulary development. Undertaking the task of enlarging children's vocabulary with "big" words is much more than introducing words and providing their meanings. But an accumulation of evidence demonstrates that this is the way vocabulary instruction is typically handled. Such evidence, along with strong findings that it takes many encounters to "own" a word, points to the need to energize vocabulary instruction.

We've had many good laughs with teachers who bring us stories about their young students' appropriation of words for their own purposes, such as *nuisance* as a label for someone who is annoying them, *vanished* when a homework paper couldn't be located, *masterpiece* to describe a completed writing assignment, and *commotion* for when someone *else* is making noise.

"... when instruction is lively and engaging, children succeed in growing their vocabularies."

It is with confidence that we say that when instruction is lively and engaging, children succeed in growing their vocabularies. How many times have we heard teachers say that they are amazed that their young children learn and use such mature words. "Kids love words," a kindergarten teacher recently told us when her class was engaged in the kind of instruction in *Steck-Vaughn Elements of Reading: Vocabulary.* As you and your class work through this program, we predict that you will agree that kids truly do love words!

Best wishes,

Isabel L. Beck Margaret G. McKeown

Isabel L. Beck Margaret G. McKeown

Isabel L. Beck, Ph.D.

Isabel Beck is a professor of education in the School of Education and a senior scientist at the Learning Research and Development Center, both at the University of Pittsburgh. Before coming to the University, she was a public school teacher in Pennsylvania, California, and North Carolina. Dr. Beck has conducted extensive research in the areas of decoding, vocabulary, and comprehension, having published approximately 100 articles and several books on those topics. Dr. Beck's work has been acknowledged by numerous awards. Most recent were the William S. Gray Award from the International Reading Association for lifetime contributions to the field and the Contributing Researcher Award from the American Federation of Teachers for bridging the gap between research and practice.

Margaret G. McKeown, Ph.D.

Margaret McKeown is a senior scientist at University of Pittsburgh's Learning Research and Development Center. Dr. McKeown's work addresses practical, current problems that classroom teachers and their students face. Her work covers the areas of instructional design and teacher professional development in reading comprehension and vocabulary. Dr. McKeown received her Ph.D. in education from the University of Pittsburgh in 1983. Her dissertation received the Most Outstanding Dissertation Award for 1985 from the International Reading Association. Dr. McKeown received a Spencer Fellowship from the National Academy of Education in 1988 for research to develop dictionary definitions for young learners. Dr. McKeown has published extensively in outlets for both research and practitioner audiences.

From the National Reading Panel

On January 8, 2002, President George W. Bush signed into law the No Child Left Behind Act of 2001. This law contains the most comprehensive reforms of the Elementary and Secondary Education Act (ESEA) since it was enacted in 1965.

One fundamental principle of the new law is an emphasis on teaching methods that have been proven effective, especially in the area of reading instruction. In 1997, as part of the Reading Excellence Act, Congress mandated a study be undertaken to analyze and report on the "status of research-based knowledge, including the effectiveness of various approaches to teaching children to read."

The Director of the National Institute of Child Health and Human Development, in cooperation with the Secretary of Education, formed a National Reading Panel (NRP) of leading authorities in reading research. The NRP held a series of public hearings, interviewed experts in the field, and screened more than 100,000 studies. The results of its work were published in 2000 in the *Report of the National Reading Panel: Teaching Children to Read.*

The NRP's report contains a comprehensive and detailed analysis of the reading research literature. It is organized into five sections—Phonemic Awareness, Phonics, Fluency, Vocabulary, and Text Comprehension—each of which represents a major building block for reading success. These have become known as the five elements of reading.

Five Elements of Reading

Vocabulary

- ***"It is clear that a large and rich vocabulary is the hallmark of an educated individual. Indeed, a large vocabulary repertoire facilitates becoming an educated person to the extent that vocabulary knowledge is strongly related to reading proficiency in particular and school achievement in general."*** **(Beck, McKeown, & Kucan, 2002, p. 1)**

- *"What is missing for many children who master phonics but don't comprehend well is vocabulary, the words they need to know in order to understand what they're reading. Thus vocabulary is the "missing link" in reading/language instruction in our school system."* (Biemiller, 2001, p. 25)

- *"Vocabulary knowledge is fundamental to reading comprehension; one cannot understand text without knowing what most of the words mean . . . [A] reader's general vocabulary knowledge is the single best predictor of how well that reader can understand text . . . Increasing vocabulary knowledge is a basic part of the process of education, both as a means and as an end."* (Nagy, 1988, p. 1)

- *"[S]tudents can be taught a strategy for identifying important vocabulary and for learning those words within the context of literature."* (Dole, Sloan, & Trathen, 1995, p. 460)

Fluency

- ***"Increasingly, it is apparent that in our zeal to develop kids' proficiency in word recognition and reading comprehension, we have been ignoring another essential. The other essential that we are referring to is fluency — the ability to read a text quickly, accurately, and with appropriate expression."*** **(Teale & Shanahan, 2001, p. 5)**

- *"Fluency has been identified as an essential link between word analysis and comprehension of text and is considered a necessary tool for learning from reading . . . ."* (Chard, Vaughn, & Tyler, 2002, p. 401)

Comprehension

- ***"Teaching children to be more strategic readers and writers involves making children aware of potential strategies, helping them to attribute success to good strategies, and helping them to choose and monitor appropriate strategies."*** **(Paris & Paris, 2001, p. 92)**

- *"The evidence is growing that elementary children can be taught to use the comprehension strategies used by excellent, mature comprehenders. Moreover, when they learn such strategies, their comprehension improves . . . ."* (Pressley, 1999, p. 96)

Phonics

- ***"Word study or phonics plays an important role in a program designed to help beginners learn to read and spell."*** **(Morris, 1999, p. 9)**

- *"Effective intervention programs for children with serious phonological weaknesses must contain explicit and intense instruction in word level skills . . . ."* (Torgesen, *et al.*, 1999, p. 590)

Phonemic Awareness

- ***"[I]nstruction that heightens phonological awareness and that emphasizes the connections to the alphabetic code promotes greater skill in word recognition—a skill essential to becoming a proficient reader."*** **(Blachman, 2000, p. 495)**

- *"The training studies settle the issue of the causal role of phonological awareness in learning to read: Phonological training reliably enhances phonological and reading skills."* (Bus & van Ijzendoorn, 1999, p. 411)

Focus on Vocabulary Instruction

Robust Vocabulary Selection

- "Trade books are superb sources of vocabulary selection . . . . A word was considered a good candidate if it seemed likely to be unfamiliar to young children but was a concept they could identify with and use in normal conversation." (Beck & McKeown, 2001, p. 18)
- "Because of the large role they play in a language user's repertoire, rich knowledge of . . . words that are of high frequency for mature language users and are found across a variety of domains . . . can have a powerful impact on verbal functioning. Thus, instruction directed toward [these] words can be most productive." (Beck, McKeown, & Kucan, 2002, p. 8)

Explicit Instruction

- "When the teacher focused students' attention on the meanings of specific words, the students were more likely to learn and retain the word meanings than when the teacher focused students' attention on deriving those same word meanings from sentence context." (Jenkins, Matlock, & Slocum, 1989, p. 228)
- "The results of this study suggest that teaching text specific vocabulary increases students' ability to understand difficult expository text. Moreover, vocabulary instruction prior to reading is effective among students of various levels of reading ability. Regardless of ability students receiving vocabulary instruction did better on the comprehension post test than subjects who did not receive vocabulary instruction." (Medo & Ryder, 1993, p. 130)

Oral Instruction and Personalization

- "Reading aloud, accompanied by explanations of unfamiliar words as they occur in the story appears to be an effective method of teaching children the meaning of new words." (Brett, Rothlein, & Hurley, 1996, p. 419)
- "[Design] questions that encourage children to talk about and connect ideas and [develop] follow-up questions that scaffold, building meaning from those ideas . . . ." (Beck & McKeown, 2001, p. 19)

Multiple Contexts

- "'Knowing' a word is to understand its core meaning and that meaning may alter in different contexts." (Osborn & Armbruster, 2001)
- "Students should be given opportunities to manipulate the words in a wide variety of ways, such as creating original contexts for the words, participating in games that require quick associations between words and meanings, and exploring different nuances of a word's meaning through discussions." (Beck, McKeown, & McCaslin, 1983, p.181)

Rich Literature

- "Texts that are effective for developing language and comprehension ability need to be conceptually challenging enough to require grappling with ideas and taking an active stance toward constructing meaning." (Beck & McKeown, 2001, p. 10)
- "[T]he finding that lower vocabulary development was associated with being in classrooms where the didactic-interactional approach was observed may implicate book choice. Given the demonstrated power of group book reading to support vocabulary and story understanding, a steady diet of books with predictable text may not be optimal." (Dickinson & Smith, 1994, pp. 118–119)

Ample Practice

- "This finding supports the notion that, with repeated exposure, young children can make use of storybooks as a rich context for word learning." (Sénéchal, 1997, p. 134)
- "More practice yielded significantly larger increments of learning. On three of the four measures of vocabulary knowledge, the high practice group demonstrated significantly more learning than the medium group, and on all four the medium practice group achieved higher scores than the low group." (Jenkins, Matlock, & Slocum, 1989, p. 228)

Bibliography

Beck, I.L., & McKeown, M.G. (2001). Text talk: Capturing the benefits of read-aloud experiences for young children. *The Reading Teacher, 55*, 10-20.

Beck, I.L., McKeown, M.G., & Kucan, L. (2002). *Bringing words to life.* New York: Guilford Press.

Beck, I.L., McKeown, M.G., & McCaslin, E.S. (1983). Vocabulary development: All contexts are not created equal. *The Elementary School Journal, 83,* 177-181.

Biemiller, A. (2001). Teaching vocabulary: Early, direct, and sequential. *American Educator, 25*, 24-28.

Blachman, B.A. (2000). Phonological awareness. In M. Kamil, P. Mosenthal, P. Pearson, & R. Barr (Eds.), *Handbook of reading research: Vol 3* (pp. 483-502). Mahwah, NJ: Erlbaum.

Brett, A., Rothlein, L., & Hurley, M. (1996). Vocabulary acquisition from listening to stories and explanations of target words. *The Elementary School Journal, 96*, 415-422.

Bus, A.G., & van Ijzendoorn, M.H., (1999). Phonological awareness and early reading: A meta-analysis of experimental training studies. *Journal of Experimental Psychology, 91,* 403-414.

Chard, D.J., Vaughn, S., & Tyler, B.J. (2002). A synthesis of research on effective interventions for building reading fluency with elementary students with learning disabilities. *Journal of Learning Disabilities, 35,* 386-406.

Dickinson, D.K., & Smith, M.W. (1994). Long-term effects of preschool teachers' book readings on low-income children's vocabulary and story comprehension. *Reading Research Quarterly, 29,* 104-122.

Dole, J.A., Sloan, C., & Trathen, W. (1995). Teaching vocabulary within the context of literature. *Journal of Reading, 38,* 452-460.

Ediger, M. (2000). Speaking activities and reading. *Reading Improvement, 37*, 137.

Fillmore, L.W., & Snow, C. (2000). What elementary teachers need to know about language. [Online] Available: http://www.cal.org/ericcll/Teachers.pdf

Harris, A.J., & Sipay, E.R. (1978). *How to increase reading ability: A guide to developmental and remedial methods.* 6th ed. New York: David McKay Company.

Jenkins, J.R., Matlock, B., & Slocum, T.A. (1989). Two approaches to vocabulary instruction: The teaching of individual word meanings and practice in deriving word meaning from context. *Reading Research Quarterly, 24,* 215-235.

[Learning First Alliance] The Content of Professional Development. (2000). Vocabulary and text comprehension. Every Child Reading: A Professional Development Guide. Learning First Alliance. [Online]. Excerpt available: http://www.readingrockets.org/article.php?ID=192

Maloch, B. (2002). Scaffolding student talk: One teacher's role in literature discussion groups. *Reading Research Quarterly, 37,* 94-112.

May, F.B., & Rizzardi, L. (2002). *Reading as communication.* 6th ed. Upper Saddle River, NJ: Merrill/Prentice Hall.

Medo, M.A., & Ryder, R.J. (1993). The effects of vocabulary instruction on readers' ability to make causal connections. *Reading Research and Instruction, 33,* 119-134.

Morris, D. (1999). *The Howard Street tutoring manual.* 2nd ed. New York: Guilford Press.

Nagy, W.E. (1988). *Teaching vocabulary to improve reading comprehension.* Urbana, IL: ERIC Clearninghouse on Reading and Communication Skills.

National Reading Panel (2000). *Teaching children to read: An evidence-based assessment of the scientific research literature on reading and its implications for reading instruction.* NIH Publication No. 00-4754. Washington, DC: National Institute of Child Health and Human Development.

Osborn, J. H., & Armbruster, B.B. (2001). Vocabulary acquisition: Direct teaching and indirect learning. *Basic Education,* 46(3). [Online] Available: http://www.c-b-e.org/be/iss0111/a2osborn.htm

Paris, S.G., & Paris, A.H. (2001). Classroom applications of research on self-regulated learning. *Educational Psychologist, 36,* 89-101.

Pressley, M. (1999). Self-regulated comprehension processing and its development through instruction. In L.B. Gambrell, L.M. Morrow, S.B. Neuman, & M. Pressley (Eds.), *Best practices in literacy instruction* (pp. 90-97). New York: Guilford Press.

[Put Reading First] Armbruster, B.B., Lehr, F., & Osborn, J. (2001). *Put reading first: The research building blocks for teaching children to read—Kindergarten through grade 3.* Washington, DC: National Institute for Literacy.

Rupley, W.H., Logan, J.W., & Nichols, W.D. (1999). Vocabulary instruction in a balanced reading program. *The Reading Teacher, 52,* 338-347.

Sénéchal, M. (1997). The differential effect of storybook reading on preschoolers' acquisition of expressive and receptive vocabulary. *Journal of Child Language, 24,* 123-138.

Stahl, S.A. (1999). *Vocabulary Development: Vol. 2.* From Reading Research to Practice Series. Cambridge, MA: Brookline Books.

Stahl, S., & Kapinus, B. (2001). *Word power: What every educator needs to know about teaching vocabulary.* Washington, DC: National Education Association.

Teale, W.H. & Shanahan, T. (2001). Ignoring the essential: Myths about fluency. *Illinois Reading Council Journal, 29,* 5-8.

Torgesen, J.K., Wagner, R.K., Rashotte, C.A., Rose, E., Lindamood, P., Conway, T., & Garvan, C. (1999). Preventing reading failure in young children with phonological processing disabilities: Group and individual responses to instruction. *Journal of Educational Psychology, 91,* 579-593.

Watts, J., & Wilkinson, B. (2002). Review of the reading research literature since the national reading panel report.

The gift of words is one of the most powerful things you can give young children today. The broader their vocabularies, the more questions they can ask, the more concepts they can ponder, the more ideas and dreams they can share.

Vocabulary

What This Program Is	What This Means for You
• The first program to systematically and explicitly teach oral language vocabulary as direct preparation for success in reading	• You can bridge the achievement gap and increase learning success for all children.
• The only program to use literature children will encounter in later years as a source for building vocabulary power NOW	• You can create learners who delight in word knowledge and who will be motivated and active readers.
• A systematic program built on the extensive and research-proven base of the work of Isabel Beck and Margaret McKeown	• You can be confident that your teaching methodologies and strategies really work for all students, including English language learners!

Just 20 minutes a day! No extra planning—fits right into your Read-Aloud time.

Weekly Plan: A trip to the classroom

Introducing the Vocabulary	Using the Vocabulary			Assessing the Vocabulary
1	2	3	4	5
Read aloud a literature selection from the Read-Aloud Anthology. Use the Vocabulary in Action page to introduce the week's vocabulary words with lively discussions that probe at children's own experiences with the words.	Use the Word Snapshots photo cards to show the vocabulary words as part of children's real-life experiences. Have children complete a Student Book activity supported by the relevant and enticing Word Chat prompts in the Teacher's Guide.	Continue the Student Book and Word Chat activities to present this week's vocabulary words in multiple contexts. The Word Challenge activity allows children to explore some words even further.	Use the graphic organizers to reinforce vocabulary meanings. Use the Your Turn to Write prompts in the Teacher's Guide to give children an opportunity to write about their experiences with the words.	After an oral review, have children complete the formal assessment in the Student Book. End the week with the Cumulative Review to help children retain their understanding of each week's vocabulary words.

Throughout the week, encourage children to use the vocabulary words as much as possible both in and out of the classroom. The Word Watcher Chart provides an incentive program that will have children seeking opportunities to use each week's vocabulary words. And the weekly home activity letters can make curriculum-aligned home involvement a reality.

Program Components

Just the right tools to make vocabulary come alive

Tote Box

Here is the perfect way to store and protect your program. One side provides easy access to the program's teacher resources: Read-Aloud Anthology, Teacher's Guide, Word Snapshots, and Word Watcher Chart and Cards. The other side offers a convenient place to store Student Books.

Read-Aloud Anthology

The Read-Aloud Anthology serves as the program's springboard. The 24 selections are rich and varied, representing some of the very best in children's literature across many genres. These stories and poems provide a rich source for the program's vivid and robust vocabulary.

Teacher's Guide

A comprehensive Teacher's Guide contains practical support, along with explicit vocabulary instruction. Step-by-step lesson prompts introduce activities that are sure to entice and delight children. Oral, visual, and physical methods help a wide audience of learners master new words.

Student Book

Student Books sustain children's interest with vibrant colors and eye-catching illustrations. A variety of appealing teacher-led activities provide ample practice opportunities. Lesson assessments offer valuable standardized test practice.

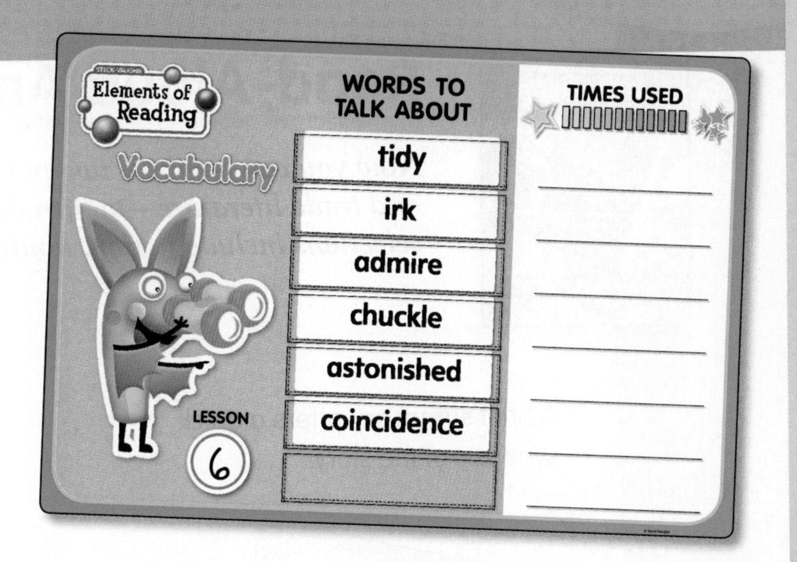

Word Watcher Chart and Word Cards

The Word Watcher Chart, a blend between a pocket chart and an erasable poster, keeps the vocabulary learning active all week. Removable cards make moving on to the next lesson a snap!

Word Snapshots

The large, colorful photo cards contain dramatic images with informative sentences that bring words to life in ways children can relate to. The real-life context of photographs helps children personalize each vocabulary word.

Also Available!

Online Assessment

Online Assessment provides diagnostic information and prescribes instruction to help you tailor your reading program to meet the needs of every child.

Professional Development

Through collaborative study groups, you can learn, practice, and refine effective instructional techniques for explicit vocabulary instruction.

Parent Place

With http://www.elementsofreading.com/parentplace parents are just a click away from activities and resources that they can use at home with their child to help reinforce important skills and strategies.

Read-Aloud Anthology

Now you can combine two powerful tools—oral language and trade literature—to introduce new words. Literature selections include fiction, nonfiction, and poetry.

A brief **summary** offers a quick synopsis of the story.

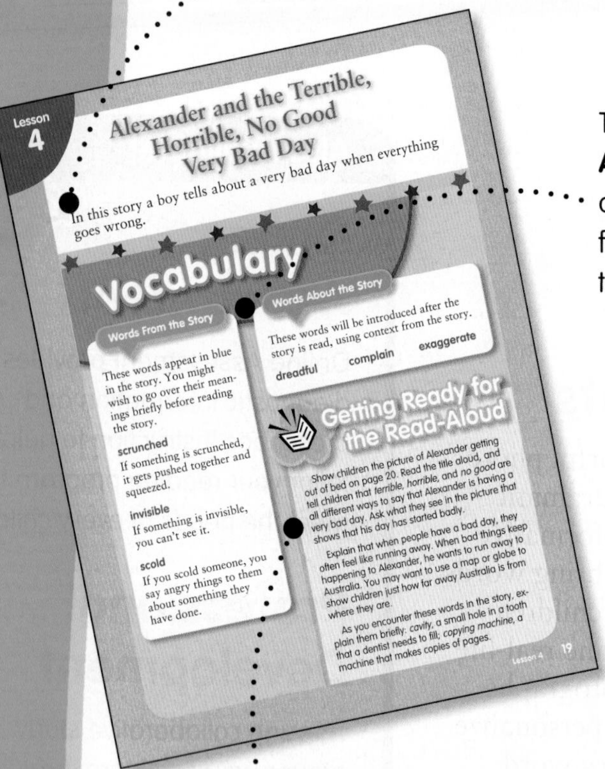

Lesson 4

Alexander and the Terrible, Horrible, No Good Very Bad Day

In this story a boy tells about a very bad day when everything goes wrong.

Vocabulary

Words From the Story

These words appear in blue in the story. You might wish to go over their meanings briefly before reading the story.

scrunched
If something is scrunched, it gets pushed together and squeezed.

invisible
If something is invisible, you can't see it.

scold
If you scold someone, you say angry things to them about something they have done.

Words About the Story

These words will be introduced after the story is read, using context from the story.

dreadful **complain** **exaggerate**

Getting Ready for the Read-Aloud

Show children the picture of Alexander getting out of bed on page 20. Read the title aloud, and tell children that *terrible, horrible,* and *no good* are all different ways to say that Alexander is having a very bad day. Ask what they see in the picture that shows that his day has started badly.

Explain that when people have a bad day, they often feel like running away. When bad things keep happening to Alexander, he wants to run away to Australia. You may want to use a map or globe to show children just how far away Australia is from where they are.

As you encounter these words in the story, explain them briefly: *cavity,* a small hole in a tooth that a dentist needs to fill; *copying machine,* a machine that makes copies of pages.

Lesson 4 19

There are **Words From the Story** and **Words About the Story.** These provide a unique opportunity to introduce words that evolve from a discussion about the story in addition to words from the story itself.

Getting Ready for the Read-Aloud sets the stage with questions that focus on the story art, ideas for building background, and easy-to-understand explanations.

Lively images capture children's attention from the moment the read-aloud begins. These colorful illustrations and photographs help engage children.

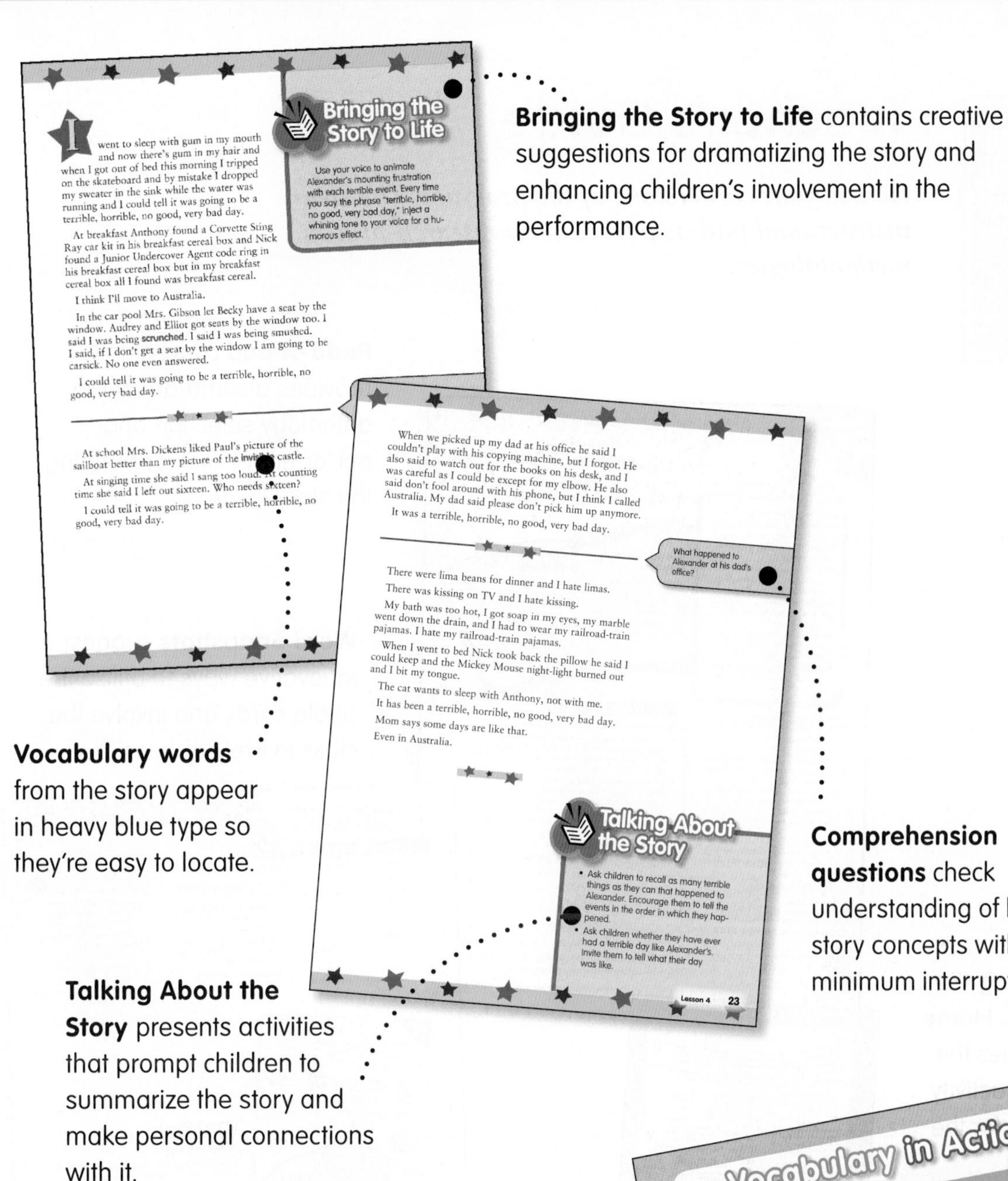

I went to sleep with gum in my mouth and now there's gum in my hair and when I got out of bed this morning I tripped on the skateboard and by mistake I dropped my sweater in the sink while the water was running and I could tell it was going to be a terrible, horrible, no good, very bad day.

At breakfast Anthony found a Corvette Sting Ray car kit in his breakfast cereal box and Nick found a Junior Undercover Agent code ring in his breakfast cereal box but in my breakfast cereal box all I found was breakfast cereal.

I think I'll move to Australia.

In the car pool Mrs. Gibson let Becky have a seat by the window. Audrey and Elliot got seats by the window too. I said I was being **scrunched**. I said I was being smushed. I said, if I don't get a seat by the window I am going to be carsick. No one even answered.

I could tell it was going to be a terrible, horrible, no good, very bad day.

At school Mrs. Dickens liked Paul's picture of the sailboat better than my picture of the **invisible** castle.

At singing time she said I sang too loud. At counting time she said I left out sixteen. Who needs sixteen?

I could tell it was going to be a terrible, horrible, no good, very bad day.

Bringing the Story to Life

Use your voice to animate Alexander's mounting frustration with each terrible event. Every time you say the phrase "terrible, horrible, no good, very bad day," inject a whining tone to your voice for a humorous effect.

When we picked up my dad at his office he said I couldn't play with his copying machine, but I forgot. He also said to watch out for the books on his desk, and I was careful as I could be except for my elbow. He also said don't fool around with his phone, but I think I called Australia. My dad said please don't pick him up anymore.

It was a terrible, horrible, no good, very bad day.

What happened to Alexander at his dad's office?

There were lima beans for dinner and I hate limas.

There was kissing on TV and I hate kissing.

My bath was too hot, I got soap in my eyes, my marble went down the drain, and I had to wear my railroad-train pajamas. I hate my railroad-train pajamas.

When I went to bed Nick took back the pillow he said I could keep and the Mickey Mouse night-light burned out and I bit my tongue.

The cat wants to sleep with Anthony, not with me.

It has been a terrible, horrible, no good, very bad day.

Mom says some days are like that.

Even in Australia.

Talking About the Story

- Ask children to recall as many terrible things as they can that happened to Alexander. Encourage them to tell the events in the order in which they happened.
- Ask children whether they have ever had a terrible day like Alexander's. Invite them to tell what their day was like.

Lesson 4 23

Bringing the Story to Life contains creative suggestions for dramatizing the story and enhancing children's involvement in the performance.

Vocabulary words from the story appear in heavy blue type so they're easy to locate.

Comprehension questions check understanding of key story concepts with minimum interruption.

Talking About the Story presents activities that prompt children to summarize the story and make personal connections with it.

Vocabulary in Action

Words From the Story

scrunched

In the story Alexander got scrunched in the car. If something is scrunched, it gets pushed together and squeezed. Let's say *scrunched* together.

- Ask a child to explain how dirty clothes might get scrunched in a laundry basket.
- Have four children act out what it would be like to be scrunched on a small bench.

invisible

Alexander drew an invisible castle. If something is invisible, you can't see it. Let's say *invisible* together.

- Ask which is invisible, air or an airplane. Why?
- Call on a child to draw a picture of someone walking an invisible dog.

scold

Alexander's mom scolded him for fighting with his brother. If you scold someone, you say angry things to them about something they have done. Let's say *scold* together.

- Ask which might you get scolded for, doing your homework or forgetting to clean your room. Explain.
- Have a child act out scolding a pet.

Words About the Story

dreadful

Alexander was having a terrible, horrible day. You could say he was having a dreadful day. If something is dreadful, it is so terrible that it could not be much worse. Let's say *dreadful* together.

- Ask which might make your day dreadful, losing a new sweater in the park or wearing a new sweater to the park. Why?
- Ask children to show the face they would make if they tasted something dreadful.

complain

Alexander talked a lot about all the bad things that happened. Another way to say that is to say he complained. Complain means to talk about how the things that are happening are bad or unfair. Let's say *complain* together.

- Ask which would make you complain, going to bed early or going to bed late. Explain.
- Call on children to complain about the kind of weather they don't like.

exaggerate

Alexander made things sound much worse than they were. This means he exaggerated. Exaggerate means to make things seem much better or much worse than they really are. Let's say *exaggerate* together.

- Ask which one is exaggerating, saying you see lots of birds or millions of birds. Why?
- Have children act out exaggerating being happy and then sad.

24 Lesson 4

Vocabulary in Action provides explicit instruction for introducing the lesson's vocabulary words. Activity prompts connect words to the story, reinforce meanings, and present opportunities for responses.

Teacher's Guide

Here is your cornerstone of the program. The clear instructional path is packed with research-proven methodologies.

Lesson 4

Alexander and the Terrible, Horrible, No Good, Very Bad Day

Vocabulary

scrunched If something is scrunched, it gets pushed together and squeezed.
invisible If something is invisible, you can't see it.
scold If you scold someone, you say angry things to them about something they have done.
dreadful If something is dreadful, it is so terrible that it could not be much worse.
complain Complain means to talk about how the things that are happening are bad or unfair.
exaggerate Exaggerate means to make things seem much better or much worse than they really are.

1 Introducing the Vocabulary

Read-Aloud

Read-Aloud Anthology, pages 19–24

In *Alexander and the Terrible, Horrible, No Good, Very Bad Day*, a boy tells about a very bad day when everything goes wrong.

Bringing the Story to Life

Use your voice to animate Alexander's mounting frustration with each terrible event. Every time you say the phrase "terrible, horrible, no good, very bad day," inject a whining tone to your voice for a humorous effect.

Word Watcher

Word Watcher Chart, Lesson 4 Word Cards

- Tell children that they will learn about these words throughout the week and that each time a child uses one of the words correctly in the classroom, you will place a mark next to the word.
- Before class begins, hide this week's word cards under six children's desks. Have children look under their desks and place word cards they find in the chart. Read each word aloud and have children repeat it. Use each word in a sentence and give the word its first tally of the week.

At a Glance

STANDARDS
Vocabulary
- Identify words that name persons, places, or things, and words that name actions
- Use vocabulary to describe ideas, feelings, and experiences

Comprehension
- Use prior knowledge to make sense of texts

Writing
- Describe connections between personal experiences and written and visual texts

LESSON RESOURCES
Read-Aloud Anthology: pp. 19–24
Student Book: pp. 14–17
Word Cards: Lesson 4
Photo Cards: 10, 13, 19–24, 27, 31, 33, 55, 82

Sending the Words Home

Blackline Master—English, page 127; Spanish, page 128

Distribute the activity letter to inform parents of the vocabulary words for this week.

Research Says...

"Prompting children to think about situations in their lives that relate to a new word increases the chances the children will recall and use the word...."
—*Bringing Words to Life*, Isabel L. Beck, et al.

16 Lesson 4

Read-Aloud conveniently provides a summary of the anthology selection and performance tips for bringing the story to life.

Word Snapshots suggest innovative ways to utilize the photo cards and involve the class in lively discussions.

2 Using the Vocabulary

Word Snapshots

Photo Cards: 10, 13, 19–24, 31, 33, 55, 82

Hold up the card pairs and ask children the following questions. Discuss which photos best show the vocabulary words.

scrunched (19 and 31) Which card shows things that are scrunched?
invisible (20 and 10) Which card shows something invisible?
scold (21 and 82) Which card shows someone being scolded?
dreadful (22 and 13) Which card shows a dreadful situation?
complain (23 and 33) Which card shows someone who is complaining?
exaggerate (24 and 55) Which card shows someone who is exaggerating?

ELL SUPPORT

Show each photo card as you pronounce the word and have children repeat it. Use realia to help explain some words. For example, have children scrunch up a piece of paper. Use the photo cards and the sentences on the backs to discuss each word.

Word Chat

Student Book, page 14

Guide children as they complete the Student Book activity. Then use children's responses and the prompts below to discuss each word.

scrunched Tell children that you will name some things and if they think the thing can be scrunched, they should say "scrunched." If not, they should say nothing.
- a mountain
- a bunch of grapes
- a house

exaggerate Tell children that you will say some things and if they think you are exaggerating, they should say "you're exaggerating!" If not, they should say nothing.
- I caught a fish THIS BIG! (Stretch your arms out to their full width.)
- I had a sandwich for lunch.
- It took me TWO DAYS to eat one grape.

dreadful Tell children that you will describe some things and if they think the thing is dreadful, they should groan and say "Ohhhh! Dreadful!" If not, they should say nothing.
- The shoestore had a sale.
- The shoestore closed for the night.
- The shoestore burned down.

Lesson 4 17

Sending the Words Home identifies the home activity letters for the lesson.

Fun with New Words

Dear Family,

scrunched
dreadful
invisible
complain
scold
exaggerate

Home letter blacklines (in both English and Spanish) provide entertaining activities that involve families in children's learning. Additional activities are available at the Parent Place website.

ELL Support offers photo card activities that target English language learners.

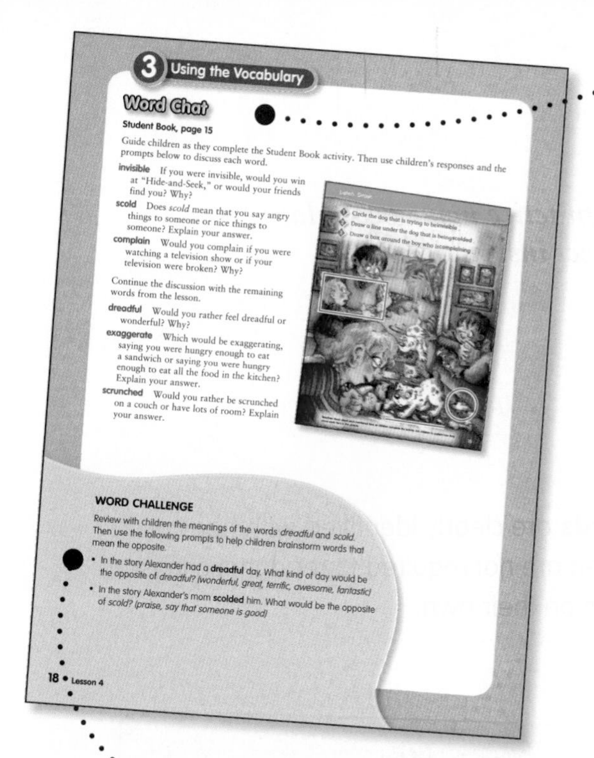

3 Using the Vocabulary

Word Chat

Student Book, page 15

Guide children as they complete the Student Book activity. Then use children's responses and the prompts below to discuss each word.

invisible If you were invisible, would you win at "Hide-and-Seek," or would your friends find you? Why?

scold Does *scold* mean that you say angry things to someone or nice things to someone? Explain your answer.

complain Would you complain if you were watching a television show or if your television were broken? Why?

Continue the discussion with the remaining words from the lesson.

dreadful Would you rather feel dreadful or wonderful? Why?

exaggerate Which would be exaggerating, saying you were hungry enough to eat a sandwich or saying you were hungry enough to eat all the food in the kitchen? Explain your answer.

scrunched Would you rather be scrunched on a couch or have lots of room? Explain your answer.

WORD CHALLENGE

Review with children the meanings of the words *dreadful* and *scold*. Then use the following prompts to help children brainstorm words that mean the opposite.

- In the story Alexander had a **dreadful** day. What kind of day would be the opposite of *dreadful? (wonderful, great, terrific, awesome, fantastic)*
- In the story Alexander's mom **scolded** him. What would be the opposite of *scold? (praise, say that someone is good)*

18 • Lesson 4

Word Chat presents increasingly challenging discussion prompts that spring from activities in the Student Book.

Word Organizers provide a method for children to visually explore word meanings and relationships. Sample answers are provided to facilitate children's responsiveness.

4 Using the Vocabulary

Word Organizers

Help your class complete the graphic organizers below. You may draw them on the board or on chart paper, or use the organizers in the back of this book to make transparencies.

Write the vocabulary word in the blue box.

invisible

1. If I were invisible, I would watch television after my bedtime.
2. If I were invisible, I would see all the movies I wanted to see.
3. If I were invisible, I would go to a toy store and play with everything.

Ask children to make up sentences about what they would do if they were invisible. You may want to model a sentence for them to get them started. Record their sentences.

After children generate sentences, ask how long they would want to be invisible. For a day? For a week?

Write the vocabulary word in the center.

dreadful: awful, terrible, bad, horrible

Ask children to think of words that mean the same or almost the same thing as dreadful. Remind them to think of the title of the read-aloud story for ideas. Record their answers.

Have children tell about some things that they think are dreadful.

Your Turn to Write

Encourage children to relate the words to their own experiences. Discuss a few of the prompts below to prepare children for writing. Have children write about one of the prompts in their journals or on a separate piece of paper.

scrunched Would you want your sandwich to get scrunched? What else wouldn't you want to get scrunched? Have you ever felt scrunched?

invisible When would it be fun to be invisible? When would it not be fun to be invisible? Can you name some things that are invisible?

scold Have you ever been scolded? How did it make you feel? Have you ever wanted to scold someone?

dreadful Did you ever have a dreadful day? What happened that made it such a bad day? What can you do to make a dreadful day better?

complain What kinds of things do you complain about? Do your friends complain about the same things or different things? Who do you talk to when you want to complain about something?

exaggerate Do you think Alexander exaggerated about how terrible his day was? Tell about a time when you exaggerated something. What did other people say to you?

Lesson 4 19

Word Challenge offers prompts that encourage children to explore synonyms, antonyms, and multiple meanings of selected vocabulary words.

Your Turn to Write provides open-ended and thought-provoking writing prompts that allow children to make personal connections with vocabulary words.

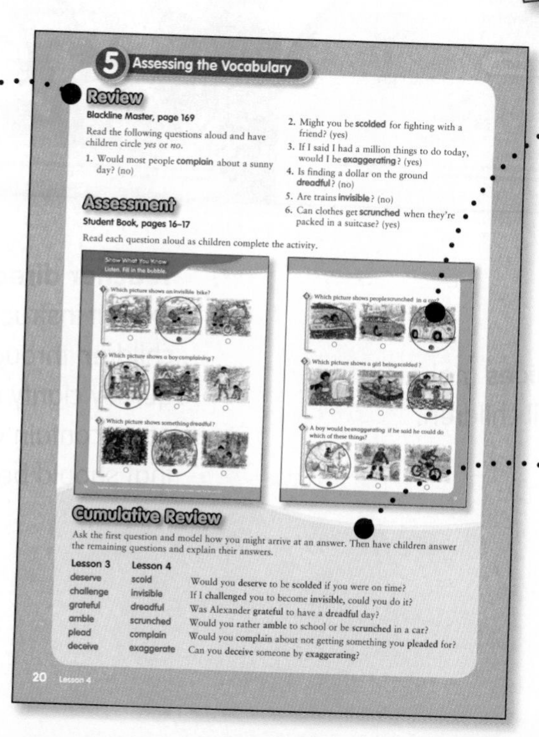

5 Assessing the Vocabulary

Review

Blackline Master, page 169

Read the following questions aloud and have children circle *yes* or *no*.

1. Would most people **complain** about a sunny day? (no)
2. Might you be **scolded** for fighting with a friend? (yes)
3. If I said I had a million things to do today, would I be **exaggerating**? (yes)
4. Is finding a dollar on the ground **dreadful**? (no)
5. Are trains **invisible**? (no)
6. Can clothes get **scrunched** when they're packed in a suitcase? (yes)

Assessment

Student Book, pages 16–17

Read each question aloud as children complete the activity.

Cumulative Review

Ask the first question and model how you might arrive at an answer. Then have children answer the remaining questions and explain their answers.

Lesson 3	Lesson 4	
deserve	scold	Would you **deserve** to be **scolded** if you were on time?
challenge	invisible	If I **challenged** you to become **invisible**, could you do it?
grateful	dreadful	Was Alexander **grateful** to have a **dreadful** day?
amble	scrunched	Would you rather **amble** to school or be **scrunched** in a car?
plead	complain	Would you **complain** about not getting something you **pleaded** for?
deceive	exaggerate	Can you **deceive** someone by **exaggerating**?

20 Lesson 4

The **Review** presents a series of yes/no questions that can be used along with the Review Answer Sheet.

Assessment activities from the Student Book appear as reduced, annotated pages at point of use.

The **Cumulative Review** presents a series of questions using words from the current and previous lessons.

Student Book

Ensure that students learn and practice new vocabulary through engaging and daily direct instruction.

Vocabulary words are clearly identified with heavy blue type. Children are not required to read these lesson vocabulary words on their own.

Lesson 4

Listen. Draw.

1 Draw a line from the word to each thing that is being scrunched.

paper chairs cups clothes

scrunched

2 Draw a line from the word to each thing that is dreadful.

weather noise flowers worm

dreadful

3 Draw a line from the word to each thing that looks like it is exaggerated.

jump lift climb fly

exaggerate

Teacher: Read aloud each numbered item. Have children draw a line to the pictures that best show each word. Let them know that there may be more than one picture for each word. Ask them why they chose the pictures they did.

14

Listen. Draw.

1 Circle the dog that is trying to be invisible.

2 Draw a line under the dog that is being scolded.

3 Draw a box around the boy who is complaining.

Teacher: Read aloud each numbered item as children complete the activity. Ask children to explain how they chose each item in the picture.

15

Illustrated answer choices make activities accessible to all children.

Teacher directions provide explicit instruction for guiding children through each activity. They quickly clarify which portions of the page contain vocabulary words that should be read by the teacher.

Show What You Know
Listen. Fill in the bubble.

1. Which picture shows an invisible bike?
2. Which picture shows a boy complaining?
3. Which picture shows something dre

16

4. Which picture shows people scrunched in a car?
5. Which picture shows a girl being scolded?
6. A boy would be exaggerating if he said he could do which of these things?

17

Assessment

Ongoing/informal assessments include the many opportunities teachers have to listen to children's discussion:

- Vocabulary in Action (in the Read-Aloud Anthology)
- Word Watcher Chart
- Word Snapshots
- Word Chats
- Word Organizers
- Your Turn to Write
- Oral Review

Formal assessments in the Student Book use a standardized test format. Authentic contexts for lesson words ensure that these assessments are accurate.

Cumulative Reviews in the Teacher's Guide assess understanding of previous and current lesson words. These often humorous or unexpected questions cause children to think deeply about word meanings.

To get maximum benefit from the Student Book . . .

- have children use the vocabulary words as they discuss their answer choices.
- keep the discussion lively and connected to children's experiences.
- guide children's discussions to ensure that they develop accurate word meanings.
- structure discussion to ensure that all children participate.

Consider extending Student Book activities by . . .

- using the Word Chats in the Teacher's Guide to facilitate further discussion of the words.
- asking children to talk about answers they didn't choose.
- having children use their hands, faces, or bodies to act out word meanings from the activities.

Word Snapshots

These photo cards are your tool to provide real-life visual support for all vocabulary words. Related activity prompts in the Teacher's Guide spark lively oral discussion. The cards also suggest many extension and enrichment activities, including:

- impromptu storytelling
- pantomimed guessing games
- comparing and contrasting images

The **photo cards** depict a common context for each word and provide a visual cue to help children recall word meaning.

A **sentence** presenting the word in context appears on the back of each card to help children infer the subtle meanings conveyed in the photo.

Word Watcher Chart

The Word Watcher Chart provides a visual incentive for children to use lesson words and a convenient way for teachers to monitor progress. See-through pockets hold each lesson's word cards. The erasable surface is perfect for tallying the number of times children use new words.

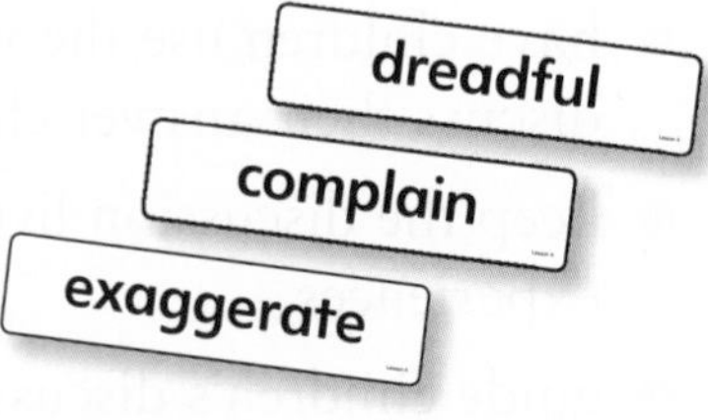

You can also use these cards to create enrichment and extension activities:

- charts to categorize words
- titles for displays of children's stories or artwork
- word walls
- word riddles

Use the **Word Watcher Certificate** in the Teacher's Guide to celebrate children's success.

Also Available!

Professional Development

The Vocabulary Professional Development Module is based on the body of research showing that teachers' knowledge and teaching skills are vital to student achievement.

Call 1-800-531-5015 to find out more.

Online Assessment

Steck-Vaughn Elements of Reading: Online Assessment is a diagnostic, prescriptive tool for classroom teachers and reading specialists. The assessment and prescriptions are tied to the specific strands of *Steck-Vaughn Elements of Reading: Vocabulary, Fluency, Comprehension,* and *Phonics.*

- Collects data using a set of reading instruments delivered online to save teacher time
- Provides a comprehensive report that gives an accurate picture of each student's abilities as well as instructional suggestions
- Provides reader-friendly reports for parents that give insight into their child's reading progress

Scope and Sequence

Level K

		Lessons																							
		1	2	3	4	5	6	7	8	9	10	11	12	13	14	15	16	17	18	19	20	21	22	23	24
Vocabulary Standards	Discuss word meaning and develop vocabulary through meaningful experiences	•	•	•	•	•	•	•	•	•	•	•	•	•	•	•	•	•	•	•	•	•	•	•	•
	Develop vocabulary by listening to and discussing selections read aloud	•	•	•	•	•	•	•	•	•	•	•	•	•	•	•	•	•	•	•	•	•	•	•	•
	Identify words that name persons, places, or things, and words that name actions	•	•	•	•	•	•	•	•	•	•	•	•	•	•	•	•	•	•	•	•	•	•	•	•
	Use vocabulary to describe ideas, feelings, and experiences	•	•	•	•	•	•	•	•	•	•	•	•	•	•	•	•	•	•	•	•	•	•	•	•
	Listen to imaginative texts in order to respond to vivid language	•	•	•	•	•	•	•	•	•	•	•	•	•	•	•	•	•	•	•	•	•	•	•	•
	Develop vocabulary by discussing characters and events from a story	•	•	•	•	•	•	•	•	•	•	•	•	•	•	•	•	•	•	•	•	•	•	•	•
	Speak to express the mood of a story by using a variety of words	•	•	•	•	•	•	•	•	•	•	•	•	•	•	•	•	•	•	•	•	•	•	•	•
	Use context to find the meaning of unknown words	•	•	•	•	•	•	•	•	•	•	•	•	•	•	•	•	•	•	•	•	•	•	•	•
	Use visual references to build upon word meaning	•	•	•	•	•	•	•	•	•	•	•	•	•	•	•	•	•	•	•	•	•	•	•	•
Comprehension Standards	Use prior knowledge to make sense of texts					•		•					•	•											
	Use pictures and context to make predictions about story content						•		•						•		•	•							
	Retell or act out order of important events in stories			•						•												•			
	Connect to life experiences the information and events in texts	•	•		•														•	•					
	Ask and answer questions about essential elements of a text															•							•		•
	Support responses with details from the text										•	•									•			•	
Writing Standards	Compose original texts			•							•								•				•		
	Dictate messages																								•
	Write to record ideas and reflections									•								•		•		•			
	Record or dictate knowledge of a topic in various ways		•			•						•				•								•	
	Describe connections between personal experiences and written and visual texts						•	•						•	•										
	Contribute ideas during a shared writing activity	•			•				•				•				•				•				
Genre	Fantasy					•	•			•					•			•						•	•
	Realistic fiction			•							•										•				
	Rhyming story		•						•			•													
	Folk tales and legends																					•			
	Nonfiction												•						•						
	Poetry and verse	•			•			•						•		•	•			•			•		

Level A

Category	Standard	1	2	3	4	5	6	7	8	9	10	11	12	13	14	15	16	17	18	19	20	21	22	23	24
		Lessons																							
Vocabulary Standards	Discuss word meaning and develop vocabulary through meaningful experiences	•	•	•	•	•	•	•	•	•	•	•	•	•	•	•	•	•	•	•	•	•	•	•	•
	Develop vocabulary by listening to and discussing selections read aloud	•	•	•	•	•	•	•	•	•	•	•	•	•	•	•	•	•	•	•	•	•	•	•	•
	Identify words that name persons, places, or things, and words that name actions	•	•	•	•	•	•	•	•	•	•	•	•	•	•	•	•	•	•	•	•	•	•	•	•
	Use visual references to build upon word meaning	•	•	•	•	•	•	•	•	•	•	•	•	•	•	•	•	•	•	•	•	•	•	•	•
	Use context to find the meaning of unknown words	•	•	•	•	•	•	•	•	•	•	•	•	•	•	•	•	•	•	•	•	•	•	•	•
	Use vocabulary to describe ideas, feelings, and experiences	•	•	•	•	•	•	•	•	•	•	•	•	•	•	•	•	•	•	•	•	•	•	•	•
	Listen to imaginative texts in order to respond to vivid language	•	•	•	•	•	•	•	•	•	•	•	•	•	•	•	•	•	•	•	•	•	•	•	•
	Develop vocabulary by discussing characters and events from a story	•	•	•	•	•	•	•	•	•	•	•	•	•	•	•	•	•	•	•	•	•	•	•	•
	Speak to express the mood of a story by using a variety of words	•	•	•	•	•	•	•	•	•	•	•	•	•	•	•	•	•	•	•	•	•	•	•	•
	Develop an understanding of diversity in language across cultures												•												
Comprehension Standards	Use prior knowledge to make sense of texts				•												•								
	Establish purposes for reading or listening (to be informed)							•										•							
	Retell or act out order of important events in stories			•							•					•					•				
	Use a variety of strategies to comprehend text						•							•					•						
	Use specific details and information from a text to answer literal questions		•										•										•		
	Make and explain inferences								•											•				•	
	Connect to life experiences the events and information in texts														•							•			•
	Distinguish between a story and a poem	•				•				•		•													
Writing Standards	Compose original texts		•								•									•				•	
	Write to record ideas and reflections						•						•									•			
	Write to discover, develop, and refine ideas			•					•							•							•		
	Write in different forms for different purposes					•				•									•						•
	Record or dictate knowledge of a topic in various ways							•							•			•							
	Write brief descriptions using sensory details	•										•					•								
	Describe connections between personal experiences and written and visual texts				•									•							•				
Genre	Fantasy		•								•			•					•		•				
	Realistic fiction				•		•						•		•								•	•	
	Rhyming story																								•
	Folk tales and legends			•					•								•			•		•			
	Nonfiction							•										•							
	Poetry and verse	•				•				•		•				•									

Level B

		Lessons																							
		1	2	3	4	5	6	7	8	9	10	11	12	13	14	15	16	17	18	19	20	21	22	23	24
Vocabulary Standards	Develop vocabulary by listening to and discussing selections read aloud	•	•	•	•	•	•	•	•	•	•	•	•	•	•	•	•	•	•	•	•	•	•	•	•
	Discuss word meaning and develop vocabulary through meaningful experiences	•	•	•	•	•	•	•	•	•	•	•	•	•	•	•	•	•	•	•	•	•	•	•	•
	Develop vocabulary by discussing characters and events from a story	•	•	•	•	•	•	•	•	•	•	•	•	•	•	•	•	•	•	•	•	•	•	•	•
	Develop vocabulary through reading	•	•	•	•	•	•	•	•	•	•	•	•	•	•	•	•	•	•	•	•	•	•	•	•
	Listen to imaginative texts in order to respond to vivid language	•	•	•	•	•	•	•	•	•	•	•	•	•	•	•	•	•	•	•	•	•	•	•	•
	Understand that word choice can shape ideas, feelings, and actions	•	•	•	•	•	•	•	•	•	•	•	•	•	•	•	•	•	•	•	•	•	•	•	•
	Use visual references to build upon word meaning	•	•	•	•	•	•	•	•	•	•	•	•	•	•	•	•	•	•	•	•	•	•	•	•
	Use context to find the meaning of unknown words	•	•	•	•	•	•	•	•	•	•	•	•	•	•	•	•	•	•	•	•	•	•	•	•
	Use vocabulary to describe ideas, feelings, and experiences	•	•	•	•	•	•	•	•	•	•	•	•	•	•	•	•	•	•	•	•	•	•	•	•
	Use context to define multiple-meaning words			•		•	•			•		•					•	•		•		•		•	•
	Use knowledge of antonyms and synonyms to determine meanings of words		•							•			•				•				•				
Comprehension Standards	Use a variety of strategies to comprehend text						•											•							
	Use prior knowledge to make sense of texts												•									•			
	Discuss texts to clarify unfamiliar words and ideas				•																•				
	Summarize information in texts										•									•					
	Connect to life experiences the information and events in texts			•										•									•		
	Make and explain inferences									•									•						
	Recognize the story problem and its resolution		•									•													•
	Analyze characters and their changes					•										•								•	
	Distinguish fiction from nonfiction								•						•										
	Recognize the musical elements of literary language	•						•									•								
Writing Standards	Use effective vocabulary in writing	•									•									•					
	Use webbing strategies to organize information							•										•							
	Write in different forms for different purposes									•									•						
	Write brief narratives that include well-chosen details			•										•									•		
	Write brief descriptions using sensory details								•				•								•				
	Write to discover, develop, and refine ideas		•									•										•			
	Write to record ideas and reflections					•											•							•	
	Write to communicate with a variety of audiences						•								•										
	Write a friendly letter				•											•									•
Genre	Fantasy										•					•					•				•
	Realistic fiction			•			•			•		•		•			•			•		•	•	•	
	Folk tales and legends				•	•							•					•	•						
	Nonfiction								•						•										
	Poetry and verse	•	•					•																	

Level C

Standards		Lessons 1	2	3	4	5	6	7	8	9	10	11	12	13	14	15	16	17	18	19	20	21	22	23	24
Vocabulary Standards	Understand that word choice can shape ideas, feelings, and actions	•	•	•	•	•	•	•	•	•	•	•	•	•	•	•	•	•	•	•	•	•	•	•	•
	Discuss word meaning and develop vocabulary through reading	•	•	•	•	•	•	•	•	•	•	•	•	•	•	•	•	•	•	•	•	•	•	•	•
	Develop vocabulary through meaningful experiences	•	•	•	•	•	•	•	•	•	•	•	•	•	•	•	•	•	•	•	•	•	•	•	•
	Use vocabulary to describe ideas, feelings, and experiences	•	•	•	•	•	•	•	•	•	•	•	•	•	•	•	•	•	•	•	•	•	•	•	•
	Develop vocabulary by listening to and discussing selections read aloud	•	•	•	•	•	•	•	•	•	•	•	•	•	•	•	•	•	•	•	•	•	•	•	•
	Use clear and specific vocabulary to communicate ideas orally	•	•	•	•	•	•	•	•	•	•	•	•	•	•	•	•	•	•	•	•	•	•	•	•
	Use visual references to build upon word meaning	•	•	•	•	•	•	•	•	•	•	•	•	•	•	•	•	•	•	•	•	•	•	•	•
	Use context to find the meaning of unknown words	•	•	•	•	•	•	•	•	•	•	•	•	•	•	•	•	•	•	•	•	•	•	•	•
	Use knowledge of antonyms and synonyms to determine the meanings of words			•				•			•				•		•				•				
	Use context to define multiple-meaning words		•				•			•		•						•				•			
	Demonstrate knowledge of levels of specificity among grade-appropriate words		•				•									•							•		
Comprehension Standards	Make and explain inferences			•				•			•						•								
	Identify main ideas and supporting details in informational texts																					•			
	Use a variety of strategies to comprehend text																	•							•
	Analyze characters and their changes		•			•								•					•						
	Recognize the story problem and its resolution															•								•	
	Use knowledge of story structure, story elements, and key vocabulary to interpret stories																				•				
	Recognize the musical elements of literary language														•					•					
	Recognize the techniques of language used in children's literature	•			•					•													•		
	Respond to questions providing appropriate elaboration						•					•													
	Connect to life experiences the information and events in texts								•				•												
Writing Standards	Write narratives that include well-chosen details		•		•			•						•					•						
	State a main idea, theme, or opinion and provide supporting details								•													•			
	Write descriptions using sensory details	•				•						•								•				•	
	Write personal and formal letters										•		•			•									
	Use organizational patterns for expository writing			•						•					•										
	Write to discover, develop, and refine ideas																•						•		
	Use effective vocabulary in writing				•		•														•				
	Use webbing strategies to organize information																	•							•
Genre	Fantasy						•	•						•					•		•				
	Realistic fiction		•			•			•		•	•					•							•	•
	Folk tales and legends			•	•					•						•		•							
	Nonfiction												•									•			
	Poetry and verse	•													•					•			•		

Level A Word List

Numbers in parentheses indicate the lesson in which a word is introduced.

A
accomplish (19)
admire (6)
admit (16)
adventurous (13)
alert (13)
amazed (12)
amble (3)
anxious (23)
appear (14)
artistic (10)
astonished (6)

B
bask (22)
boast (20)

C
capture (2)
caution (11)
certain (8)
challenge (3)
chuckle (6)
clumsy (2)
coincidence (6)
comforting (1)
commotion (24)
complain (4)
conflict (24)
contemplate (22)
convince (8)
creative (17)
crouch (10)
cunning (16)

D
deceive (3)
delicate (19)
delightful (2)
deserve (3)
destroy (7)
determined (21)
disguise (8)
dissolve (11)
disturb (7)
dreadful (4)
dull (13)
dwell (7)

E
eager (13)
elated (22)
enhance (19)
enormous (20)
entertain (17)
exaggerate (4)
exchange (23)
expression (1)

F
fad (17)
fierce (2)
flatter (20)
fleet (1)
frantic (21)
fret (24)
frighten (20)
furious (16)

G
gather (17)
ghastly (11)
glimmer (1)
glimpse (15)
gobble (9)
grand (15)
grateful (3)
gullible (16)

H
harmony (24)
haul (22)
household (17)
humble (20)

I
injured (22)
inquire (10)
investigate (19)
invisible (4)
irk (6)

L
leisure (14)
lively (1)
longs (16)

M
mandatory (18)
memorize (23)
mighty (20)
mound (9)

N
nibble (10)

O
observant (15)
observe (7)
outgoing (14)
outsmart (8)

P
palate (12)
pasture (18)
patient (10)
perform (5)
petrified (13)
plead (3)
pleasant (15)
preposterous (11)
pride (5)
protest (24)
provide (18)

Q
quiver (8)

R
realize (16)
rearrange (12)
regret (23)
relax (14)
relief (23)
rely (13)
rescue (2)
resourceful (14)
ridiculous (5)
romp (17)

S
savory (21)
scamper (21)
scold (4)
scrap (18)
scrumptious (8)
scrunched (4)
seasonal (22)
serenade (5)
shelter (7)
shrewd (21)
skyscraper (15)
sliver (12)
sloppy (9)
sly (11)
soothe (24)
spangled (5)
sprinkle (9)
squiggle (9)
stare (23)
strain (15)
stunned (21)
surplus (12)
survive (7)
suspend (5)
suspense (2)
swift (11)

T
tempting (18)
tidy (6)
tremendous (12)
tribute (9)
tumble (14)

V
variety (19)
vast (19)
velvet (18)
versatile (1)

W
wander (10)

*What are the **essential** elements of reading that will prepare children to achieve their full **academic potential?***

With the goal of teaching all children to read well by the end of third grade, the National Reading Panel of leading authorities in reading research identified five essential elements of effective reading instruction. The panel determined that explicit and systematic instruction must be provided in these five key areas, each of which represents a major building block for reading success:

Vocabulary
The addition of new words to a child's store of word meanings.

Fluency
The ability to read a text quickly, accurately, and with expression.

Phonics
The acquisition of letter-sound correspondences and their use to read and spell words.

Phonemic Awareness
The ability to hear, identify, and manipulate the individual sounds in spoken words.

Comprehension
The use of complex processes and strategies to construct, evaluate, and respond to meaning conveyed in one or more texts.

A rich vocabulary is the hallmark of a proficient reader.

— Isabel L. Beck, Ph.D., and Margaret G. McKeown, Ph.D.

"Kids love words," a wise kindergarten teacher once said. That basic premise is a guiding force in any sound vocabulary program. For only if children take pleasure in knowing and using words will they spend the mental effort necessary to develop their knowledge. And vocabulary knowledge is essential to success in school and beyond.

Tips for Effective Vocabulary Instruction

Read aloud to children literature that contains rich vocabulary and engaging story lines.

Choose words for explicit instruction that bring action and description to language.

Personalize the vocabulary by having children relate their own experiences to the vocabulary words.

Facilitate lively discussions about the words to make them memorable.

Use photos and illustrations to show robust, rich vocabulary words in real-life contexts.

Provide ample practice to give children the repeated encounters needed to own each new word.

Explicit vocabulary instruction is best suited for words that can add to language ability.

Although many words are learned through implicit reading, robust, language-enhancing words (such as *astonished*, *delicate*, and *soothe*) are the best choices for explicit instruction. Knowledge of these types of words exponentially increases children's overall language ability.

Just providing information will not result in deep or sustained knowledge of a word.

When teaching a new word, it must be explained in a meaningful way that children can relate to. An explanation should be both memorable and fully comprehensible. The explanation, after all, is the vehicle a teacher has to interpret a set of unfamiliar letters into a familiar concept.

Providing direct instruction in vocabulary after a read-aloud provides a strong context from which to introduce word meaning.

Stopping the flow of a story to introduce, teach, and practice vocabulary only devalues the literature from which the words are extracted. Instead, fully enjoy the literature itself. Once the story is firmly in the child's understanding, there is a strong context from which to introduce vocabulary meanings.

Research Says . . .

"Oral vocabulary is a key to learning to make the transition from oral to written forms."
—National Reading Panel

Effective instruction must provide examples of vocabulary words in multiple contexts.

To teach a word in only one context, even a rich and robust context, denies a child the opportunity to gain full ownership of its meaning. Instead, introduce words in one context (i.e., introduce *scrunched* as a child scrunched in a car), but then provide ample exposures to the word in as many contexts as possible (i.e., scrunched paper, scrunched cans, etc.).

Frequent encounters with new words are essential if the words are to become a permanent part of the child's vocabulary repertoire.

Even when vocabulary words are introduced in lively and memorable ways, they are rarely retained unless children have frequent encounters with the words. In one week, it may take as many as six to eight encounters with a word before it becomes part of a child's accessible vocabulary.

A Trip to the Classroom

Mr. Lopez has structured his day to include 20 minutes of oral vocabulary instruction each day. This whole-class, teacher-led instruction time follows a consistent pattern that results in notable oral language achievement.

Day 1 Mr. Lopez reads aloud an engaging piece of **literature**. He then introduces the week's vocabulary words with a lively discussion and questions that probe at children's own experiences with the words.

Day 2 Mr. Lopez uses photos that show that **robust**, rich vocabulary words are a part of children's real-life experiences. Mr. Lopez then has children complete an engaging activity with the words that is supported by relevant and fun discussions.

Day 3 Mr. Lopez presents activities and encourages discussions that highlight this week's vocabulary words in **multiple contexts**.

Day 4 Mr. Lopez uses **graphic organizers** to reinforce vocabulary meanings. He then gives the children an opportunity to write about their experiences with one or more of the vocabulary words.

Day 5 Mr. Lopez gives an oral review of the words and then has children complete a formal **assessment**. He ends the week with a cumulative review, which allows children to think about the previous week's words in relation to this week's words.

Throughout the week, Mr. Lopez uses a tally chart to encourage children to use the vocabulary words. He has adopted this methodology because he can apply it to any set of vocabulary words chosen from his reading program or encountered in a natural context. He can feel certain that these 20 minutes each day contribute to his children's overall reading proficiency and test performance.

*Teaching oral reading **fluency** leads to clear and substantial improvement in silent reading comprehension.*

— Timothy Shanahan, Ph.D.

Fluency—the ability to read a text quickly, accurately, and with appropriate expression—has been referred to as the most neglected reading skill of all. To be good readers, students must read fluently, and programs that emphasize only two elements—word recognition and comprehension—are likely to be inferior because they don't do enough to build fluency.

Tips for Effective Fluency Instruction

Model fluent oral reading to help students hear what a text should sound like.

Have students read and reread each text to the point that it sounds good.

Provide ample time for students to read and reread texts because students learn to read by reading.

Show pauses visually by drawing lines to mark them in sentences.

Provide practice with high-frequency words and phonics to help students build word recognition and decoding speed.

Wait when a child makes a mistake so that the child has time to catch and correct the error.

Oral reading practice builds fluency skills.

The trick to good teaching is often to get the thinking "out of the head" and into the physical and sensory space. Oral reading practice requires students to read all of the words and it allows both student and teacher to hear the reading.

Good fluency instruction requires that students reread text repeatedly until they can read it well.

Reading a text over and over allows students to become fluent. Too many students never get the chance to work with a text to the point that they can read it well. This deprives them of any sense of success and keeps them from developing basic reading skills. Repeated practice has been found to improve students' ability to read other texts fluently.

Just encouraging students to read more has not been proven to improve fluency or reading comprehension.

As of yet, studies have failed to demonstrate a consistent relationship between increased reading and improved fluency or comprehension. It is imperative that valuable instructional time be devoted to those things proven to improve reading achievement.

Research Says . . .

"Fluency is one of several critical factors neccesary for reading comprehension."
—National Reading Panel

Students benefit from guidance when they read.

Practice is a great idea, but practice with guidance or coaching is almost always superior to working on one's own. Studies indicate that students make better reading gains when they receive sound coaching from teachers, parents, volunteers, and even other students.

Fluency practice is most efficient, and probably most effective, when students work with books at or near their reading level.

Students often struggle with fluency because the texts they are reading are simply too hard—too hard to enjoy, to understand, or to learn from. Fluency develops most quickly when students have the opportunity to practice materials that are "slightly difficult." If the materials are too easy, not much is learned. If the materials are too hard, students struggle to make progress. Goldilocks knew what she was talking about: Students need books that are "just right."

A Trip to the Classroom

Mr. Lopez devotes 30 minutes of his daily reading instruction time to fluency. This whole-class, teacher-led fluency time follows a consistent routine.

Day 1 Mr. Lopez presents the book students will be reading and reads the book aloud as students follow along. As he reads, he models key fluency skills students will focus on in the coming days. He then engages students in a discussion of the book's content and how he read the book.

Day 2 Mr. Lopez has students engage in repeated readings of the book. He also has them complete an activity addressing high-frequency words in the book.

Day 3 Mr. Lopez takes students through the book, providing explicit instruction in word knowledge and fluency. He then has the students read the book again.

Day 4 Mr. Lopez has students work in pairs to read a passage from the book two or more times. Pair members use a fluency checklist to evaluate each other's last reading of the book. Students then practice their phrasing by marking pauses.

Day 5 Mr. Lopez assesses students' fluency progress by listening to each student read the passage to him. Alternatively, he has students tape their reading, listen to it, and assess it.

Throughout the week, Mr. Lopez asks students questions to monitor their comprehension. He also has them practice reading high-frequency words. In the week that follows, Mr. Lopez has students apply the fluency skills they learned to their regular classroom reading materials. He periodically sends home a copy of a book for students to share with family members.

Phonics and phonemic awareness instruction allows students to develop accurate, automatic knowledge of letter-sound relationships and spelling patterns—the foundation of skillful reading and fluent writing.

— Darrell Morris, Ed.D., and Janet W. Bloodgood, Ph.D.

In order for a phonics program to be successful, it is fundamental to first find out where the child is functioning in phonics ability and then teach that child at his or her own developmental level. Phonics instruction need not be rote and drill-like. Instead, concepts can be taught in a problem-solving format and reinforced through enjoyable games and activities.

Conceptual Foundation for Effective Phonics and Phonemic Awareness Instruction:

Focus on sounds of written words.

Relate patterns and letters to sounds through sorts and games.

Decode words through the manipulation of letter sounds and patterns.

Connect to reading through application of phonics and phonemic awareness patterns in daily literacy experiences.

Connect to written language through labeling and writing.

Providing early and explicit, systematic instruction in phonics and word study improves a child's ability to break the code.

Systematic phonics instruction helps children learn to read by teaching them how to use the alphabetic system. Phonics knowledge facilitates word prediction, for readers can figure out words new to them by using letter-sound cues in conjunction with context clues. Systematic phonics instruction boosts growth in reading fluency and comprehension.

Phonics instruction is effective when it is taught through picture sorts, word sorts, and games.

Sorting pictures and words in order to introduce patterns helps children figure out categorizing principles. The sorting activities are repeated until the children are accurate and automatic when they read and write the word patterns. In addition, children have ample chances to practice these patterns with games such as Bingo and Concentration.

Research Says . . .

"Systematic phonics instruction has been used widely over a long period of time with positive results."
—National Reading Panel

Providing instruction in phonemic awareness strategies in conjunction with concepts of print can aid in learning to read.

Phonemic awareness training means helping children to focus on, hear, and identify discrete sounds in spoken words. The combination of explicit phonemic awareness training and letter-sound correspondence prepares children to read words. They begin to read words by applying their phonemic-awareness skills to identify first letters and then match them to the corresponding sounds. In addition, when phonemic awareness instruction is combined with teaching the concept of word, children begin to make sense of print.

Current findings tell us that small-group instruction is a highly effective way to learn phonics and phonemic awareness skills.

Working with small, flexible groups allows for ongoing assessment and for tailoring instruction. Groups can work at their optimum learning levels. Whether a group needs additional help or is ready to move on to the next concept, the teacher will be able to respond quickly. The pace of instruction is flexible, allowing children time to learn concepts.

A Trip to the Classroom

Mr. Lopez has structured class time to include explicit phonics instruction each day. He determines each child's skill level and then arranges children in small groups for instruction.

Focus on Sounds Mr. Lopez uses the engaging language poster to focus children's attention on specific sounds and words. He guides the children in a search for objects and actions for the target sounds and helps the group connect the words to contextual meaning through discussion of the poster scene.

Teach Patterns Mr. Lopez provides explicit instruction by modeling a picture sort to help the group become familiar with the week's target words. Then Mr. Lopez guides the children to uncover the phonics and spelling patterns.

Practice Mr. Lopez helps reinforce and practice the word patterns in the lesson with fun games and independent word sorts. He has the children write in their Phonics Notebooks to demonstrate their knowledge of the target word sounds and spelling patterns.

Apply Patterns Mr. Lopez guides children to manipulate letters and blend sounds to make words that use the patterns they have been learning.

Assess and Apply Throughout the week, Mr. Lopez has differentiated his instruction based on frequent and ongoing assessment of the group. At the end of the set of lessons, Mr. Lopez uses a formal assessment to determine the group's progress. He also has children apply the phonics skills by having them read the decodable stories and write sentences using the target patterns.

When children read independently with thorough comprehension, they develop confidence in their abilities.

— Scott Paris, Ph.D.

Children love it when they can read a text, understand it, and share it. But they need to learn that comprehension is neither simple nor automatic. They should know that there are multiple layers of meaning in any given text. Comprehension may require re-reading, reflection, asking questions, and many other reading strategies. By teaching children to employ reading strategies, we empower them to become better readers and better learners.

Tips for Effective Comprehension Instruction

Model effective comprehension strategies by thinking aloud and describing how you use a given strategy.

Teach children to actively monitor comprehension by generating and answering questions as they read.

Explicitly model for children how to reread to check comprehension or to get deeper understanding.

Explain when, how, and why strategies are appropriate to enable children to use them selectively.

Multiple readings of a text helps children comprehend thoroughly.

Practice reduces decoding demands and allows children to spend more energy thinking about the meaning and connections among sentences. Re-reading encourages children to search text selectively and to master the ideas fully.

Explicit instruction of comprehension strategies promotes comprehension.

Teachers should explain what strategies are, how to use them, when they should be applied, and why they are effective. Teachers can model appropriate strategies that can be used before, during, and after reading to construct meaning.

Scaffolded support ensures comprehension success.

Teachers can provide hints and help as needed during reading so that children learn to use strategies on their own. Parents, peers, and software can also provide scaffolded support to apply strategies.

Research Says . . .

"The instruction of cognitive strategies improves reading comprehension in readers with a range of abilities."
—National Reading Panel

Instruction should motivate students to make meaning.

Comprehension is fostered when readers ask and answer questions, when they discuss their interpretations with others, and when they write in response to reading. Thinking hard about text meaning can be creative, satisfying, and fun.

Comprehension instruction should be based on a variety of authentic texts that allow readers to construct many connections.

Children need to build meaning across diverse genres. The texts should be challenging and informative to foster cumulative and conceptual learning about interesting topics. Texts should promote connections between text-text, text-self, and text-world.

A Trip to the Classroom

Mr. Lopez has organized his class time to include explicit comprehension instruction, applied practice, and assessment each week. He begins with whole-class instruction. Then, children work to apply strategies through multiple readings of the text and hands-on activities. Finally, he returns to whole-class instruction to review the comprehension focus and assess children's understanding.

Day 1 Mr. Lopez reads a selection with the class, introducing the comprehension focus, and modeling the use of appropriate reading strategies throughout the selection.

Days 2–4 Children circulate through three applied instruction centers—a scaffolded software center, a science or social studies center, and a writing center.

In the software center, children receive the scaffolded support they need to re-read the text at different levels, answering increasingly challenging questions, and gaining deeper and fuller understanding of the content.

In the science or social studies center, children practice applying the comprehension focus as well as the science or social studies content of the lesson. The hands-on activities further solidify understanding of the topic and promote inquisitive thinking.

The writing center offers a place for children to reflect on the comprehension focus, apply it in a different context, and create their own work implementing what they've learned.

Day 5 Mr. Lopez asks children to provide a summary of the story and to discuss what they learned in the various centers. He uses the discussion to review the comprehension focus and content focus of the lesson. He then uses the report generated from the scaffolded software, discussion questions, and the children's writing sample as opportunities to assess children's understanding. He ends the lesson with a cumulative review that asks children to apply the comprehension strategy of a previous lesson to this week's story.

How are the essential ***elements of reading*** *connected?*

As mandated by the National Reading Panel, explicit and systematic instruction must be provided in each of the five essential elements of reading. In addition, important skill connections should be made to integrate the elements.

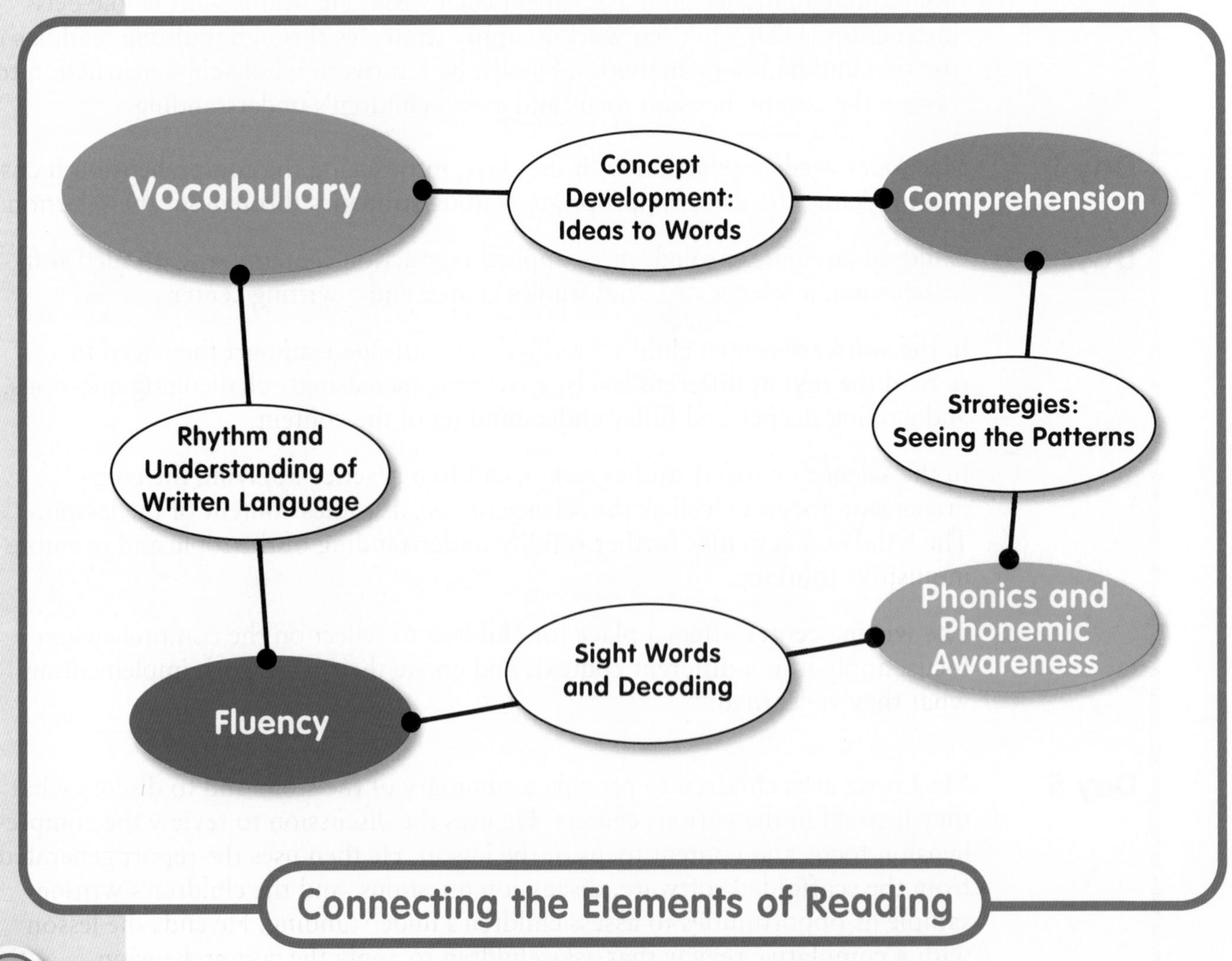

To put the elements of reading in a broader context...

No Child Left Behind Checklist	
Diagnostic Assessment	✓
Explicit Instruction	✓
Home Involvement	✓
Professional Development	✓

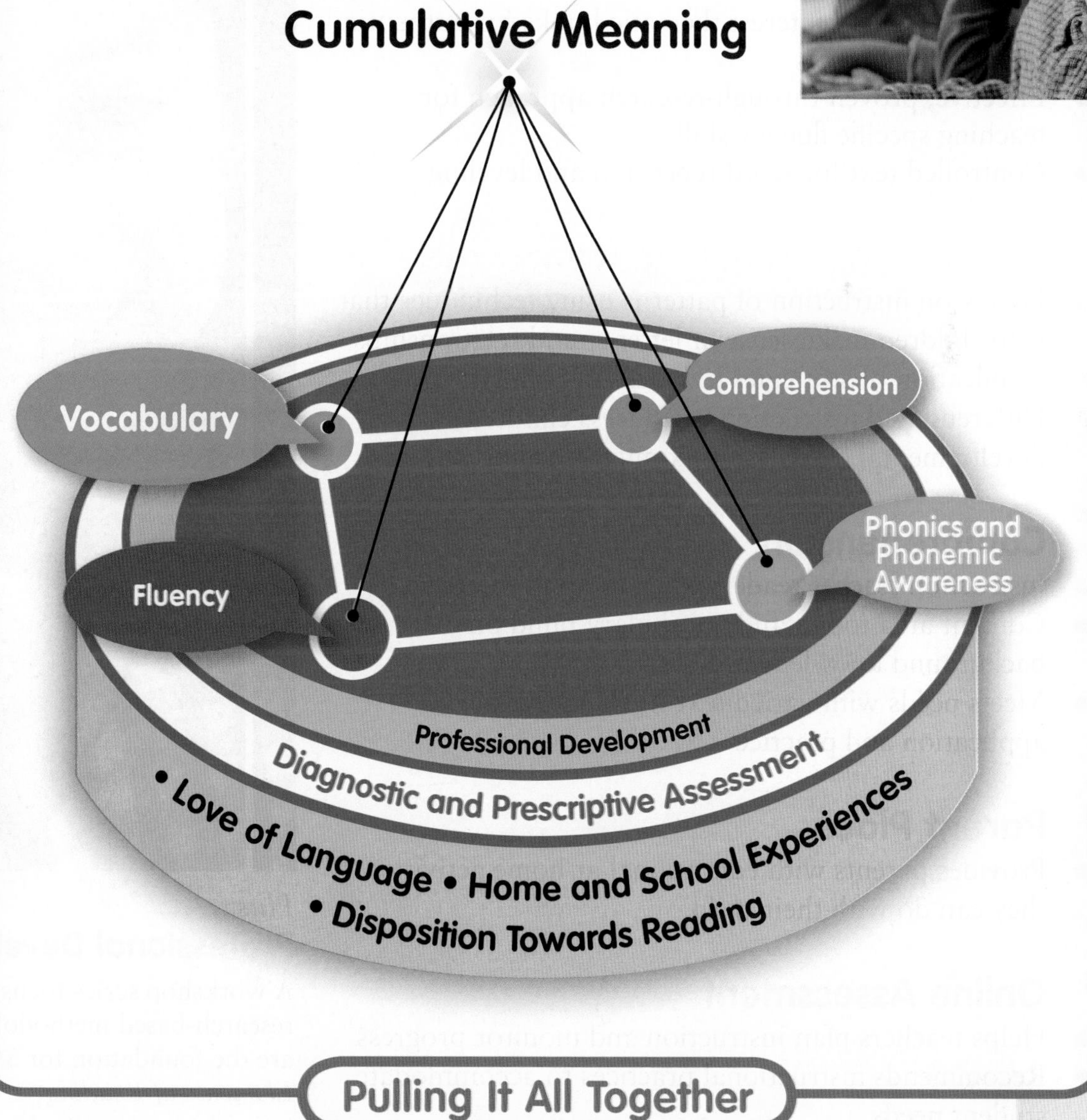

Pulling It All Together

NRP-Focused Instruction

A deliberate research-based cohesive system for increasing overall reading achievement with a unique skills matrix that builds and spirals for success

Vocabulary

- Systematic approach to oral language vocabulary—the foundation to reading success
- Authentic literature to build the broad vocabulary essential to future reading proficiency
- In-depth opportunities for practice and discussion—the keys to vocabulary and reading growth

Fluency

- Full-length, high-interest thematic books for authentic reading experiences
- Effective, proven-through-research approach for teaching specific fluency skills
- Controlled text for word repetition and leveling

Phonics and Phonemic Awareness

- Hands-on instruction of patterns using techniques that help children make sense of letter-sound relationships
- Application of strategies to words in context
- Differentiated instruction to address children's developmental needs for maximum learning

Comprehension

- Instruction teaches readers when to apply strategies
- Content area topics and vocabulary build on background knowledge
- Meets needs with varied text levels for strategy application and practice

Parent Place

- Provides parents with educational at-home activities they can do with their child.

Online Assessment

- Helps teachers plan instruction and monitor progress
- Recommends instructional practices to accommodate student needs
- Reports keep teachers and parents informed

Plus . . .

Professional Development

A workshop series focusing on the research-based methodologies that are the foundation for *Steck-Vaughn Elements of Reading*

Words Are Like Faces

Vocabulary

comforting Something comforting makes you feel better when you are sad or afraid.

fleet A person or animal that is fleet moves fast.

glimmer To glimmer is to shine or twinkle softly.

expression Your expression is the look on your face that shows what you are feeling.

lively Someone or something that is lively is full of life.

versatile If someone or something is versatile, it can do many different things.

At a Glance

STANDARDS

Vocabulary
- Develop vocabulary by listening to and discussing selections read aloud
- Use context to find the meaning of unknown words

Comprehension
- Distinguish between a story and a poem

Writing
- Write brief descriptions using sensory details

LESSON RESOURCES

Read-Aloud Anthology: pp. 1–6
Student Book: pp. 2–5
Word Cards: Lesson 1
Photo Cards: 1–6

1 Introducing the Vocabulary

Read-Aloud

Read-Aloud Anthology, pages 1–6

The poem "Words Are Like Faces" is a celebration of words, exploring the range of emotions that words express as well as the wonderful sounds they make.

Bringing the Poem to Life

As you read this poem, bring out its rhythm and savor the sounds of each word. Use exaggerated expressions that reflect the emotions described in the poem. You may read the entire poem once, and then read it again, pausing to ask questions.

Word Watcher

Word Watcher Chart, Lesson 1 Word Cards

- Tell children that they will learn about these words throughout the week and that each time a child uses one of the words correctly in the classroom, you will place a mark next to the word.
- Place the word cards face down on a table. Call on a volunteer to choose one of the cards and give it to you. Say the word and a sentence using the word. Then have children say the word with you. Help the volunteer place the card in the chart and give the word its first tally of the week. Continue with the other cards.

Sending the Words Home

Blackline Master—English, page 121; Spanish, page 122

Distribute the activity letter to inform parents of the vocabulary words for this week.

Research Says...

"Reading aloud to children teaches vocabulary in one of the most natural ways possible. Words that are puzzling can be easily explained in the context of the story."

—*Reading as Communication*, Frank B. May and Louis Rizzardi

2 Using the Vocabulary

Word Snapshots

Photo Cards: 1–6

Discuss each photo card from this lesson individually. Read the sentence on the back of the card and ask children to share personal experiences similar to those depicted in the cards. Then display the cards in the groups indicated below and have children tell a story using all three cards in a group.

Group 1	Group 2
comforting	**fleet**
expression	**glimmer**
lively	**versatile**

ELL SUPPORT

Discuss the photo cards and how the words relate to the poem. Hold up one photo card and have children say the word with you. Then ask children to brainstorm other ways the word might be used. Continue with the other words.

glimmer Tell children that you will describe some things and if they think that the thing can glimmer, they should say "glimmer." If not, they should say nothing.

- an ocean at sunset
- a black shirt
- a diamond ring

Word Chat

Student Book, page 2

Guide children as they complete the Student Book activity. Then use children's responses and the prompts below to discuss each word.

versatile Tell children that you will describe a person and if they think that this person is versatile, they should pat their heads, rub their bellies, and say "versatile." If not, they should say nothing.

- Jim is good at painting and singing.
- Nancy can't watch television when she does her homework.
- Kate knows how to cook eggs and how to make orange juice.

lively Tell children that you will describe some things and if they think you are describing something lively, they should say "lively." If not, they should say nothing.

- The hamster ran around and around on its wheel for hours without getting tired.
- Alice danced all night long.
- Max dragged his feet as he walked down the sidewalk.

3 Using the Vocabulary

Word Chat

Student Book, page 3

Guide children as they complete the Student Book activity. Then use children's responses and the prompts below to discuss each word.

comforting If someone is comforting, do they make you feel safe or scared? Why?

expression Is your expression the look on your face or the color of your hair? Explain.

fleet Is a fleet person more like a slow turtle or more like a fast rabbit? Why is that?

Continue the discussion with the remaining words from the lesson.

glimmer If something glimmers, is it dark or does it twinkle? Explain your choice.

versatile Which is more versatile, a hat that can also be used as a bowl or a hat that only covers your head? Tell why.

lively Would a person who is lively be tired all the time or always ready to play? Explain.

WORD CHALLENGE

Explain to children that the word *fleet* has more than one meaning. They have already learned that it means "moving fast." Tell them that another meaning is "a group of boats or ships." Then provide the following prompts and ask children which meaning the word *fleet* has in each prompt.

- The **fleet** of fishing boats sailed off early in the morning. (a group of boats or ships)
- The **fleet** deer ran through the forest. (moving fast)

4 Using the Vocabulary

Word Organizers

Help your class complete the graphic organizers below. You may draw them on the board or on chart paper, or use the organizers in the back of this book to make transparencies.

Write the vocabulary word in the center.

expression

happy

angry

scared

tired

surprised

sad

Review the meaning of expression *with children. Ask children to think of some different expressions people can show on their faces. Record their answers, modeling sample answers when necessary.*

Invite children to demonstrate the six expressions and discuss when they might use these expressions.

Write the words shown in blue boxes to begin.

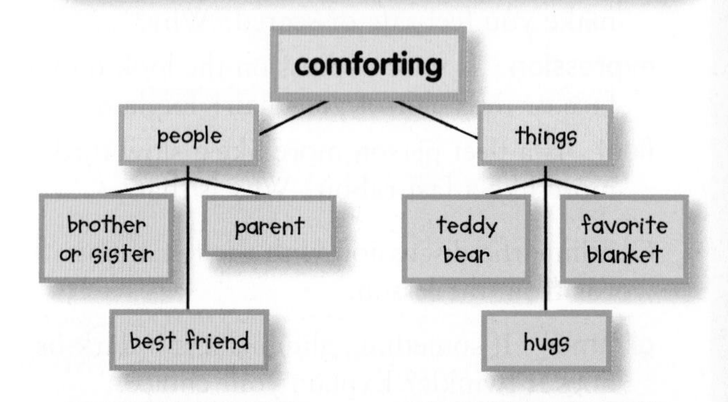

Ask children to name people who are comforting and record their answers. Model sample answers as needed.

Ask children to tell what these people do when they are comforting someone or something.

Ask children to name things that can be comforting. Record their answers, modeling sample answers as needed.

Discuss what makes these things and people comforting.

Your Turn to Write

Encourage children to relate the words to their own experiences. Discuss a few of the prompts below to prepare children for writing. Have children write about one of the prompts in their journals or on a separate piece of paper.

comforting What are some things that are comforting to you? Have you ever been comforting to another person? What did you say and do?

fleet Are you a fleet person, or would you like to be? What animals are fleet? How does being fleet help them?

glimmer What are some things outside that glimmer? Can you find something in our classroom that glimmers? How does it look?

expression What would put a happy expression on your face? When might you have a sad expression? Can you always tell how someone feels by their expression? Why or why not?

lively Who do you know that is lively? How does a lively person act? What are some animals that are lively?

versatile Do you know any versatile people? What different things can they do? What are some machines that are versatile?

5 Assessing the Vocabulary

Review

Blackline Master, page 169

Read the following questions aloud and have children circle *yes* or *no*.

1. Is a turtle a **fleet** animal? (no)
2. Is a computer a **versatile** machine? (yes)
3. Might a candle **glimmer**? (yes)
4. If you are sad, do you have a happy **expression** on your face? (no)
5. Would a **lively** person fall asleep at their desk? (no)
6. Is a pair of scissors very **comforting**? (no)

Assessment

Student Book, pages 4–5

Read each question aloud as children complete the activity.

Cumulative Review

Ask the first question and model how you might arrive at an answer. Then have children answer the remaining questions and explain their answers.

Why might someone with a sad **expression** need **comforting**?
If a puppy is **lively**, might he also be **fleet**?
Is it **comforting** to see the stars **glimmer**?
Is a **fleet** person more **versatile** than others?
If you have a happy **expression**, might your eyes **glimmer**?
Might a **lively** person also be **versatile**?

Lesson 2

Big Al

Vocabulary

delightful If you say someone or something is delightful, you mean that it is very pleasant.

clumsy A clumsy person has trouble moving or handling things and often trips over or breaks them.

capture If you capture someone or something, you catch it and keep it from getting away.

fierce A fierce animal or person behaves in a mean way and often looks for a fight.

rescue When you rescue someone, you save them from something bad happening.

suspense Suspense is the feeling you get when you know something is about to happen very soon.

At a Glance

STANDARDS

Vocabulary
- Discuss word meaning and develop vocabulary through meaningful experiences
- Listen to imaginative texts in order to respond to vivid language

Comprehension
- Use specific details and information from a text to answer literal questions

Writing
- Compose original texts

LESSON RESOURCES

Read-Aloud Anthology: pp. 7–12
Student Book: pp. 6–9
Word Cards: Lesson 2
Photo Cards: 7–12, 32, 64, 74, 84, 125, 131

1 Introducing the Vocabulary

Read-Aloud

Read-Aloud Anthology, pages 7–12

In *Big Al* all the little fish are afraid of Big Al, until they discover what a wonderful friend a big fish can be!

Bringing the Story to Life

Emphasize the words *little, big,* and *TEETH* in the third paragraph. When you get to the part where Big Al sneezes, act out a giant sneeze that would be worthy of Big Al!

Word Watcher

Word Watcher Chart, Lesson 2 Word Cards

- Tell children that they will learn about these words throughout the week and that each time a child uses one of the words correctly in the classroom, you will place a mark next to the word.
- Hold up each word card, and use the word in a sentence. Then give clues: Find words that begin with *c (clumsy* and *capture)*. Find words that end with *e (capture, fierce, rescue, suspense)*. Find the word with the most letters *(delightful)*. As children locate each word, say it together and give it its first tally of the week.

Sending the Words Home

Blackline Master—English, page 123; Spanish, page 124

Distribute the activity letter to inform parents of the vocabulary words for this week.

Research Says...

"As children [develop] reading and writing competence, we need to [use] their listening and speaking competencies to enhance their vocabulary development."

—Bringing Words to Life, Isabel L. Beck, *et al.*

2 Using the Vocabulary

Word Snapshots

Photo Cards: 7–12, 32, 64, 74, 84, 125, 131

Hold up the card pairs and ask children the following questions. Discuss which photos show activities the children enjoy and why.

delightful (7 and 32) Which card shows girls having a delightful time?

clumsy (8 and 84) Which card shows someone looking clumsy?

capture (9 and 64) Which card shows an animal that has been captured?

fierce (10 and 74) Which card shows an animal looking fierce?

rescue (11 and 125) Which card shows a person rescuing someone?

suspense (12 and 131) Which card gives you a feeling of suspense?

ELL SUPPORT

Show children the photo cards, one at a time. Pronounce each vocabulary word and have children pronounce it with you. Read the sentence on the back of each card. Then use each word in a sentence and have children take turns acting out the words.

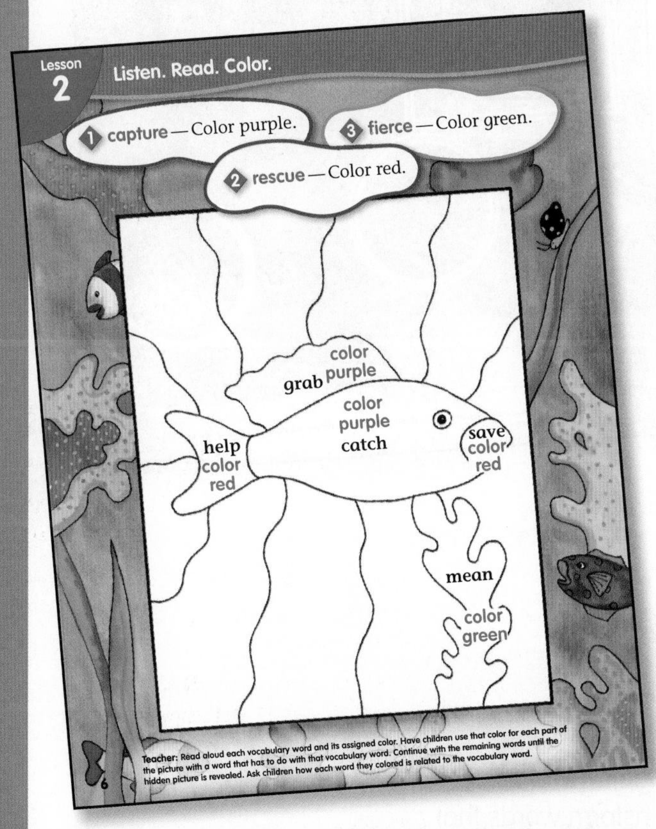

fierce Tell children that you will describe an animal, and if they think you are describing an animal being fierce, they should make a scary frown and say "Grrrrr. Fierce!" If not, they should say nothing.

- The lion growled at the zebras nearby.
- The puppy jumped on my lap and licked my face.
- The mama grizzly bear showed her teeth when a deer came near her cubs.

Word Chat

Student Book, page 6

Guide children as they complete the Student Book activity. Then use children's responses and the prompts below to discuss each word.

capture Tell children that you will describe a situation and if they think it describes animals that have been captured, they should clasp their hands and say "captured." If not, they should say nothing.

- There are many beautiful and colorful birds in the jungle.
- I see six birds flying over a mountain.
- The birds at the zoo are kept in a large, comfortable cage.

rescue Tell children that you will describe a situation and if they think it describes someone who needs to be rescued, they should say "rescue." If not, they should say nothing.

- Jack took the train to the city to go to work.
- Jack's boat turned over and he found himself in ice-cold water without a life jacket!
- Jack drove to the supermarket to go shopping.

3 Using the Vocabulary

Word Chat

Student Book, page 7

Guide children as they complete the Student Book activity. Then use children's responses and the prompts below to discuss each word.

suspense Would you be in suspense if you were watching a person in a movie walk slowly through a scary, dark house? Why or why not?

clumsy Would you feel clumsy if you carefully put a vase on a table or if you knocked a vase off a table and it fell into a hundred pieces? Explain.

delightful If you were eating a delightful dinner, would you be smiling or crying? Why is that?

Continue the discussion with the remaining words from the lesson.

capture If a spider captured a fly, would it keep it or let it go? Explain what you mean.

rescue If you rescue someone, would they thank you or be angry with you? Why?

fierce If a fierce animal stood next to you, would you be bored or scared? Explain your answer.

WORD CHALLENGE

Review with children the meanings of the words *delightful* and *fierce*. Then use the following prompts to help children brainstorm words that mean the opposite.

- In the story Big Al scared the other fish because he looked so **fierce**. But Big Al was really the opposite of *fierce*. Can you think of some words to describe him? *(kind, gentle, friendly, nice, loving)*
- In the story Big Al had a **delightful** time with the fish until he sneezed. Can you think of some words that mean the opposite of *delightful*? *(bad, awful, terrible, horrible)*

4 Using the Vocabulary

Word Organizers

Help your class complete the graphic organizers below. You may draw them on the board or on chart paper, or use the organizers in the back of this book to make transparencies.

Write the words shown in blue boxes to begin.

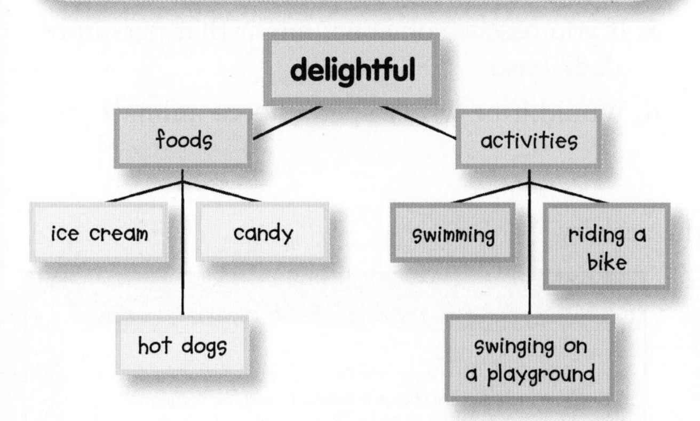

Write the vocabulary word in the center.

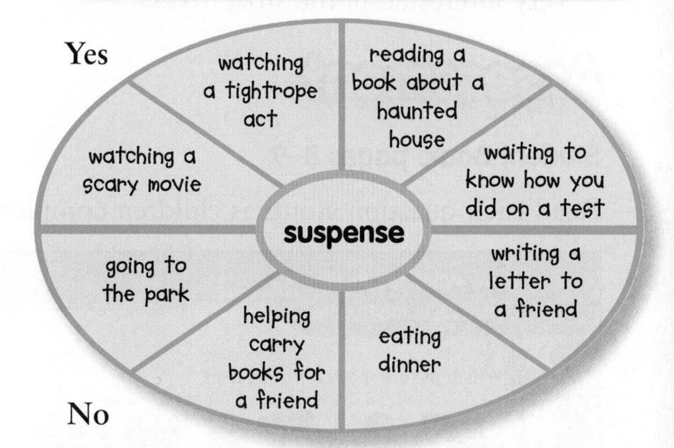

Ask children to name foods they think are delightful. Record their answers, modeling sample answers as needed.
Ask what makes these foods delightful.

Ask children to name activities they think are delightful and record their answers. Model sample answers as needed.
Ask what are some activities that are not delightful.

Say each of the activities listed on this organizer. After you say each one, ask children to tell you whether to write the activity in the top of the oval (meaning yes, it is suspenseful) or in the bottom of the oval (meaning no, it is not suspenseful). As children explain their answers, write the activity in the appropriate place in the organizer.

Your Turn to Write

Encourage children to relate the words to their own experiences. Discuss a few of the prompts below to prepare children for writing. Have children write about one of the prompts in their journals or on a separate piece of paper.

delightful Describe a delightful day. What would you do? Who would be with you?

clumsy Have you ever felt clumsy? What did you do? How did you feel about it?

capture Have you ever played a game where you were captured? How did it make you feel? Did you get to capture someone else?

fierce Have you ever seen a fierce animal? How did the animal act? Did it scare you?

rescue Have you ever been rescued? What happened? Have you ever seen another person being rescued?

suspense What stories have you heard that kept you in suspense? Have you seen any movies that kept you in suspense? Describe what happened to make you feel that way.

5 Assessing the Vocabulary

Review

Blackline Master, page 169

Read the following questions aloud and have children circle *yes* or *no*.

1. If a story keeps you in **suspense**, are you very interested in the story? (yes)
2. Might a **clumsy** person often drop things? (yes)
3. If a party is **delightful**, do you want to leave? (no)
4. If you **capture** a grasshopper, can it easily hop away? (no)
5. If you **rescue** someone, might that person be glad? (yes)
6. Would it be wise to pet a **fierce** animal? (no)

Assessment

Student Book, pages 8–9

Read each question aloud as children complete the activity.

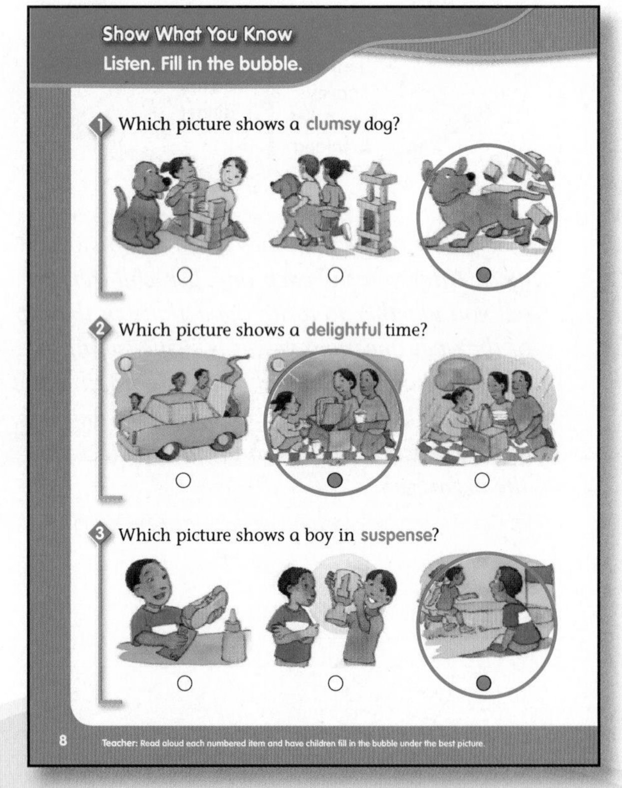

Cumulative Review

Ask the first question and model how you might arrive at an answer. Then have children answer the remaining questions and explain their answers.

Lesson 1	Lesson 2	
expression	suspense	What **expression** might you have if you are in **suspense**?
comforting	fierce	Would it be **comforting** to meet a **fierce** bear?
fleet	clumsy	Can someone who is **fleet** also be **clumsy**?
lively	delightful	If you were having a **delightful** day, would you feel **lively**?
glimmer	capture	Could you **capture** a **glimmer** of light?
versatile	rescue	How did Big Al show he was **versatile** when he **rescued** the fish?

One Good Turn Deserves Another

Vocabulary

deserve If you deserve something, you should get it because of what you have done.

grateful If you are grateful for something that someone has given you or done for you, you are pleased and wish to thank the person.

amble When you amble somewhere, you walk there slowly and in a restful way.

plead If you plead with someone, you beg them to do something for you that will help you out.

deceive If you deceive someone, you make them believe something that is not true.

challenge If you challenge someone, you ask them to do something that is difficult or that you think they cannot do.

At a Glance

STANDARDS

Vocabulary
- Develop vocabulary by discussing characters and events from a story
- Speak to express the mood of a story by using a variety of words

Comprehension
- Retell or act out order of important events in stories

Writing
- Write to discover, develop, and refine ideas

LESSON RESOURCES

Read-Aloud Anthology: pp. 13–18
Student Book: pp. 10–13
Word Cards: Lesson 3
Photo Cards: 13–18

1 Introducing the Vocabulary

Read-Aloud

Read-Aloud Anthology, pages 13–18

In the Mexican folk tale *One Good Turn Deserves Another*, a mouse saves a snake's life and, with the help of a coyote, proves that one good turn deserves another.

Bringing the Story to Life

As you read the part of the snake, extend the *s* in words like *ssso* to make the snake hiss. Use a high, squeaky voice for the mouse. For the crow, use a bored, matter-of-fact voice. Read the armadillo's words with a slow, lumbering voice. Make the coyote's voice tricky or mischievous.

Word Watcher

Word Watcher Chart, Lesson 3 Word Cards

- Tell children that they will learn about these words throughout the week and that each time a child uses one of the words correctly in the classroom, you will place a mark next to the word.
- Line up the word cards along the board ledge. Ask six children to come up and pick a word that they want to learn. As each child hands you their word card, say the word and use it in a sentence. Have the class repeat the word as you put the card in the chart and give it its first tally of the week.

Sending the Words Home

Blackline Master—English, page 125; Spanish, page 126

Distribute the activity letter to inform parents of the vocabulary words for this week.

Research Says...

"...help your students develop vocabulary [by fostering] word consciousness—an awareness of and interest in words, their meanings, and their power."

—Put Reading First

2 Using the Vocabulary

Word Snapshots

Photo Cards: 13–18

Hold up one of the photo cards for all the class to see. Read the sentence on the back of the card. Then call on volunteers to use the vocabulary word in a sentence of their own. Record the sentences on the board. Repeat this activity for all of the words in the lesson.

Then display the photo cards on the board ledge and quiz the class by saying each vocabulary word and having children point to the correct picture.

ELL SUPPORT

Show the photo cards and discuss with children how the words relate to the story. Hold up each card, say the word, and have children repeat it. Then ask children yes/no questions about each word. For example, for *deserve* say *If you work hard all day, do you deserve to rest?*

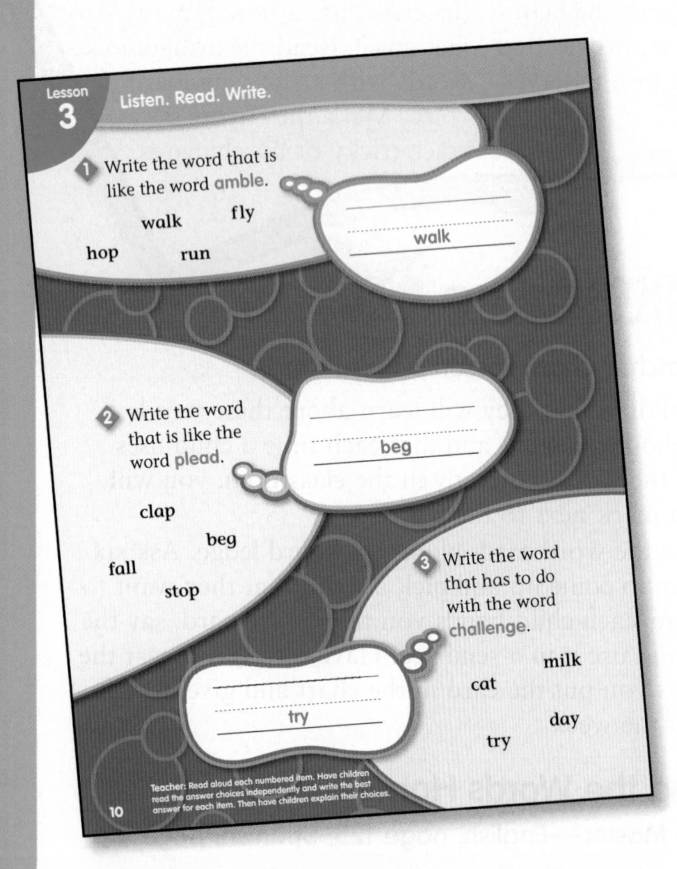

challenge Tell children that you will describe an activity and if they think doing it would challenge them, they should say "challenge." If not, they should say nothing.

- climbing Mount Everest, the tallest mountain in the world
- driving to school yourself
- listening to a story

Word Chat

Student Book, page 10

Guide children as they complete the Student Book activity. Then use children's responses and the prompts below to discuss each word.

amble Tell children that you will describe a situation and if they think it describes someone ambling, they should say "amble." If not, they should say nothing.

- Jen hurried to tell her friend the news.
- Victor and his family spent all day wandering around the new park.
- Max ran to catch the school bus.

plead Tell children that you will describe a situation and if they think it describes someone pleading, they should say "plead." If not, they should say nothing.

- Tran and his dad played catch.
- Nora asked her brother ten times to play tag with her.
- Jason begged to see a new movie about dinosaurs.

3 Using the Vocabulary

Word Chat

Student Book, page 11

Guide children as they complete the Student Book activity. Then use children's responses and the prompts below to discuss each word.

For each vocabulary word, provide children with the first part of a sentence that includes the vocabulary word. Have children provide an ending for the sentence that shows they know what the new word means.

deserve Kim thought she deserved to play outside because....

deceive People do not like to be deceived because....

grateful Sean was grateful to the doctor for....

challenge Pat liked to challenge her brother to....

Continue the discussion with the remaining words from the lesson.

amble Justin ambled across the field because....

plead Keiko pleaded with her parents to....

Listen. Circle.

1 deserve plead

2 deceive amble

3 amble grateful

4 deceive challenge

Teacher: Read aloud the two vocabulary words for each picture. Ask children to circle the word that best goes with each picture. Ask children how the word they chose goes with the picture.

11

WORD CHALLENGE

Review with children the meanings of the words *deceive* and *grateful.* Then use the following prompts to help children brainstorm words that mean the same or almost the same thing.

- Recall how the coyote **deceived** the snake in the story. Can you think of any words that mean the same or almost the same thing as *deceive*? *(trick, fool, lie)*
- In the story the mouse thought the snake should have been **grateful** that she saved his life. Can you think of any words that mean the same or almost the same thing as *grateful*? *(thankful, pleased)*

4 Using the Vocabulary

Word Organizers

Help your class complete the graphic organizers below. You may draw them on the board or on chart paper, or use the organizers in the back of this book to make transparencies.

Write the vocabulary word in the blue box.

deserve

1. We deserve to have a party because we finished our school work.
2. I deserve to get a puppy because I know how to care for a pet.
3. I deserve to stay up late on Saturday because I clean my room every day.

Ask children to think of sentences about things they deserve and tell why they deserve them. You may want to start them off by modeling a sentence for them. Then record their sentences.

After children generate sentences, have them tell if they think they will get what they deserve.

Write the vocabulary word in the diamond.

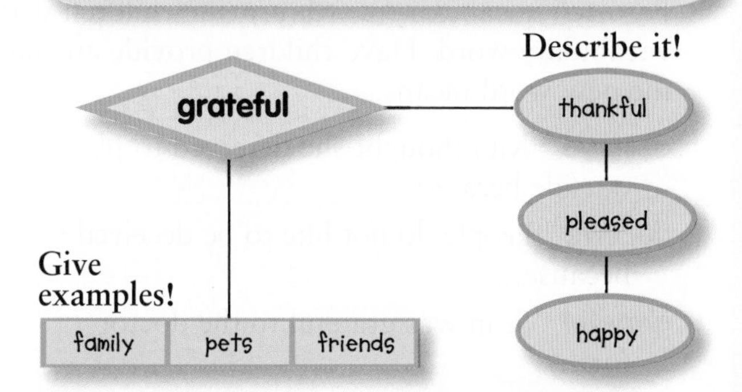

Ask children to think of other words to describe what grateful *means. Model sample answers as needed, and record their answers in the ovals.*

Invite children to name things they are grateful for and have them explain why. Record their answers in the boxes, modeling sample answers as necessary.

Your Turn to Write

Encourage children to relate the words to their own experiences. Discuss a few of the prompts below to prepare children for writing. Have children write about one of the prompts in their journals or on a separate piece of paper.

deserve Can you think of someone who deserves something nice? Why does that person deserve it? When was the last time you got something that you deserved?

grateful Have you ever been grateful for something? How did you show you were grateful? Has anyone ever been grateful to you for something you did?

amble When was the last time you ambled somewhere? Why didn't you walk quickly? Can you think of a time when it wouldn't be a good idea to amble?

plead When have you pleaded for something? What was it? Why did you want it so badly? Has anyone ever pleaded with you for something?

deceive Has anyone ever deceived you? What happened and how did you feel? Have you ever deceived someone else? How did that make you feel?

challenge Have you ever challenged someone? Has anyone ever challenged you to do something? Were you able to do it?

5 Assessing the Vocabulary

Review

Blackline Master, page 169

Read the following questions aloud and have children circle *yes* or *no*.

1. If you **challenge** your friends to count to a million and back, do you think they will be able to do it? (no)
2. Do people always get everything they **deserve**? (no)
3. If you **plead** for something, do you care if you get it? (yes)
4. If you **amble**, are you in a hurry? (no)
5. Would a **grateful** person say "thank you"? (yes)
6. If you **deceive** someone, do you tell the person the truth? (no)

Assessment

Student Book, pages 12–13

Read each question aloud as children complete the activity.

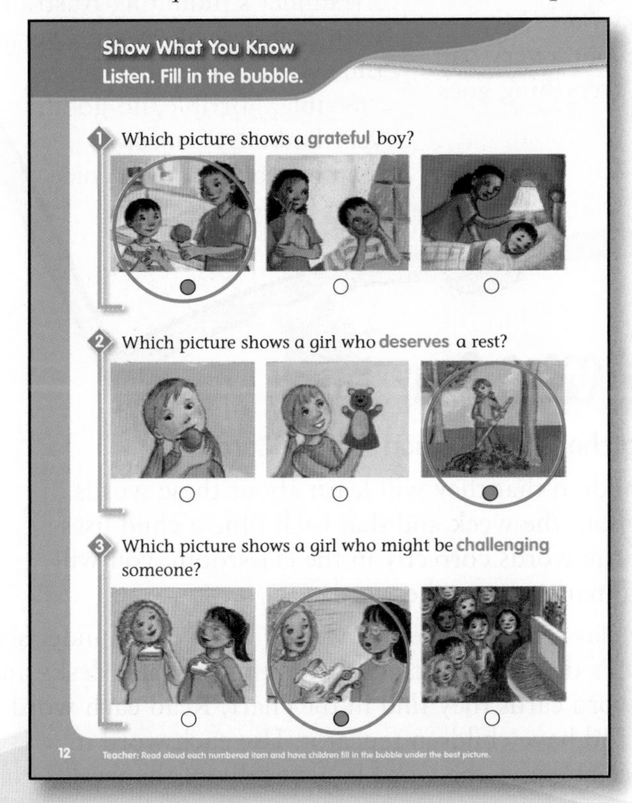

Cumulative Review

Ask the first question and model how you might arrive at an answer. Then have children answer the remaining questions and explain their answers.

Lesson 2	Lesson 3	
fierce	challenge	Would you pet a **fierce** animal if someone **challenged** you to?
rescue	grateful	If someone **rescued** you, would you be **grateful**?
suspense	plead	Would you **plead** to know a story's ending if you were in **suspense**?
delightful	amble	Could it be **delightful** to **amble** with a friend?
clumsy	deserve	Does a **clumsy** pet **deserve** a hug?
capture	deceive	In a game, can you **deceive** someone and then **capture** them?

Lesson 4

Alexander and the Terrible, Horrible, No Good, Very Bad Day

Vocabulary

scrunched If something is scrunched, it gets pushed together and squeezed.

invisible If something is invisible, you can't see it.

scold If you scold someone, you say angry things to them about something they have done.

dreadful If something is dreadful, it is so terrible that it could not be much worse.

complain Complain means to talk about how the things that are happening are bad or unfair.

exaggerate Exaggerate means to make things seem much better or much worse than they really are.

At a Glance

STANDARDS

Vocabulary
- Identify words that name persons, places, or things, and words that name actions
- Use vocabulary to describe ideas, feelings, and experiences

Comprehension
- Use prior knowledge to make sense of texts

Writing
- Describe connections between personal experiences and written and visual texts

LESSON RESOURCES

Read-Aloud Anthology: pp. 19–24	Word Cards: Lesson 4
Student Book: pp. 14–17	Photo Cards: 10, 13, 19–24, 31, 33, 55, 82

1 Introducing the Vocabulary

Read-Aloud

Read-Aloud Anthology, pages 19–24

In *Alexander and the Terrible, Horrible, No Good, Very Bad Day*, a boy tells about a very bad day when everything goes wrong.

Bringing the Story to Life

Use your voice to animate Alexander's mounting frustration with each terrible event. Every time you say the phrase "terrible, horrible, no good, very bad day," inject a whining tone to your voice for a humorous effect.

Word Watcher

Word Watcher Chart, Lesson 4 Word Cards

- Tell children that they will learn about these words throughout the week and that each time a child uses one of the words correctly in the classroom, you will place a mark next to the word.
- Before class begins, hide this week's word cards under six children's desks. Have children look under their desks and place word cards they find in the chart. Read each word aloud and have children repeat it. Use each word in a sentence and give the word its first tally of the week.

Sending the Words Home

Blackline Master—English, page 127; Spanish, page 128

Distribute the activity letter to inform parents of the vocabulary words for this week.

Research Says...

"Prompting children to think about situations in their lives that relate to a new word increases the chances the children will recall and use the word...."

—*Bringing Words to Life,* Isabel L. Beck, *et al.*

2 Using the Vocabulary

Word Snapshots

Photo Cards: 10, 13, 19–24, 31, 33, 55, 82

Hold up the card pairs and ask children the following questions. Discuss which photos best show the vocabulary words.

scrunched (19 and 31) Which card shows things that are scrunched?

invisible (20 and 10) Which card shows something invisible?

scold (21 and 82) Which card shows someone being scolded?

dreadful (22 and 13) Which card shows a dreadful situation?

complain (23 and 33) Which card shows someone who is complaining?

exaggerate (24 and 55) Which card shows someone who is exaggerating?

ELL SUPPORT

Show each photo card as you pronounce the word and have children repeat it. Use realia to help explain some words. For example, have children scrunch up a piece of paper. Use the photo cards and the sentences on the backs to discuss each word.

Lesson 4

Listen. Draw.

1 Draw a line from the word to each thing that is being scrunched.

paper
chairs
cups
scrunched
clothes

2 Draw a line from the word to each thing that is dreadful.

weather
noise
dreadful
flowers
worm

3 Draw a line from the word to each thing that looks like it is exaggerated.

jump
exaggerate
lift
climb
fly

Teacher: Read aloud each numbered item. Have children draw a line to the pictures that best show each word. Let them know that there may be more than one picture for each word. Ask them why they chose the pictures they did.

14

exaggerate Tell children that you will say some things and if they think you are exaggerating, they should say "You're exaggerating!" If not, they should say nothing.

- I caught a fish THIS BIG! (Stretch your arms out to their full width.)
- I had a sandwich for lunch.
- It took me TWO DAYS to eat one grape.

Word Chat

Student Book, page 14

Guide children as they complete the Student Book activity. Then use children's responses and the prompts below to discuss each word.

scrunched Tell children that you will name some things and if they think the thing can be scrunched, they should say "scrunched." If not, they should say nothing.

- a mountain
- a bunch of grapes
- a house

dreadful Tell children that you will describe some things and if they think the thing is dreadful, they should groan and say "Ohhhh! Dreadful!" If not, they should say nothing.

- The shoestore had a sale.
- The shoestore closed for the night.
- The shoestore burned down.

3 Using the Vocabulary

Word Chat

Student Book, page 15

Guide children as they complete the Student Book activity. Then use children's responses and the prompts below to discuss each word.

invisible If you were invisible, would you win at "Hide-and-Seek," or would your friends find you? Why?

scold Does *scold* mean that you say angry things to someone or nice things to someone? Explain your answer.

complain Would you complain if you were watching a television show or if your television were broken? Why?

Continue the discussion with the remaining words from the lesson.

dreadful Would you rather feel dreadful or wonderful? Why?

exaggerate Which would be exaggerating, saying you were hungry enough to eat a sandwich or saying you were hungry enough to eat all the food in the kitchen? Explain your answer.

scrunched Would you rather be scrunched on a couch or have lots of room? Explain your answer.

WORD CHALLENGE

Review with children the meanings of the words *dreadful* and *scold*. Then use the following prompts to help children brainstorm words that mean the opposite.

- In the story Alexander had a **dreadful** day. What kind of day would be the opposite of *dreadful? (wonderful, great, terrific, awesome, fantastic)*
- In the story Alexander's mom **scolded** him. What would be the opposite of *scold? (praise, say that someone is good)*

4 Using the Vocabulary

Word Organizers

Help your class complete the graphic organizers below. You may draw them on the board or on chart paper, or use the organizers in the back of this book to make transparencies.

Write the vocabulary word in the blue box.

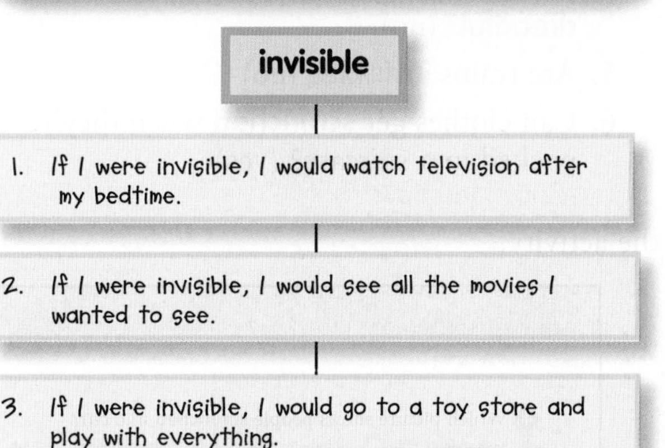

Ask children to make up sentences about what they would do if they were invisible. You may want to model a sentence for them to get them started. Record their sentences.

After children generate sentences, ask how long they would want to be invisible. For a day? For a week?

Write the vocabulary word in the center.

Ask children to think of words that mean the same or almost the same thing as dreadful. *Remind them to think of the title of the read-aloud story for ideas. Record their answers.*

Have children tell about some things that they think are dreadful.

Your Turn to Write

Encourage children to relate the words to their own experiences. Discuss a few of the prompts below to prepare children for writing. Have children write about one of the prompts in their journals or on a separate piece of paper.

scrunched Would you want your sandwich to get scrunched? What else wouldn't you want to get scrunched? Have you ever felt scrunched?

invisible When would it be fun to be invisible? When would it not be fun to be invisible? Can you name some things that are invisible?

scold Have you ever been scolded? How did it make you feel? Have you ever wanted to scold someone?

dreadful Did you ever have a dreadful day? What happened that made it such a bad day? What can you do to make a dreadful day better?

complain What kinds of things do you complain about? Do your friends complain about the same things or different things? Who do you talk to when you want to complain about something?

exaggerate Do you think Alexander exaggerated about how terrible his day was? Tell about a time when you exaggerated something. What did other people say to you?

5 Assessing the Vocabulary

Review

Blackline Master, page 169

Read the following questions aloud and have children circle *yes* or *no*.

1. Would most people **complain** about a sunny day? (no)
2. Might you be **scolded** for fighting with a friend? (yes)
3. If I said I had a million things to do today, would I be **exaggerating**? (yes)
4. Is finding a dollar on the ground **dreadful**? (no)
5. Are trains **invisible**? (no)
6. Can clothes get **scrunched** when they're packed in a suitcase? (yes)

Assessment

Student Book, pages 16–17

Read each question aloud as children complete the activity.

Show What You Know
Listen. Fill in the bubble.

1. Which picture shows an invisible bike?
2. Which picture shows a boy complaining?
3. Which picture shows something dreadful?

16 Teacher: Read aloud each numbered item and have children fill in the bubble under the best picture.

4. Which picture shows people scrunched in a car?
5. Which picture shows a girl being scolded?
6. A boy would be exaggerating if he said he could do which of these things?

17

Cumulative Review

Ask the first question and model how you might arrive at an answer. Then have children answer the remaining questions and explain their answers.

Lesson 3	Lesson 4	
deserve	scold	Would you **deserve** to be **scolded** if you were on time?
challenge	invisible	If I **challenged** you to become **invisible**, could you do it?
grateful	dreadful	Was Alexander **grateful** to have a **dreadful** day?
amble	scrunched	Would you rather **amble** to school or be **scrunched** in a car?
plead	complain	Would you **complain** about not getting something you **pleaded** for?
deceive	exaggerate	Can you **deceive** someone by **exaggerating**?

Lesson 5

The Frogs Wore Red Suspenders

Vocabulary

suspend When you suspend something, you hold it up or hang it up off the ground.

serenade If you serenade someone, you sing or play a song for them on a musical instrument.

spangled Something that is spangled is covered with small, shiny things.

pride Pride is the feeling you get when you have done something well.

ridiculous Something ridiculous is very foolish and makes no sense.

perform When you perform, you do something like sing, dance, play an instrument, or speak in front of a group.

At a Glance

STANDARDS

Vocabulary
- Use visual references to build upon word meaning
- Use vocabulary to describe ideas, feelings, and experiences

Comprehension
- Distinguish between a story and a poem

Writing
- Write in different forms for different purposes

LESSON RESOURCES

Read-Aloud Anthology: pp. 25–28
Student Book: pp. 18–21
Word Cards: Lesson 5
Photo Cards: 25–30

1 Introducing the Vocabulary

Read-Aloud

Read-Aloud Anthology, pages 25–28

In the silly poem "The Frogs Wore Red Suspenders," a group of animals puts on an unusual performance.

Bringing the Poem to Life

Have fun reading this poem. Use your voice to express surprise at the animal costumes, to dramatize the croaking and oinking, and to demonstrate the sighs of the ducks and chickens. On the last line, act out the birds' pride.

Word Watcher

Word Watcher Chart, Lesson 5 Word Cards

- Tell children that they will learn about these words throughout the week and that each time a child uses one of the words correctly in the classroom, you will place a mark next to the word.
- Place the cards for this week's words in a pile, facedown. Have a child choose a card. Say the word and have the children repeat it. Then say a sentence with the vocabulary word and place the first tally of the week by the word. Continue with the other cards.

Sending the Words Home

Blackline Master—English, page 129; Spanish, page 130

Distribute the activity letter to inform parents of the vocabulary words for this week.

Research Says...

"Within the sociocultural perspective language plays a vital role, enabling learners to gain, process, organize, and evaluate knowledge."

—*Reading Research Quarterly*, Beth Maloch

2 Using the Vocabulary

Word Snapshots

Photo Cards: 25–30

Have children stand in a circle, facing one another. One at a time, give each photo card to a child in the circle, saying the vocabulary word and the sentence on the back of the card. With all the photos facing the inside of the circle, say one of the vocabulary words and have the children point to the card that shows that word. Continue until all the words have been used. After children identify each card correctly, ask how they knew that was the correct card.

ELL SUPPORT

Hold up one photo card at a time. Pronounce each vocabulary word and have children say the word with you. Place the photos along the board ledge. Say a vocabulary word and a sentence using the word. Have children find the photo for each word and repeat each word with you.

ridiculous Tell children that you will describe a situation and if they think someone or something is ridiculous, they should make a silly face and say "ridiculous." If not, they should say nothing.

- Justin poured ketchup all over his chocolate chip cookies.
- Andy skinned his knee and needed a bandage.
- Lindsey put on a sweater, a jacket, a heavy coat, and three pairs of mittens to go to the swimming pool.

Word Chat

Student Book, page 18

Guide children as they complete the Student Book activity. Then use children's responses and the prompts below to discuss each word.

serenade Tell children you will describe a situation and if they think someone is serenading someone, they should sing "La la la! Serenade!" If not, they should say nothing.

- The baby cried for a bottle.
- Julia sang the new song she learned to her mom.
- Nick practiced playing the guitar.

suspend Tell children that you will describe a situation and if they think something is being suspended, they should say "suspend." If not, they should say nothing.

- Bob's kite got stuck in a tree and hung from the branches.
- Emily dropped her books all over the floor.
- We hung balloons from the ceiling for our party.

Word Chat

Student Book, page 19

Guide children as they complete the Student Book activity. Then use children's responses and the prompts below to discuss each word.

After children complete the pages, briefly remind them of all the words in this lesson. (You might want to refer to the Word Watcher Chart or display the corresponding photo cards.) Explain that you are going to say a word or a phrase and that children should say the vocabulary word that comes to mind. After each response, have children give reasons for their choice.

sparkly dress **(spangled)**
dancer on stage **(perform)**
winning a race **(pride)**
cow wearing sunglasses **(ridiculous)**

Continue the discussion with the remaining words from the lesson.

singing outside someone's window **(serenade)**
yo-yo **(suspend)**

WORD CHALLENGE

Remind children that to suspend something means "to hang it," or "to hold it up." The word *suspend* can also have another meaning. It can mean "to stop for a while." If a person asked you to suspend talking, would they want you to hang your talking from the ceiling, or would they want you to stop talking for a while? (stop talking for a while) Listen to some sentences and say whether *suspend* means "to hold something up" or "to stop."

- I need a string to **suspend** the artwork. (hold it up)
- It got dark, so we had to **suspend** the game. (stop)
- Max used a rope to **suspend** the wet laundry. (hold it up)
- Tori had to **suspend** working to eat lunch. (stop)
- The circus tent was **suspended** by a pole. (hold it up)

4 Using the Vocabulary

Word Organizers

Help your class complete the graphic organizers below. You may draw them on the board or on chart paper, or use the organizers in the back of this book to make transparencies.

Write the vocabulary word in the diamond.

Describe it!

perform

acting

singing

dancing

Give examples!

a play	a talent show	a ballet

Encourage children to describe different ways they could perform. Record their suggestions, modeling sample answers as necessary.

Ask children which type of performing they enjoy most and why.

Invite children to name things that they might perform in. Record appropriate answers.

Write the vocabulary word in the center.

Ask children to name things that would give them pride. Record their answers in the top half of the circle, modeling sample answers when necessary.

Ask children why these things would give them pride.

Ask children to name things that would not give them pride. You might wish to provide sample answers and have children tell whether each belongs in the bottom half of the circle or not. Record appropriate answers.

Ask children why these things would not give them pride.

Your Turn to Write

Encourage children to relate the words to their own experiences. Discuss a few of the prompts below to prepare children for writing. Have children write about one of the prompts in their journals or on a separate piece of paper.

suspend What decorations would you like to suspend from the ceiling of your room? How would you suspend them? What things are suspended in the classroom right now?

serenade Do you think a serenade would make someone feel good? Who would you like to serenade? How would you serenade someone?

spangled Do you think spangled things are beautiful? What have you seen that is spangled?

pride What have you done that made you feel pride? Is pride a good feeling? How can you make your parents feel pride in you?

ridiculous Have you ever done something ridiculous? How did it make you feel? What is the most ridiculous thing you've ever seen?

perform Have you ever performed for someone? What did you do? Do you like to watch other people perform?

5 Assessing the Vocabulary

Review

Blackline Master, page 169

Read the following questions aloud and have children circle *yes* or *no*.

1. Could you **suspend** a swing from a tree branch? (yes)
2. Can people hear a **serenade**? (yes)
3. Is spinach **spangled**? (no)
4. Do you feel **pride** when someone tells you that you did a good job? (yes)
5. Is it **ridiculous** to ride a bus to school? (no)
6. Can a skateboarder **perform** tricks? (yes)

Assessment

Student Book, pages 20–21

Read each question aloud as children complete the activity.

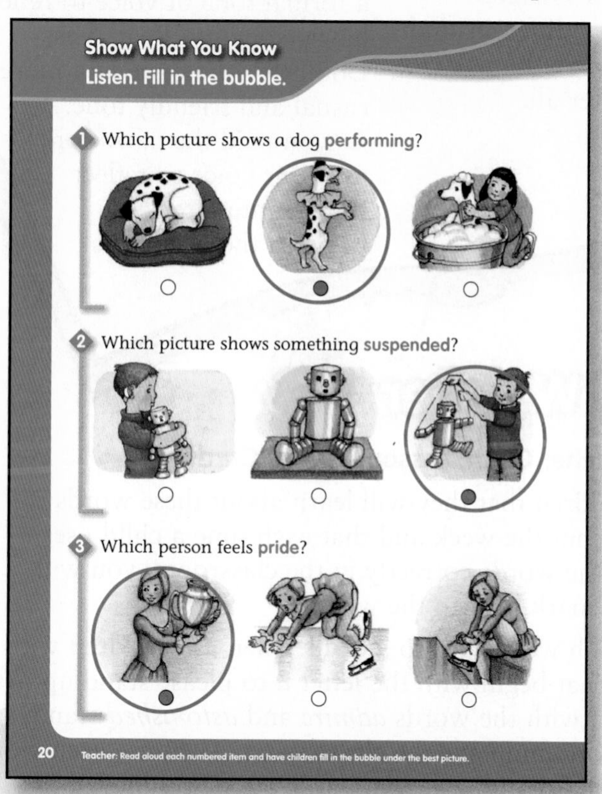

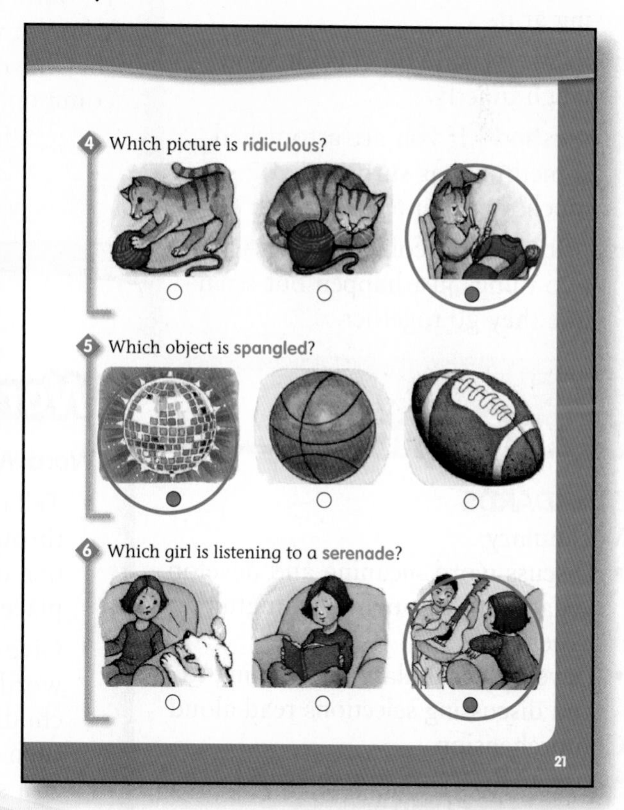

Cumulative Review

Ask the first question and model how you might arrive at an answer. Then have children answer the remaining questions and explain their answers.

Lesson 4	Lesson 5	
complain	spangled	Would you **complain** if your sandwich were **spangled**?
exaggerate	ridiculous	Is it **ridiculous** to **exaggerate** how tall you are?
invisible	perform	Can you **perform** a trick juggling **invisible** balls?
scold	pride	Do you feel **pride** if someone **scolds** you?
dreadful	serenade	How would you like to hear a **dreadful serenade**?
scrunched	suspend	Can you **suspend** something that is **scrunched**?

Lesson 6

Mr. Bizbee and Miss Doolittle

Vocabulary

tidy Something that is tidy is very neat and clean.

irk If you irk someone, you make them a little bit angry.

admire When you admire someone, you look up to them and want to be like them. When you admire something, you like looking at it.

chuckle When you chuckle, you laugh quietly.

astonished If you are astonished, something has surprised you so much that you feel shocked.

coincidence A coincidence is when two things just happen but seem like they go together.

At a Glance

STANDARDS

Vocabulary
- Discuss word meaning and develop vocabulary through meaningful experiences
- Develop vocabulary by listening to and discussing selections read aloud

Comprehension
- Use a variety of strategies to comprehend text

Writing
- Write to record ideas and reflections

LESSON RESOURCES

Read-Aloud Anthology: pp. 29–35	**Word Cards:** Lesson 6
Student Book: pp. 22–25	**Photo Cards:** 14, 18, 31–36, 52–53, 73, 139

1 Introducing the Vocabulary

Read-Aloud

Read-Aloud Anthology, pages 29–35

In *Mr. Bizbee and Miss Doolittle*, two neighbors who are very different find they have some things in common after all.

Bringing the Story to Life

Read Mr. Bizbee's dialogue in a formal tone of voice to reflect his personality. Read Miss Doolittle's dialogue in a more casual and friendly tone. As you read the narration, use your voice to reflect the mounting tension between the neighbors.

Word Watcher

Word Watcher Chart, Lesson 6 Word Cards

- Tell children that they will learn about these words throughout the week and that each time a child uses one of the words correctly in the classroom, you will place a mark next to the word.
- Give each word card to a child. Then ask children with words that begin with the letter *a* to please stand up. As children with the words *admire* and *astonished* stand, say each word and have the class repeat. Then use each word in a sentence and give the words the first tallies of the week. Follow the same procedure for the letters *c*, *i*, and *t*.

Sending the Words Home

Blackline Master—English, page 131; Spanish, page 132

Distribute the activity letter to inform parents of the vocabulary words for this week.

Research Says...

"Students learn new words better when they encounter them often and in various contexts. The more children see, hear, and work with specific words, the better they seem to learn them."

—Put Reading First

2 Using the Vocabulary

Word Snapshots

Photo Cards: 14, 18, 31–36, 52–53, 73, 139

Hold up the card pairs and ask children the following questions. Ask children to explain each of their choices.

tidy (31 and 53) Which card shows a tidy room?

irk (32 and 14) Which card shows a person irking another person?

admire (33 and 18) Which card shows someone admiring another person?

chuckle (34 and 52) Which card shows people chuckling?

astonished (35 and 73) Which card shows a boy who is astonished?

coincidence (36 and 139) Which card shows a coincidence?

ELL SUPPORT

Show children each photo card, saying the word and the sentence on the back. Act out the different words and have children name which vocabulary word you are acting out. For example, for *tidy* show children that you are making your desk neat and clean.

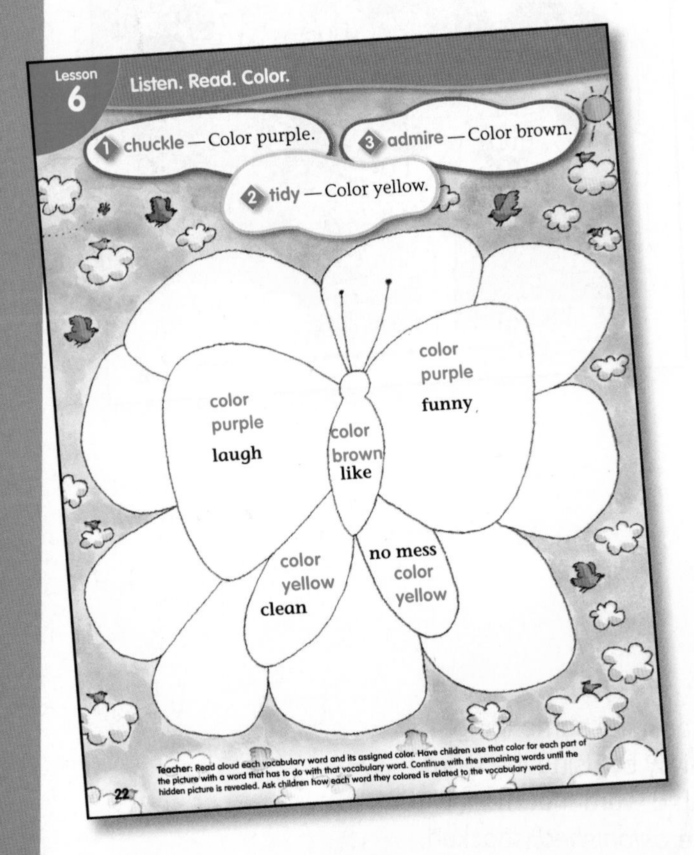

Word Chat

Student Book, page 22

Guide children as they complete the Student Book activity. Then use children's responses and the prompts below to discuss each word.

chuckle Tell children that you will describe a situation and if they think they would chuckle in that situation, they should say "chuckle" and then chuckle. If not, they should say nothing.

- Your friend forgets your birthday.
- Your friend breaks your toy.
- Your friend tells a joke.

tidy Tell children that you will describe a place and if they think you are describing a tidy place, they should say "tidy." If not, they should say nothing.

- Jan's family just moved into their house. There were boxes and furniture everywhere, and everything was dusty.
- Jan made her bed and dusted her furniture. She put her games and toys away neatly and straightened the books on her shelves.
- Jan and her brother baked a cake. There was flour on the walls and counters. When they looked up, they saw frosting on the ceiling!

admire Tell children that you will name some people and things and if they admire the person or thing, they should say "admire." If not, they should say nothing.

- Mom
- jewelry
- trucks

3 Using the Vocabulary

Word Chat

Student Book, page 23

Guide children as they complete the Student Book activity. Then use children's responses and the prompts below to discuss each word.

astonished If you were astonished, would you be very surprised or very sleepy? Explain.

coincidence Which would be a coincidence, two neighbors that had the same last name or two sisters that had the same last name? Why is that?

irk If someone irks you, would you say "thank you" or "Please stop it!"? Explain.

Continue the discussion with the remaining words from the lesson.

tidy If you kept your room tidy, would your mother be angry or happy? Why?

admire Would you admire a person if they took something that belonged to you? Why or why not?

chuckle Would you chuckle if your puppy did a trick or if he were sick? Explain your answer.

WORD CHALLENGE

Challenge children to think of words that mean almost the same thing as some of the words in this lesson. Model the activity by using the word ***astonished*** in a sentence and then replacing it with a word that means nearly the same thing. You could say that you were *astonished* (shocked, amazed) when there was a snowstorm in the spring.

- Ask children to think of words that mean almost the same thing as ***tidy*** *(clean, neat)* and make up sentences.
- Ask children to think of words that mean almost the same thing as ***chuckle*** *(laugh, giggle)* and make up sentences.

4 Using the Vocabulary

Word Organizers

Help your class complete the graphic organizers below. You may draw them on the board or on chart paper, or use the organizers in the back of this book to make transparencies.

Write the vocabulary word in the blue box.

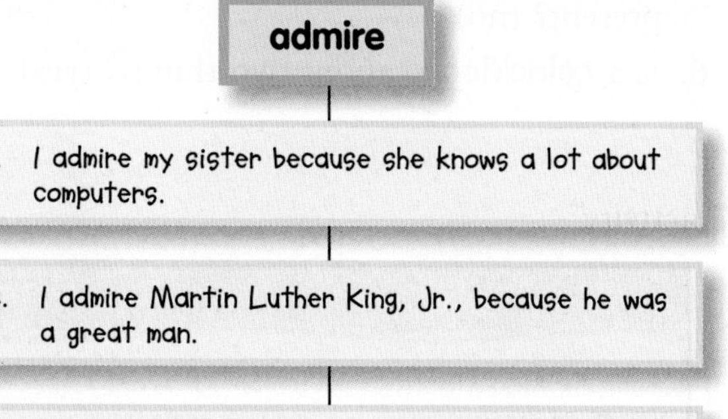

Ask children to make up sentences about someone or something they admire and tell why. You may want to model a sentence for them. Record their sentences.

Ask children what they can do so that people will admire them.

Write the vocabulary word in the center.

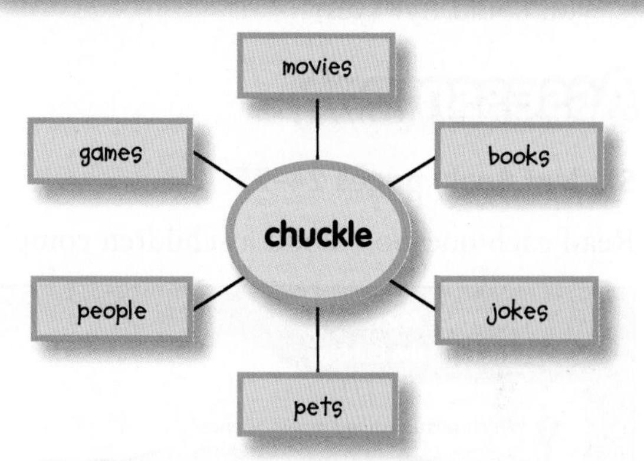

Ask children to think of times when they chuckle. Ask them what things make them chuckle. Record their answers.

Have children tell about the last time they chuckled.

Your Turn to Write

Encourage children to relate the words to their own experiences. Discuss a few of the prompts below to prepare children for writing. Have children write about one of the prompts in their journals or on a separate piece of paper.

tidy What things do you do to help keep our classroom tidy? What things do you do to help keep your home tidy? Do you like a room that is tidy?

irk Have you ever irked someone? What did you do to bother them? Has someone ever irked you?

admire What are some things about you that other people admire? Tell about something a friend has done that you admire.

chuckle Can you think of a joke or a funny story that makes you chuckle? Do you know someone who often makes you chuckle? Describe what that person is like.

astonished Describe how your face looks when you are astonished. Has anything ever happened that astonished you? Describe what happened and tell how it made you feel.

coincidence What makes a coincidence so special? Has a coincidence ever happened to you or someone you know? Tell what happened and how you or the other person felt about it.

5 Assessing the Vocabulary

Review

Blackline Master, page 169

Read the following questions aloud and have children circle *yes* or *no*.

1. Might you be **astonished** if you found out you could fly? (yes)
2. Would you **admire** someone who you thought was mean? (no)
3. Might you **chuckle** if you watched a funny movie? (yes)
4. Should everyone help keep our classroom **tidy**? (yes)
5. Would someone **irk** you if they bought you a present? (no)
6. Is a **coincidence** about two things? (yes)

Assessment

Student Book, pages 24–25

Read each question aloud as children complete the activity.

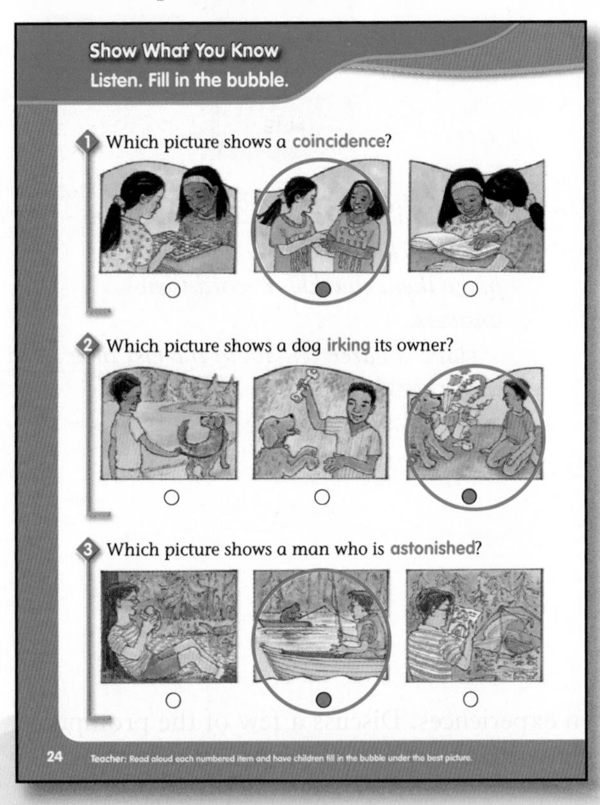
Show What You Know
Listen. Fill in the bubble.

1 Which picture shows a coincidence?

2 Which picture shows a dog irking its owner?

3 Which picture shows a man who is astonished?

24 Teacher: Read aloud each numbered item and have children fill in the bubble under the best picture.

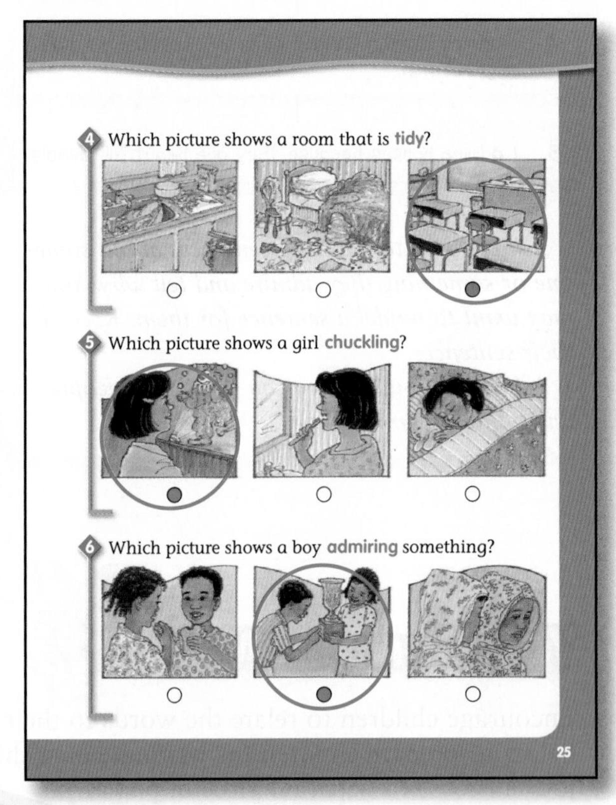
4 Which picture shows a room that is tidy?

5 Which picture shows a girl chuckling?

6 Which picture shows a boy admiring something?

25

Cumulative Review

Ask the first question and model how you might arrive at an answer. Then have children answer the remaining questions and explain their answers.

Lesson 5	Lesson 6	
spangled	admire	Why might you **admire** a **spangled** jacket?
ridiculous	coincidence	Do you think a **coincidence** is **ridiculous**?
suspend	chuckle	Would you **chuckle** if clowns were **suspended** from the ceiling?
pride	tidy	Do you feel **pride** when you keep your room **tidy**?
serenade	irk	Would it **irk** you to be **serenaded** when you were trying to read?
perform	astonished	Would you be **astonished** to see your best friend **perform** on TV?

Lesson 7

One Small Garden

Vocabulary

survive To survive is to continue to live, even through difficult times and events.

shelter To shelter something is to keep it from getting hurt by the sun or the weather.

disturb When you disturb someone or something, you bother or upset it in some way.

destroy To destroy something is to break or hurt it so badly that it can't be fixed.

observe To observe something is to watch it very closely.

dwell If you dwell somewhere, you live there.

At a Glance

STANDARDS

Vocabulary
- Use context to find the meaning of unknown words
- Speak to express the mood of a story by using a variety of words

Comprehension
- Establish purposes for reading or listening (to be informed)

Writing
- Record or dictate knowledge of a topic in various ways

LESSON RESOURCES

Read-Aloud Anthology: pp. 36–43
Student Book: pp. 26–29
Word Cards: Lesson 7
Photo Cards: 37–42

1 Introducing the Vocabulary

Read-Aloud

Read-Aloud Anthology, pages 36–43

This excerpt from the nonfiction story *One Small Garden* solves a mystery about a family of raccoons that comes and goes in a garden.

Bringing the Story to Life

Pause frequently to be sure children understand what is happening. As you read, sketch the garage roof, the tree, and the fence on the board. Use a raccoon cutout to show how the raccoons moved.

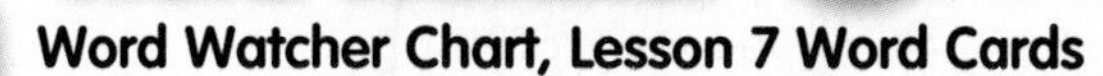

Word Watcher

Word Watcher Chart, Lesson 7 Word Cards

- Tell children that they will learn about these words throughout the week and that each time a child uses one of the words correctly in the classroom, you will place a mark next to the word.
- Draw a tree on the board and fasten the cards to the tree's branches. Have children pluck the words one by one and bring them to you. Have children say each word with you. Use it in a sentence and place the first tally of the week by the word.

Sending the Words Home

Blackline Master—English, page 133; Spanish, page 134

Distribute the activity letter to inform parents of the vocabulary words for this week.

Research Says...

"Vocabulary expands when children have numerous opportunities to encounter new words and examples...in rich contextual settings."

—*The Reading Teacher*, William H. Rupley, *et al.*

2 Using the Vocabulary

Word Snapshots

Photo Cards: 37–42

Read the sentence on the back of each card as you give photo cards to six children. Then say the sentences below, which use each word in a different context. For each sentence, have the child with that card hold it up and repeat the word.

survive Living things need food and water to survive.

shelter A large umbrella sheltered the children from the rain.

disturb A loud noise can disturb a baby's nap.

destroy The strong wind destroyed the kite.

observe The boy sat at the pond to observe the frog.

dwell People need a safe place to dwell.

ELL SUPPORT

Hold up one photo card at a time. Pronounce each vocabulary word and have children say the word with you. Place the photos along the board ledge. Say a vocabulary word and a sentence using the word. Have children find the photo for each word and repeat each word with you.

Word Chat

Student Book, page 26

Guide children as they complete the Student Book activity. Then use children's responses and the prompts below to discuss each word.

Divide the class into two groups. Assign the first word to one group and the second word to the other. Explain that you will say a sentence with a missing word, and the group that has the word that fits the sentence should say their word aloud.

survive/disturb

- My dad might get mad if we ______ him. (disturb)
- The tree broke, but the birds will ______ . (survive)
- I knocked over the fishbowl, but the goldfish will ______ . (survive)
- Mother is reading a book. If we turn on the TV, we will ______ her. (disturb)

shelter/destroy

- If rain falls on a book, it can ______ the book. (destroy)
- A shady tree can ______ us from the sun. (shelter)
- If you stomp on the flowers, you will ______ them. (destroy)
- In the rain, an umbrella will ______ us. (shelter)

Word Chat

Student Book, page 27

Guide children as they complete the Student Book activity. Then use children's responses and the prompts below to discuss each word.

After children complete the pages, briefly remind them of all the words in this lesson. (You might want to refer to the Word Watcher Chart or display the corresponding photo cards.) Explain that you are going to say a word or a phrase and that children should say the vocabulary word that comes to mind. After each response, have children give reasons for their choice.

a loud crashing noise at night **(disturb)**

an apartment building **(dwell)**

microscope **(observe)**

Continue the discussion with the remaining words from the lesson.

a roof **(shelter)**

being rescued from the ocean **(survive)**

smash **(destroy)**

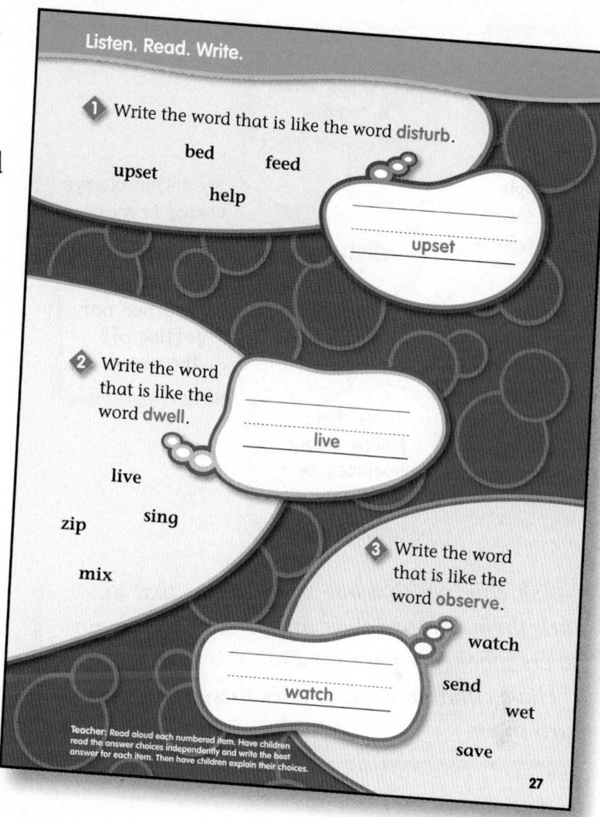

WORD CHALLENGE

Point out that the narrator of the story discovered that the raccoons dwelled in the hollow tree. The word *dwell* means "to live in a place." Explain that if children know the meaning of the word *dwell*, they can use it to figure out the meaning of some other words that are made from the word *dwell*. Ask the following questions.

- If I say the tree was a **dwelling** for the raccoons, what is a **dwelling**? (a house, a place to live)
- If I say that bats are cave **dwellers**, what is a **dweller**? (a person or thing that lives in a place)

Ask children to play "What Dweller Dwells in This Dwelling?" Name a dwelling and ask what dweller might dwell there.

- cave (a bear, a bat, a fox)
- nest (a bird, a rabbit)
- a hole (a rabbit, a prairie dog, a ground squirrel)

4 Using the Vocabulary

Word Organizers

Help your class complete the graphic organizers below. You may draw them on the board or on chart paper, or use the organizers in the back of this book to make transparencies.

Write the vocabulary word in the center.

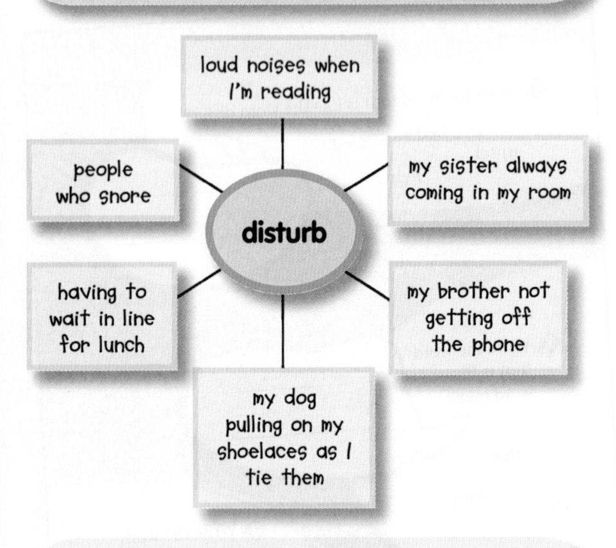

Ask children to name some things that disturb them. Record their answers, modeling answers whenever necessary.
Have children explain why these things disturb them.

Write the words shown in blue boxes to begin.

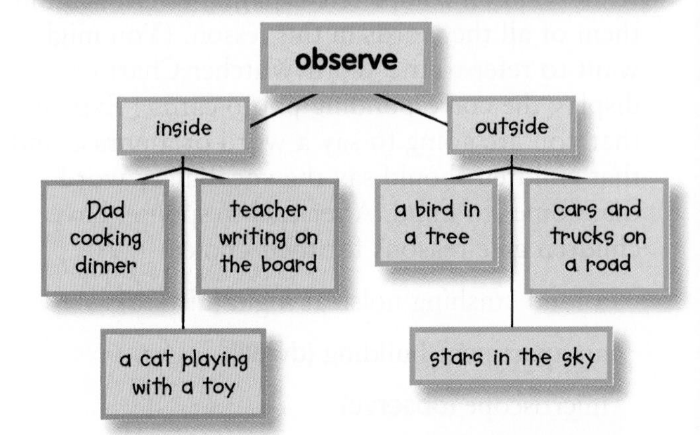

Ask children to name some things that they might observe inside. Record their answers, modeling sample answers if needed.

Ask children to name some things that they might observe outside. Record their answers, modeling sample answers if needed.

Ask how observing something might be different from just looking at it.

Your Turn to Write

Encourage children to relate the words to their own experiences. Discuss a few of the prompts below to prepare children for writing. Have children write about one of the prompts in their journals or on a separate piece of paper.

survive Have you ever survived something difficult in your life? What did you do?

shelter When are some times when you have needed to be sheltered? How would you shelter your pet from a storm?

disturb Has someone ever disturbed you while you were watching your favorite program? What do you do when someone disturbs you? What do you do that might disturb a friend?

destroy Have you ever accidentally destroyed something? What can you do to protect something you care about from being destroyed?

observe Have you ever observed people walking by on the street? What things do you like to observe when you are riding in a car?

dwell If you could dwell in a special place, where would you go? Who would dwell there with you?

5 Assessing the Vocabulary

Review

Blackline Master, page 169

Read the following questions aloud and have children circle *yes* or *no*.

1. Might a grizzly bear **dwell** under your bed? (no)
2. Can you fix a toy that is **destroyed**? (no)
3. Does food help you **survive**? (yes)
4. Can you **observe** flowers in a garden? (yes)
5. Is a car **sheltered** in a garage? (yes)
6. Does a rock in your shoe **disturb** you? (yes)

Assessment

Student Book, pages 28–29

Read each question aloud as children complete the activity.

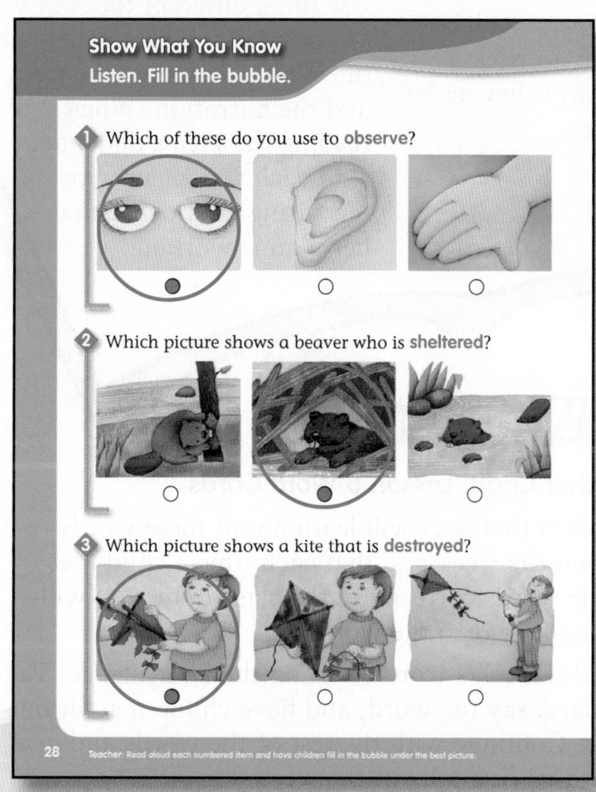

Cumulative Review

Ask the first question and model how you might arrive at an answer. Then have children answer the remaining questions and explain their answers.

Lesson 6	Lesson 7	
tidy	dwell	Do you like to **dwell** in a **tidy** place?
irk	destroy	Would it **irk** you if someone **destroyed** your painting?
chuckle	disturb	Would you **chuckle** if someone **disturbed** your dinner?
admire	observe	Can you **observe** something that you **admire**?
astonished	survive	Would you be **astonished** if a toy **survived** the washing machine?
coincidence	shelter	Would it be a **coincidence** if you ran into a friend looking for **shelter** from the rain?

Lesson 8

The Hen and the Apple Tree

Vocabulary

certain If you are certain about something, you strongly believe that it is true.

quiver To quiver means to shake a tiny bit.

outsmart When you outsmart someone, you trick them or beat them by doing something clever.

disguise A disguise is something you wear to make you look like someone or something else.

scrumptious Something scrumptious is so delicious that you don't want to stop eating it.

convince If you convince someone, you talk them into believing something or doing something.

At a Glance

STANDARDS

Vocabulary
- Use visual references to build upon word meaning
- Listen to imaginative texts in order to respond to vivid language

Comprehension
- Make and explain inferences

Writing
- Write to discover, develop, and refine ideas

LESSON RESOURCES

Read-Aloud Anthology: pp. 44–48

Student Book: pp. 30–33

Word Cards: Lesson 8

Photo Cards: 43–48, 61, 82, 100, 110, 127, 132

1 Introducing the Vocabulary

Read-Aloud

Read-Aloud Anthology, pages 44–48

In the fable *The Hen and the Apple Tree*, a wolf tries unsuccessfully to trick a clever hen into believing he is an apple tree.

Bringing the Story to Life

Use three different tones of voice as you read the Hen's dialogue, the Wolf's dialogue (the tree), and the narration. When reading the Hen's dialogue, read each statement with increasing confidence that her plan is working.

Word Watcher

Word Watcher Chart, Lesson 8 Word Cards

- Tell children that they will learn about these words throughout the week and that each time a child uses one of the words correctly in the classroom, you will place a mark next to the word.
- Line up this week's word cards on the board ledge. Take a word card, say the word, and have children act it out with you. Continue with the rest of the words and give each word its first tally of the week.

Sending the Words Home

Blackline Master—English, page 135; Spanish, page 136

Distribute the activity letter to inform parents of the vocabulary words for this week.

Research Says...

"Children learn words best when they are provided with instruction over an extended period of time and when that instruction has them work actively with the words."

—Put Reading First

2 Using the Vocabulary

Word Snapshots

Photo Cards: 43–48, 61, 82, 100, 110, 127, 132

Hold up each card pair and read the sentence on the back of the photo card from this lesson. Ask children to choose which card the sentence represents and to explain their choice.

certain (43 and 132)
quiver (44 and 110)
outsmart (45 and 100)
disguise (46 and 127)
scrumptious (47 and 61)
convince (48 and 82)

ELL SUPPORT

Show children one photo card at a time. Say each word and have children repeat it. Then ask a yes/no question for each word. For example, for *disguise* ask, *Is the boy wearing a disguise?*

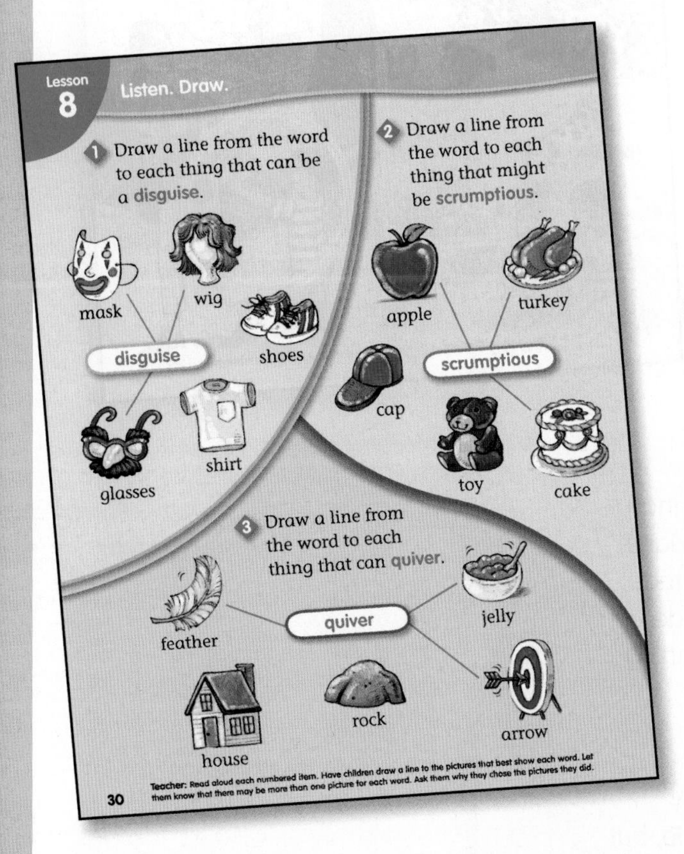
Lesson 8

Listen. Draw.

1 Draw a line from the word to each thing that can be a disguise.

mask, wig, shoes, glasses, shirt — disguise

2 Draw a line from the word to each thing that might be scrumptious.

apple, turkey, cap, toy, cake — scrumptious

3 Draw a line from the word to each thing that can quiver.

feather, jelly, house, rock, arrow — quiver

Teacher: Read aloud each numbered item. Have children draw a line to the pictures that best show each word. Let them know that there may be more than one picture for each word. Ask them why they chose the pictures they did.

30

quiver Tell children that you will say some things and if they think a thing can quiver, they should shake a little bit and say "quiver." If not, they should say nothing.

- a desk
- a book
- a flower

Word Chat

Student Book, page 30

Guide children as they complete the Student Book activity. Then use children's responses and the prompts below to discuss each word.

disguise Tell children that you will describe a girl and if they think the girl is wearing a disguise, they should say "disguise." If not, they should say nothing.

- A girl is wearing jeans and a sweater.
- A girl is wearing a pair of large sunglasses and a wig.
- A girl is wearing a necklace.

scrumptious Tell children that you will say some things and if they think a thing is scrumptious, they should lick their lips and say "Yum! Scrumptious!" If not, they should say nothing.

- pie with ice cream on top
- a cute puppy
- a new bike

3 Using the Vocabulary

Word Chat

Student Book, page 31

Guide children as they complete the Student Book activity. Then use children's responses and the prompts below to discuss each word.

certain Does *certain* mean that you don't know the answer at all? Why or why not?

convince Does *convince* mean that you make someone laugh really hard? Explain your answer.

outsmart Does *outsmart* mean that you explain something carefully with a lot of details? Why or why not?

Continue the discussion with the remaining words from the lesson.

quiver Does *quiver* mean that someone stands very still? Why is that?

disguise Is a disguise something you wear to stay warm? Explain your answer.

scrumptious Does *scrumptious* mean that something is very cold? Explain.

WORD CHALLENGE

Explain to children that the word *certain* has more than one meaning. They have already learned that it means "strongly believing that something is true." Explain that another meaning is "some, but not all." Then provide the following prompts and ask children which meaning *certain* has in each prompt.

- I'm **certain** that it's going to rain today. (strongly believing that something is true)
- **Certain** plants need a lot of water to grow. (some, but not all)
- Tom was **certain** about the answer. (strongly believing that something is true)
- Lisa will take **certain** clothes on her vacation. (some, but not all)

4 Using the Vocabulary

Word Organizers

Help your class complete the graphic organizers below. You may draw them on the board or on chart paper, or use the organizers in the back of this book to make transparencies.

Write the vocabulary word in the center.

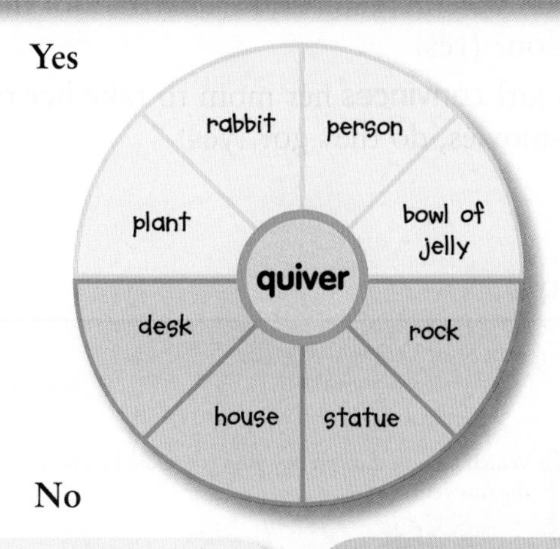

Ask children to name things that can quiver. Record their answers in the top half of the circle. Model sample answers as necessary.

Ask children to tell about a time when they saw something quiver.

Have children name objects that can't quiver. Record their answers on the bottom half of the circle.

Ask children to explain why these things can't quiver.

Write the vocabulary word in the diamond.

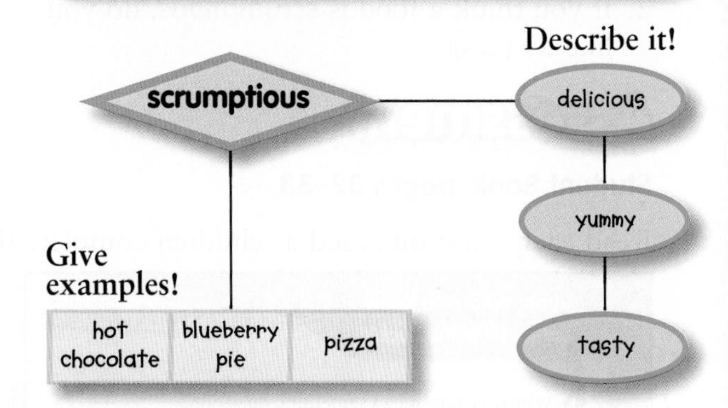

Ask children to think of other words to describe scrumptious. *Use sample answers as models, and record their answers.*

Ask children to name foods they think are scrumptious and record their answers. Model sample answers if needed.

Have children explain what makes these foods scrumptious.

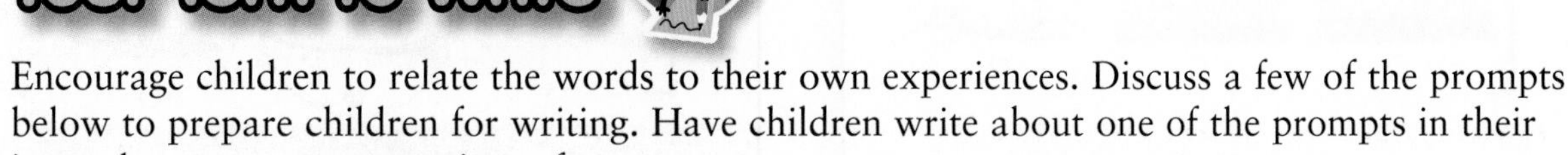

Encourage children to relate the words to their own experiences. Discuss a few of the prompts below to prepare children for writing. Have children write about one of the prompts in their journals or on a separate piece of paper.

certain Tell me something that you are certain about. What makes you so sure that it is true? Tell about a time when you felt certain.

quiver What would make a tree quiver? Show me what a quivering tree would look like. What other things can quiver?

outsmart Tell about a time when you outsmarted someone. Tell about a time when someone outsmarted you. What did that person do and how did it feel?

disguise Why would someone wear a disguise? Have you ever worn a disguise? Describe what it looked like.

scrumptious Name a food that you think is scrumptious. What makes the food scrumptious? How often do you eat that food?

convince Tell about a time when you tried to convince someone to do something or to go somewhere. Did you convince them? Has anyone ever tried to convince you to do something?

5 Assessing the Vocabulary

Review

Blackline Master, page 169

Read the following questions aloud and have children circle *yes* or *no*.

1. Can a large rock **quiver**? (no)
2. If you think a food is **scrumptious**, do you like it? (yes)
3. Are most people **certain** about how old they are? (yes)
4. Do you wear a **disguise** when you go to school? (no)
5. If you **outsmart** someone, do you fool the person? (yes)
6. If a girl **convinces** her mom to take her to the movies, do they go? (yes)

Assessment

Student Book, pages 32–33

Read each question aloud as children complete the activity.

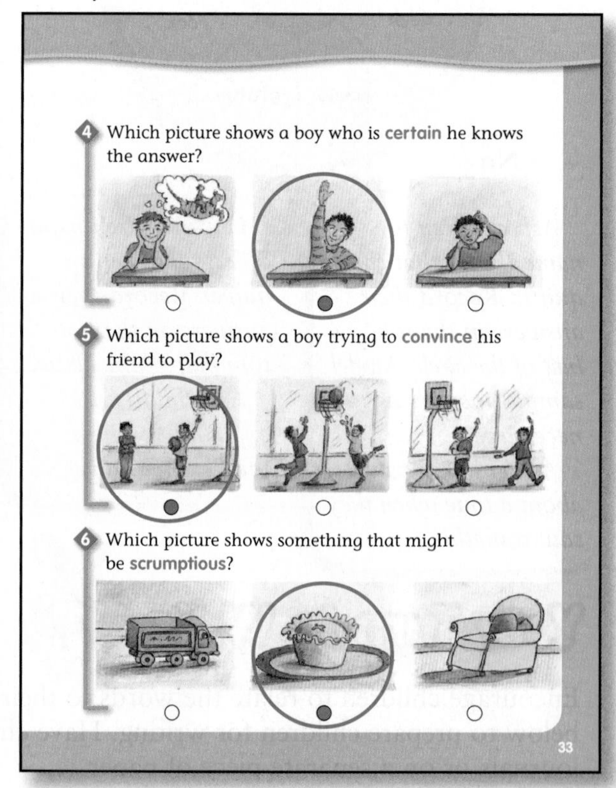

Cumulative Review

Ask the first question and model how you might arrive at an answer. Then have children answer the remaining questions and explain their answers.

Lesson 7	Lesson 8	
disturb	certain	Are you **certain** that you don't **disturb** others at the movies?
observe	disguise	Why might you **observe** a person who was wearing a **disguise**?
survive	outsmart	Might a mouse **survive** by **outsmarting** a cat?
destroy	scrumptious	Would you **destroy** a **scrumptious** cake?
dwell	quiver	Can a bird **dwell** in a tree that **quivers**?
shelter	convince	Could someone **convince** you to **shelter** a lion?

Spaghetti! Spaghetti!

Vocabulary

sprinkle When you sprinkle something, you scatter tiny pieces of it over something else.

mound A mound of something is a big, round pile.

squiggle A squiggle is a line that bends and curves.

gobble When you gobble food, you eat it quickly and greedily.

sloppy If something is sloppy, it is messy and careless.

tribute A tribute is something you say or do to show how important you think someone or something is.

At a Glance

STANDARDS

Vocabulary
- Develop vocabulary by listening to and discussing selections read aloud
- Identify words that name persons, places, or things, and words that name actions

Comprehension
- Distinguish between a story and a poem

Writing
- Write in different forms for different purposes

LESSON RESOURCES

Read-Aloud Anthology: pp. 49–52
Student Book: pp. 34–37
Word Cards: Lesson 9
Photo Cards: 31, 49–54, 70, 72, 99, 113, 134

1 Introducing the Vocabulary

Read-Aloud

Read-Aloud Anthology, pages 49–52

In the poem "Spaghetti! Spaghetti!" a boy tells what he loves so much about his favorite food—spaghetti!

Bringing the Poem to Life

Read the poem with exaggerated expression. Emphasize rhyming words and words like *slurpy, slishy,* and *sloshy*. When you read the phrase "Spaghetti! Spaghetti!" have children shout the words with you.

Word Watcher

Word Watcher Chart, Lesson 9 Word Cards

- Tell children that they will learn about these words throughout the week and that each time a child uses one of the words correctly in the classroom, you will place a mark next to the word.
- Line up the word cards on the board ledge. Read each word aloud and have children repeat it. Then point to each card and say a sentence that uses that word such as, *I like to* sprinkle *raisins on my cereal.* Continue with the other words and give each word its first tally of the week.

Sending the Words Home

Blackline Master—English, page 137; Spanish, page 138

Distribute the activity letter to inform parents of the vocabulary words for this week.

Research Says...

"Because vocabulary instruction is an ongoing process, a teacher needs to be able to vary the delivery of that instruction. This involves using different approaches during the school year."

—*Vocabulary Development,* Steven A. Stahl

2 Using the Vocabulary

Word Snapshots

Photo Cards: 31, 49–54, 70, 72, 99, 113, 134

Hold up the card pairs and ask children the following questions. After each question, ask children to explain their choices.

sprinkle (49 and 113)
Which card shows someone sprinkling something?

mound (50 and 70)
Which card shows a mound?

squiggle (51 and 134)
Which card shows a squiggle?

gobble (52 and 99)
Which card shows someone gobbling food?

sloppy (53 and 31)
Which card shows a room that looks sloppy?

tribute (54 and 72)
Which card shows a tribute?

ELL SUPPORT

Discuss the photo cards and how the words relate to the poem. Hold up each photo card. Have children talk about how each photo shows what each word means.

Lesson 9

Listen. Read. Circle.

squiggle
sloppy
mound

1 Joe wanted to help out in the yard.
He began to rake the leaves.
He raked all morning.
By noon, the yard was clean.
All the leaves had been raked into a big, round pile.

sprinkle
gobble
tribute

2 Ann and Mary love the chicken soup that Mom cooks.
This morning they smelled the soup when they woke up.
They waited and waited for the soup to be ready.
Finally, they heard Mom say, "Come and eat!"
Ann and Mary ran to the table.
They ate all the soup up right away!

Teacher: For each story, read aloud the vocabulary words and then have children read the story independently. Have children circle the vocabulary word that best describes the story. Ask children why the word they chose was the best one for each story.

34

tribute Tell children that you will describe some situations and if they think someone or something is being given a tribute, they should salute you and say "tribute." If not, they should say nothing.

- Max wrote a beautiful song to honor the firefighters.
- The class wrote a poem for the teacher.
- My neighbor cut down her rose bush.

Word Chat

Student Book, page 34

Guide children as they complete the Student Book activity. Then use children's responses and the prompts below to discuss each word.

mound Tell children that you will describe different situations and if they think you are describing a mound, they should move their arms to look like they are making a mound while they say "mound." If not, they should say nothing.

- I poured a glass of water on the floor.
- The bulldozer pushed a bunch of dirt together into one big pile.
- She plopped ten, huge spoonfuls of jelly into a clear bowl.

gobble Tell children that you will describe some foods and if they think they would want to gobble that food, they should smack their lips and say "gobble." If not, they should say nothing.

- warm apple pie
- scrambled rotten eggs
- roast chicken with gravy

Word Chat

Student Book, page 35

Guide children as they complete the Student Book activity. Then use children's responses and the prompts below to discuss each word.

tribute Who would you give a tribute to, a woman who robbed a bank or a woman who caught a bank robber? Why?

sprinkle Which sprinkles from the sky, rain drops or rainbows? Why is that?

squiggle If you walk in a squiggle, are you walking straight toward where you are going or are you walking in a bending and curving path? Explain.

sloppy If you were sloppy, would the front of your shirt be clean and tucked in or would it be covered with messy food stains? Why?

Continue the discussion with the remaining words from the lesson.

mound Which would you stand on to be taller, a mound or the flat ground? Explain why you say that.

gobble When would you gobble your food, when you had plenty of time to eat or when you were in a hurry? Why?

WORD CHALLENGE

Review with children the meaning of the word *sloppy*. Use the following prompts to help children brainstorm words that mean the opposite. Point out that the word *sloppy* has several words with an opposite meaning.

- After I played in the slimy pond, I looked **sloppy**. But after I took a bath, I looked ______ . (clean)
- After we spilled juice on the kitchen floor, it looked **sloppy**. But after we mopped the juice up, the floor looked ______ . (neat, dry)

4 Using the Vocabulary

Word Organizers

Help your class complete the graphic organizers below. You may draw them on the board or on chart paper, or use the organizers in the back of this book to make transparencies.

Write the vocabulary word in the center.

Yes

noodle
curly hair
string
shoelace
squiggle
soccer ball
baseball hat
apple
ruler

No

Ask children to name things that could be squiggle-shaped. Model sample answers as needed and record their answers in the top half of the circle.

Ask children why these objects can look like squiggles.

Ask children to name things that could not be squiggle-shaped. Record their answers in the bottom half of the circle, providing sample answers if needed.

Ask children why these objects cannot look like squiggles.

Write the words shown in blue boxes to begin.

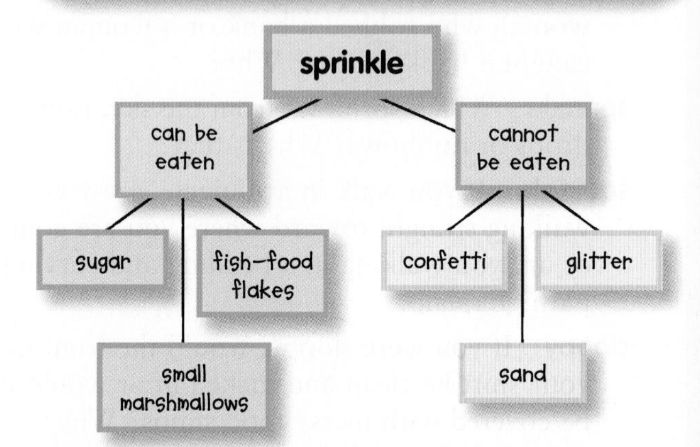

Ask children to name things that can be sprinkled and eaten. Record their answers, modeling sample answers as needed.

Ask children to name things that can be sprinkled but cannot be eaten. Offer sample answers if necessary, and record appropriate answers.

Ask children to explain what all the answers recorded have in common and why they can be sprinkled.

Your Turn to Write

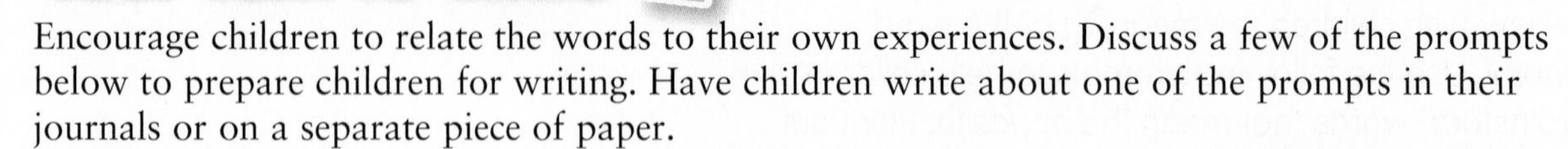

Encourage children to relate the words to their own experiences. Discuss a few of the prompts below to prepare children for writing. Have children write about one of the prompts in their journals or on a separate piece of paper.

sprinkle What things do you sprinkle on food? What things would you sprinkle if you were making something pretty?

mound Have you ever had a mound of food on your plate? Can you think of some animals that build mounds?

squiggle Do you like to draw or paint squiggles? How is a squiggle different from a straight line? Can you find a squiggle in our classroom?

gobble Do you ever gobble food? How do you feel afterwards? What animals gobble their food?

sloppy Are there times when you look sloppy? Would you describe your room as sloppy?

tribute What are different ways to make a tribute? Who would you like to write a tribute to? What makes that person special?

5 Assessing the Vocabulary

Review

Blackline Master, page 169

Read the following questions aloud and have children circle *yes* or *no*.

1. Might you look **sloppy** after painting? (yes)
2. Would you want to give a **tribute** to a mean person? (no)
3. Can a cloud **sprinkle** rain? (yes)
4. Is a **mound** flat? (no)
5. If you really like what you're eating, might you **gobble** it? (yes)
6. Is a road that bends and curves shaped like a **squiggle**? (yes)

Assessment

Student Book, pages 36–37

Read each question aloud as children complete the activity.

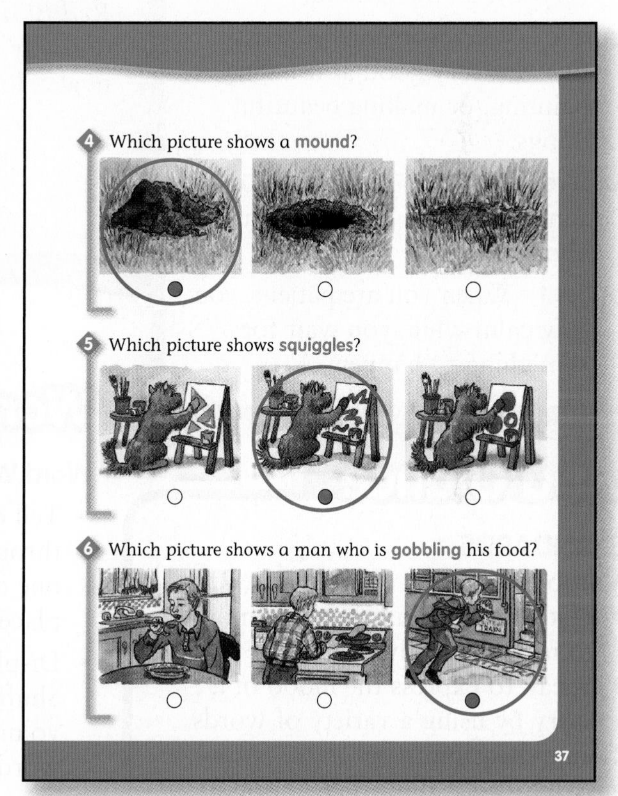

Cumulative Review

Ask the first question and model how you might arrive at an answer. Then have children answer the remaining questions and explain their answers.

Lesson 8	Lesson 9	
certain	sprinkle	Might you be **certain** you want to **sprinkle** nuts on your ice cream?
quiver	mound	Can a **mound** of spaghetti **quiver**?
outsmart	squiggle	Can you **outsmart** someone by walking in a **squiggle**?
scrumptious	gobble	If something tastes **scrumptious**, do you **gobble** it?
disguise	sloppy	Does being **sloppy** make a good **disguise**?
convince	tribute	Can a **tribute convince** people that something is important?

Lesson 10

The Lion and the Little Red Bird

Vocabulary

wander When you wander, you walk around as if you had no special place to go.

nibble When you nibble food, you eat it in tiny bites.

crouch When you crouch, you bend your knees and get down very low to the ground.

artistic When someone is artistic, they are very good at drawing, painting, or making beautiful things.

inquire When you inquire about something, you ask questions about it.

patient When you are patient, you stay calm while you wait for something to happen.

At a Glance

STANDARDS

Vocabulary
- Listen to imaginative texts in order to respond to vivid language
- Speak to express the mood of a story by using a variety of words

Comprehension
- Retell or act out order of important events in stories

Writing
- Compose original texts

LESSON RESOURCES

Read-Aloud Anthology: pp. 53–58

Student Book: pp. 38–41

Word Cards: Lesson 10

Photo Cards: 55–60

1 Introducing the Vocabulary

Read-Aloud

Read-Aloud Anthology, pages 53–58

In *The Lion and the Little Red Bird*, a little bird finds out why a lion's tail is a new color each day.

Bringing the Story to Life

Place emphasis on the color words that foreshadow the upcoming color of the lion's tail. Before revealing each new color of the lion's tail, pause to build suspense. Then announce the color with a flourish.

Word Watcher

Word Watcher Chart, Lesson 10 Word Cards

- Tell children that they will learn about these words throughout the week and that each time a child uses one of the words correctly in the classroom, you will place a mark next to the word.
- Display word cards one at a time and say each word. Shuffle the cards and place them facedown in a pile. Ask volunteers to draw a card and give it to you. Say the word, use it in a sentence, and make a tally mark.

Sending the Words Home

Blackline Master—English, page 139; Spanish, page 140

Distribute the activity letter to inform parents of the vocabulary words for this week.

Research Says...

"...with interactive reading, vocabulary is reinforced through providing children with multiple opportunities to interact with new vocabulary words."

—"Review of the Reading Research Literature Since the National Reading Panel Report," Jennifer Watts and Bill Wilkinson

2 Using the Vocabulary

Word Snapshots

Photo Cards: 55–60

Display the photo cards and ask pairs of children to make up a short story about a card. Provide the following story starters.

wander My uncle likes to wander through the fields near his house, because....

nibble My pet rat likes to nibble on lettuce, because....

crouch Sam had to crouch down low to draw on the sidewalk. Then....

artistic Amy is very artistic. She paints beautiful pictures of flowers and....

inquire Malika raised her hand to inquire about where to put her work and then....

patient Everyone was patient waiting for water because....

ELL SUPPORT

Hold up the photo card for each vocabulary word as you say that word and provide a facial expression or pantomime clue. Then say each word again in random order. Have children repeat the word and provide the facial expression or pantomime connected with the word's meaning.

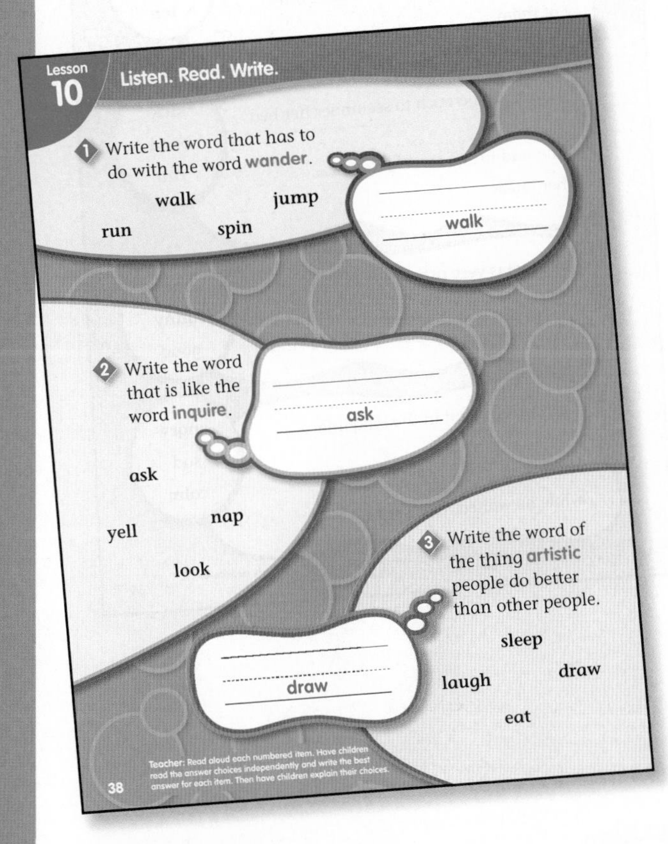

artistic/patient

- A person who carves a beautiful statue out of stone is ______ . (artistic)
- If you can draw a picture that looks like someone, you are ______ . (artistic)
- When you wait two hours for a cake to bake, you are ______ . (patient)
- If you can easily wait for the chocolate chip cookies to cool down before eating them, you are ______ . (patient)

Word Chat

Student Book, page 38

Guide children as they complete the Student Book activity. Then use children's responses and the prompts below to discuss each word.

Divide the class into two groups. Assign the first word to one group and the second word to the other. Explain that you will say a sentence with a missing word, and the group that has the word that fits the sentence should say their word aloud.

wander/inquire

- Someone who is in no rush might ______ . (wander)
- If you get lost, you can find a police officer and ______ . (inquire)
- When you need information, you can ______ . (inquire)
- When you're in a hurry, it's not a good idea to ______ . (wander)

3 Using the Vocabulary

Word Chat

Student Book, page 39

Guide children as they complete the Student Book activity. Then use children's responses and the prompts below to discuss each word.

nibble Does nibble mean that you take giant bites? Why or why not?

crouch Does crouch mean that you jump over something? Explain your answer.

artistic Are paintings in a museum painted by someone who is artistic? Why or why not?

patient Does patient mean that someone is angry? Explain what you mean.

Continue the discussion with the remaining words from the lesson.

wander Does wander mean that you jump up and down? Explain your answer.

inquire Does inquire mean that someone asks for information? Why or why not?

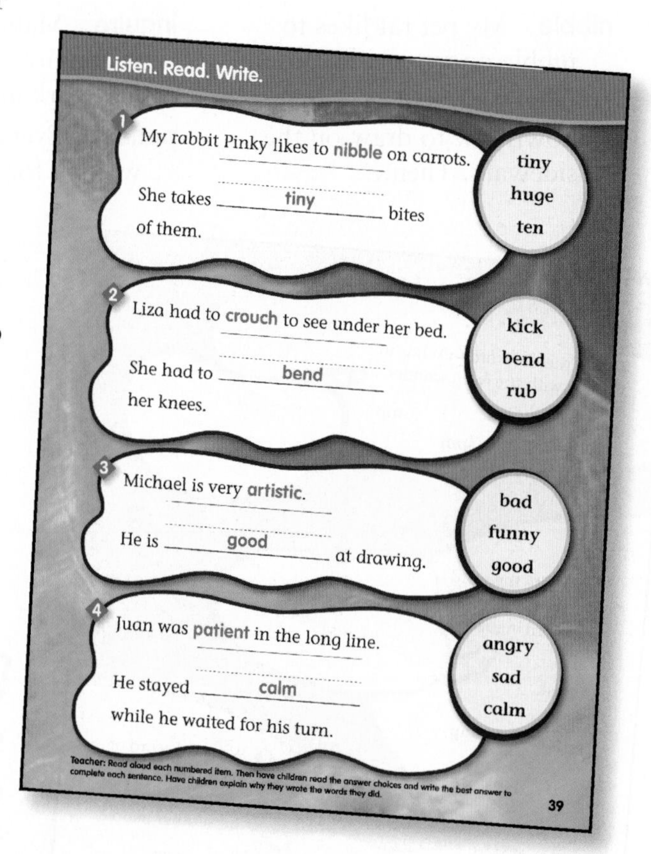
Listen. Read. Write.

1 My rabbit Pinky likes to **nibble** on carrots.
She takes tiny bites of them.
tiny / huge / ten

2 Liza had to **crouch** to see under her bed.
She had to bend her knees.
kick / bend / rub

3 Michael is very **artistic**.
He is good at drawing.
bad / funny / good

4 Juan was **patient** in the long line.
He stayed calm while he waited for his turn.
angry / sad / calm

Teacher: Read aloud each numbered item. Then have children read the answer choices and write the best answer to complete each sentence. Have children explain why they wrote the words they did.

39

WORD CHALLENGE

Tell children that sometimes a word can have more than one meaning. For example, the word *patient* can mean "to stay calm while you wait for something to happen." But *patient* can also mean "a person who is being treated by a doctor, dentist, or nurse." Read each of the following sentences aloud and ask children which of those meanings fits in each sentence.

- It was hard to be **patient** while I waited for the first day of school. (to stay calm)
- The doctor asked his **patient** how she was feeling. (person being treated)
- The nurse asked the **patients** in the waiting room to fill out some forms. (person being treated)
- I tried to be **patient** while I waited for my dentist to finish his phone call. (to stay calm)

4 Using the Vocabulary

Word Organizers

Help your class complete the graphic organizers below. You may draw them on the board or on chart paper, or use the organizers in the back of this book to make transparencies.

Write the word in the blue diamond.

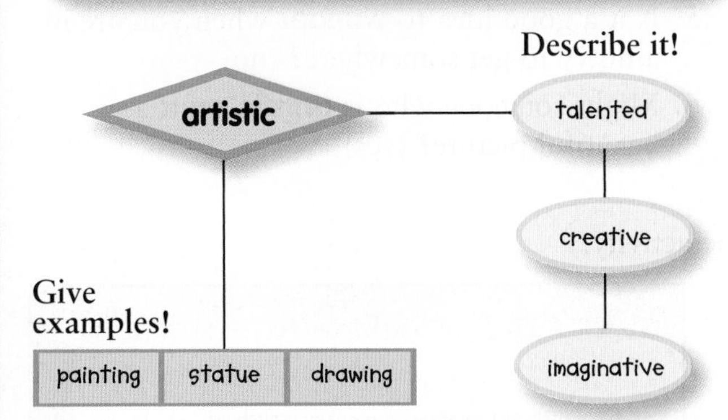

Write the vocabulary word in the center.

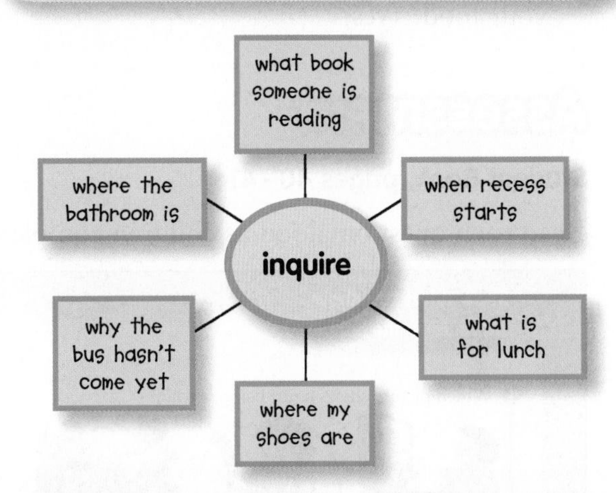

Ask children for other words to describe people who are artistic. Model sample answers if needed and record their answers.

Have children tell about someone they know who is artistic.

Ask children to name things an artistic person might make. Record their answers, providing sample answers if needed.

Ask children which is their favorite artistic item and why.

Ask children what things they might inquire about. Record their answers, modeling answers whenever necessary.

Ask children if there is anything that they inquire about every day. Have them explain their answers.

Your Turn to Write

Encourage children to relate the words to their own experiences. Discuss a few of the prompts below to prepare children for writing. Have children write about one of the prompts in their journals or on a separate piece of paper.

wander Have you ever wandered around somewhere? Where would be fun to wander around? When is it not a good idea to wander?

nibble What kind of animals might nibble their food? What kinds of animals probably never nibble their food? Why?

crouch Describe what you look like when you crouch. What are some places where you might have to crouch? Why?

artistic Tell about a time you saw beautiful, artistic things. What did you see? What do you think the people who made those things are like?

inquire What are some things that people inquire about? Tell about some things you have inquired about. What did you learn?

patient What are some times when it would be hard to be patient? Explain about a time when you had to be patient. Why was it important to be patient?

5 Assessing the Vocabulary

Review

Blackline Master, page 169

Read the following questions aloud and have children circle *yes* or *no*.

1. If you weren't hungry, might you **nibble** your food? (yes)
2. Do people **inquire** when they need information? (yes)
3. Does someone who is **patient** complain about having to wait? (no)
4. Might you have to **crouch** down inside a playhouse with a very low ceiling? (yes)
5. Is it a good idea to **wander** when you are in a hurry to get somewhere? (no)
6. Might someone who is **artistic** paint a beautiful picture? (yes)

Assessment

Student Book, pages 40–41

Read each question aloud as children complete the activity.

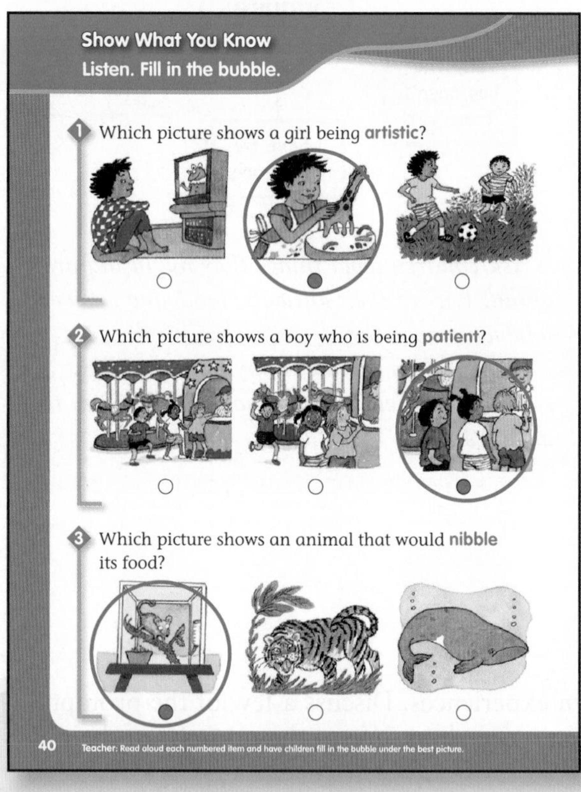

Show What You Know
Listen. Fill in the bubble.

1 Which picture shows a girl being **artistic**?

2 Which picture shows a boy who is being **patient**?

3 Which picture shows an animal that would **nibble** its food?

40 Teacher: Read aloud each numbered item and have children fill in the bubble under the best picture.

4 Which picture shows a monkey **crouching**?

5 Which picture shows someone who is **wandering**?

6 Which picture shows a boy who wants to **inquire** about something?

41

Cumulative Review

Ask the first question and model how you might arrive at an answer. Then have children answer the remaining questions and explain their answers.

Lesson 9	Lesson 10	
gobble	nibble	Does a hungry bear **nibble** its food, or does it **gobble** it?
sloppy	artistic	Would an **artistic** person paint a **sloppy** picture?
squiggle	wander	When you **wander**, is your path a **squiggle** or a straight line?
mound	crouch	Might you **crouch** down to hide behind a **mound** of dirt?
sprinkle	inquire	Would you **inquire** about why bakers **sprinkle** sugar on cookies?
tribute	patient	Might you give a **tribute** to thank someone who is extremely **patient**?

Herbert Glerbett

Vocabulary

dissolve When something dissolves, it melts and disappears.

ghastly If something is ghastly, it is the scariest thing you can think of.

sly Someone who is sly is wise and might do things in a sneaky way to get what they want.

swift Something that is swift moves fast.

preposterous Something preposterous is so strange that it couldn't possibly be true.

caution When you caution someone, you warn that person of danger.

At a Glance

STANDARDS

Vocabulary
- Discuss word meaning and develop vocabulary through meaningful experiences
- Develop vocabulary by discussing characters and events from a story

Comprehension
- Distinguish between a story and a poem

Writing
- Write brief descriptions using sensory details

LESSON RESOURCES

Read-Aloud Anthology: pp. 59–62
Student Book: pp. 42–45
Word Cards: Lesson 11
Photo Cards: 61–66

1 Introducing the Vocabulary

Read-Aloud

Read-Aloud Anthology, pages 59–62

The fantasy poem "Herbert Glerbett" tells about the surprising thing that happened to a boy who ate too much of his favorite food.

Bringing the Poem to Life

Read the first two stanzas in a lively, conversational tone. Then slow your reading and use a horrified tone to read stanza three. Read stanza four as if you are giving advice that children should take seriously.

Word Watcher

Word Watcher Chart, Lesson 11 Word Cards

- Tell children that they will learn about these words throughout the week and that each time a child uses one of the words correctly in the classroom, you will place a mark next to the word.
- Divide children into six groups. Give each group a card. Have each group hold up its card. Say the word and have that group of children repeat it after you. Then use the word in a sentence and give the word its first tally of the week.

Sending the Words Home

Blackline Master—English, page 141; Spanish, page 142

Distribute the activity letter to inform parents of the vocabulary words for this week.

Research Says...

"Vocabulary plays an important part in learning to read. As beginning readers, children use the words they have heard to make sense of the words they see in print."

—Put Reading First

2 Using the Vocabulary

Word Snapshots

Photo Cards: 61–66

Hold up each card and read the sentence on the back of the card. Then ask the following questions.

dissolve How can you tell the tablet is dissolving?

ghastly What is ghastly about this creature?

sly Who is being sly in this picture? How do you know?

swift How can you tell this animal is moving swiftly?

preposterous What is preposterous about this picture?

caution Why is the crossing guard cautioning drivers and children?

ELL SUPPORT

Discuss each vocabulary word. Pronounce each word and have children repeat after you. Then line the photo cards along the board ledge. Tell children a sentence using a vocabulary word. Have a child find the photo card that illustrates your sentence. Then ask the child to pantomime the word. Continue with the other words.

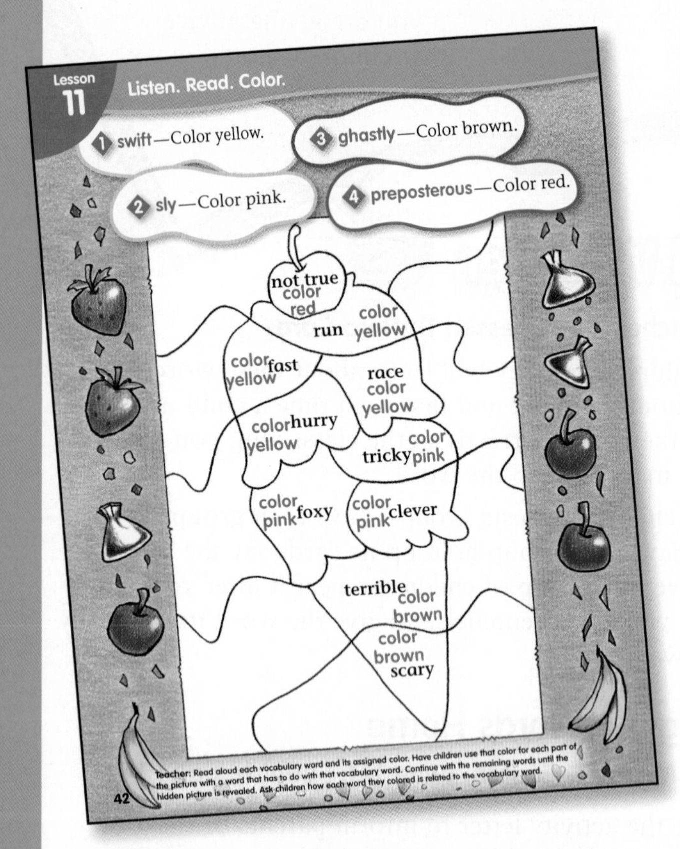

Word Chat

Student Book, page 42

Guide children as they complete the Student Book activity. Then use children's responses and the prompts below to discuss each word.

swift Tell children that you will name a thing and if they think this thing is swift, they should say "swift." If not, they should say nothing.

- a flying airplane
- a man carrying a huge bag of heavy rocks

sly Tell children that you will describe a person and if they think the person is sly, they should say "sly." If not, they should say nothing.

- Ally fell asleep. She snored through the whole movie.
- Sue told her little brother Ben that washing dishes was fun. Ben said he would wash the dishes for her.

preposterous Tell children that you will describe a situation and if they think the situation is preposterous, they should say "Pshaw! Preposterous!" If not, they should say nothing.

- This morning my shoes tried to run away from me.
- My dog reads me stories at night.

ghastly Tell children that you will describe a thing and if they think it is ghastly, they should look scared and whisper "ghastly." If not, they should say nothing.

- a hand that walks by itself on its fingers and taps on windows
- a huge bat that builds a nest in your hair

3 Using the Vocabulary

Word Chat

Student Book, page 43

Guide children as they complete the Student Book activity. Then use children's responses and the prompts below to discuss each word.

After children complete the page, briefly remind them of all the words in this lesson. (You might want to refer to the Word Watcher Chart or display the corresponding photo cards.) Explain that you are going to say a word or a phrase and that children should say the vocabulary word that comes to mind. After each response, have children give reasons for their choice.

warn a friend in danger **(caution)**
melt away **(dissolve)**

Continue the discussion with the remaining words from the lesson.

very scary costume **(ghastly)**
tricky fox **(sly)**
running fast **(swift)**
unbelievable story **(preposterous)**

WORD CHALLENGE

Remind children that they have learned that *dissolve* means "to melt and disappear." Explain that the word can also mean "to have a feeling slowly go away." The sentences below use the word *dissolve* to describe feelings slowly going away. Read each sentence aloud. Then have children supply additional sentences using this meaning of the word.

- Jessie's joy **dissolved** when he found out he didn't make the soccer team.
- Amy's fear of the dark **dissolved** when she got older.

4 Using the Vocabulary

Word Organizers

Help your class complete the graphic organizers below. You may draw them on the board or on chart paper, or use the organizers in the back of this book to make transparencies.

Write the vocabulary word in the center.

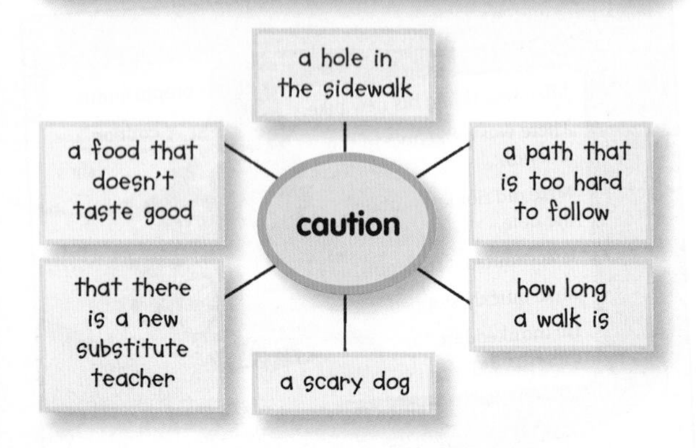

Ask children to name some things that they might caution someone about. Record their answers, providing sample answers as needed.

Have children talk about a time when they had to caution someone or when they were cautioned by someone.

Write the words shown in blue boxes to begin.

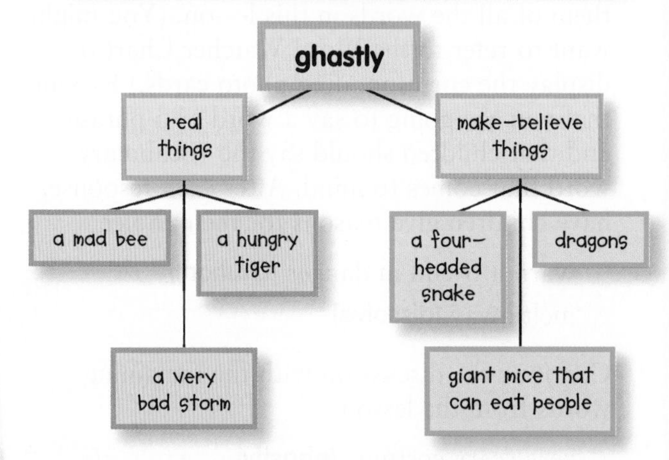

Ask children to name some things in real life that they think are ghastly. Record their answers, modeling sample answers as needed.

Ask children to explain why they think these things are ghastly.

Ask children to name some make-believe things that they think are ghastly. Model answers if necessary, and record appropriate responses.

Ask children to explain why they think these things are ghastly.

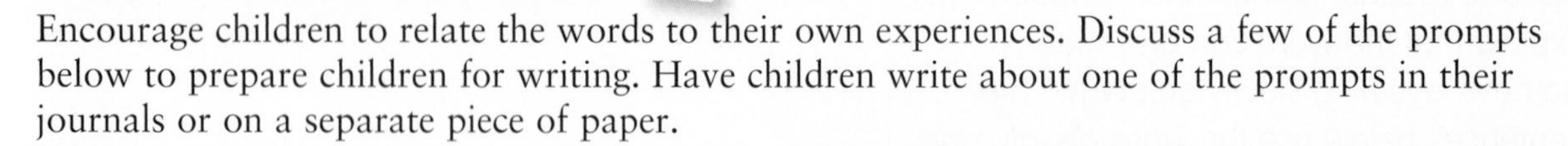

Your Turn to Write

Encourage children to relate the words to their own experiences. Discuss a few of the prompts below to prepare children for writing. Have children write about one of the prompts in their journals or on a separate piece of paper.

dissolve What are some things you can dissolve in water or milk to make tasty drinks? What are some ways you could dissolve a big block of ice?

ghastly Tell about a ghastly character in a movie or television show you saw. What is something ghastly? What might the person do when he or she sees the ghastly thing?

sly How might a sly dog get a snack it was not supposed to have? Is it a good or bad thing to be sly? Why or why not?

swift What are some things that make people move swiftly? What might make you move swiftly?

preposterous Tell a preposterous tale about something happening at school. What is the most preposterous thing you ever heard? Why?

caution What are some things people caution you about? Why do they caution you about these things? What might you caution a younger child about?

5 Assessing the Vocabulary

Review

Blackline Master, page 169

Read the following questions aloud and have children circle *yes* or *no*.

1. Does a turtle move **swiftly**? (no)
2. Would it be **preposterous** if someone told you that a zebra would be a new student in your school? (yes)
3. Might you **caution** someone about eating a rotten egg sandwich? (yes)
4. Would you be **sly** if you tricked your sister into doing your chores? (yes)
5. Could you **dissolve** chocolate syrup in milk? (yes)
6. Would it be **ghastly** to hear a tiny kitten meow from behind a door? (no)

Assessment

Student Book, pages 44–45

Read each question aloud as children complete the activity.

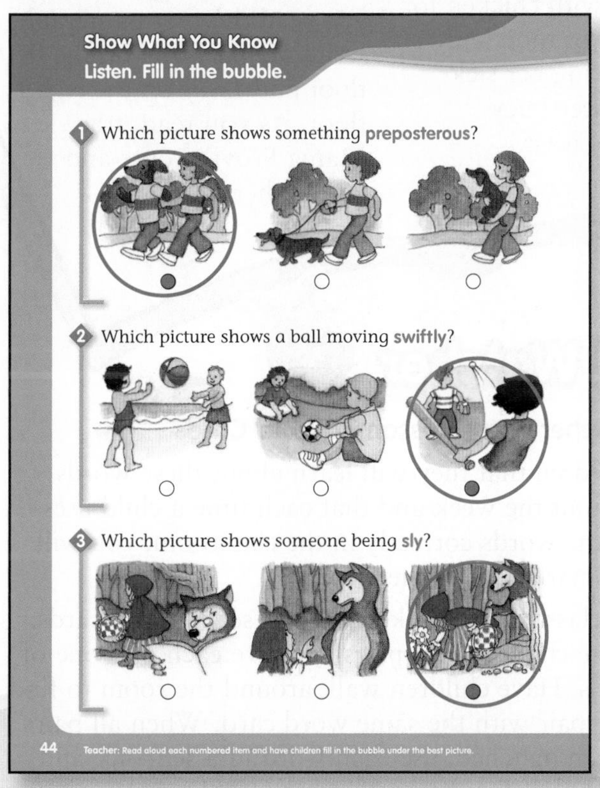

Show What You Know
Listen. Fill in the bubble.

1. Which picture shows something **preposterous**?
2. Which picture shows a ball moving **swiftly**?
3. Which picture shows someone being **sly**?

44 Teacher: Read aloud each numbered item and have children fill in the bubble under the best picture.

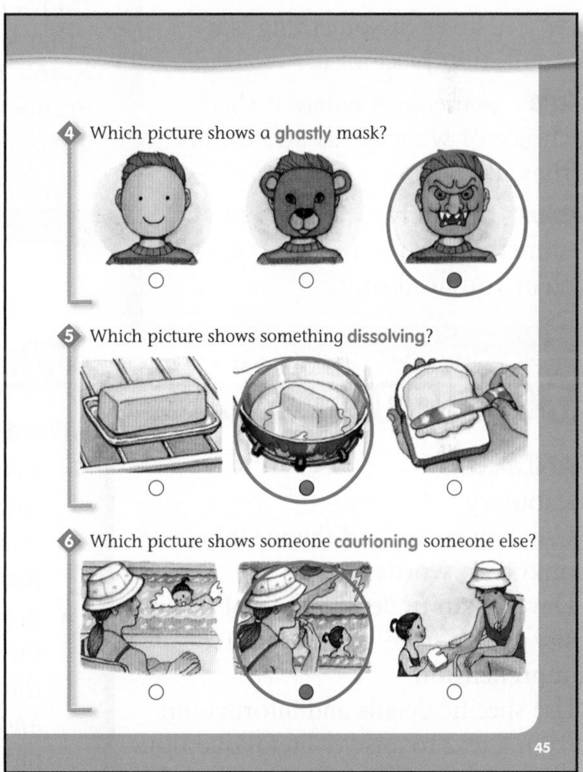

4. Which picture shows a **ghastly** mask?
5. Which picture shows something **dissolving**?
6. Which picture shows someone **cautioning** someone else?

45

Cumulative Review

Ask the first question and model how you might arrive at an answer. Then have children answer the remaining questions and explain their answers.

Lesson 10	Lesson 11	
wander	caution	Might someone **caution** you about **wandering** too far from home?
nibble	dissolve	Could you **nibble** on something that had **dissolved**?
crouch	sly	Might a **sly** person **crouch** behind something?
artistic	ghastly	Is it **ghastly** to be **artistic**?
inquire	swift	Might you **inquire** about whether someone left a room **swiftly**?
patient	preposterous	Might you need to be **patient** to listen to a **preposterous** story?

Lesson 12

Mama Provi and the Pot of Rice

Vocabulary

tremendous If something is tremendous, it is very large or in a very large amount.

amazed If something has amazed you, it has surprised you very much.

rearrange If you rearrange things, you change the way in which they are organized or ordered.

sliver A sliver of something is a small, thin piece of it.

palate Someone's palate is their choice of what foods and drinks they like.

surplus You have a surplus of something when you have more than you need of it.

At a Glance

STANDARDS

Vocabulary
- Use context to find the meanings of unknown words
- Develop an understanding of diversity in language across cultures

Comprehension
- Use specific details and information from a text to answer literal questions

Writing
- Write to record ideas and reflections

LESSON RESOURCES

Read-Aloud Anthology: pp. 63–70
Student Book: pp. 46–49
Word Cards: Lesson 12
Photo Cards: 67–72

1 Introducing the Vocabulary

Read-Aloud

Read-Aloud Anthology, pages 63–70

In *Mama Provi and the Pot of Rice*, Mama Provi trades rice with chicken for other kinds of food and is able to bring her sick granddaughter Lucy a wonderful feast.

Bringing the Story to Life

Draw on the board an apartment building with eight floors. After you read the first paragraph, write *Mama Provi* on the first floor and *Lucy* on the eighth floor. As you read, trace Mama Provi's route and act out her knocking.

Word Watcher

Word Watcher Chart, Lesson 12 Word Cards

- Tell children that they will learn about these words throughout the week and that each time a child uses one of the words correctly in the classroom, you will place a mark next to the word.
- Before class begins, make a second set of word cards. Organize children into pairs and give each pair one of the cards. Have children walk around the room to find another pair with the same word card. When all pairs have been matched, use each word in a sentence and give each word its first tally of the week.

Sending the Words Home

Blackline Master—English, page 143; Spanish, page 144

Distribute the activity letter to inform parents of the vocabulary words for this week.

Research Says...

"One of the oldest findings in educational research is the strong relationship between vocabulary knowledge and reading comprehension."

—*Vocabulary Development,* Steven A. Stahl

2 Using the Vocabulary

Word Snapshots

Photo Cards: 67–72

Hold up one of the photo cards for the class to see. Read the sentence on the back of the card. Then call on volunteers to use the vocabulary word in a sentence of their own. Record the sentences on the board. Repeat this activity for all of the words in the lesson.

Then display the photo cards on the board ledge and quiz the class by saying each vocabulary word and having children point to the correct picture.

ELL SUPPORT

Hold up one photo card at a time. Pronounce the vocabulary word and have children say the word with you. Read the sentences on the back of each card, and place the cards along the board ledge. Say each vocabulary word, and have children find the matching card.

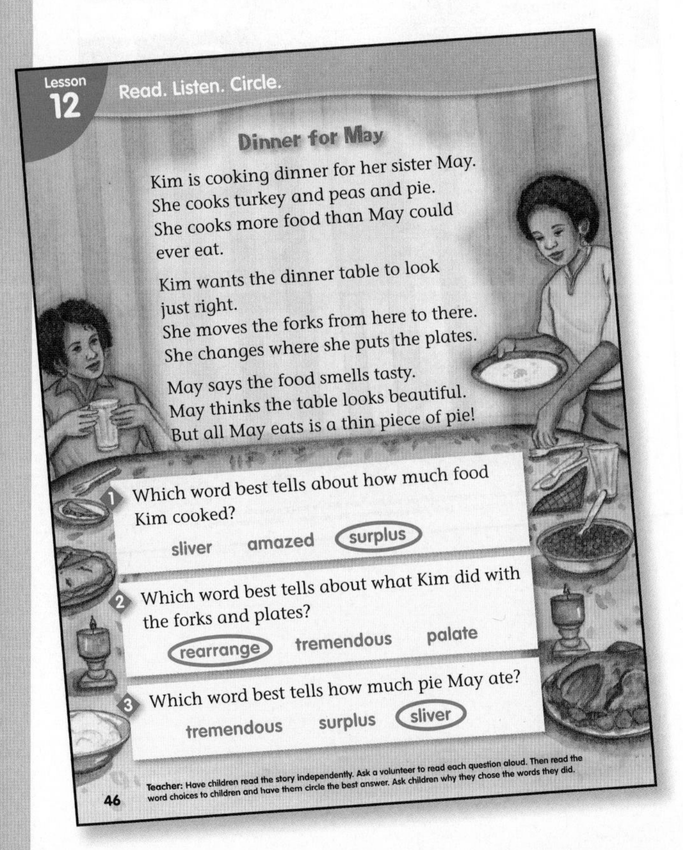

Lesson 12 Read. Listen. Circle.

Dinner for May

Kim is cooking dinner for her sister May.
She cooks turkey and peas and pie.
She cooks more food than May could ever eat.

Kim wants the dinner table to look just right.
She moves the forks from here to there.
She changes where she puts the plates.

May says the food smells tasty.
May thinks the table looks beautiful.
But all May eats is a thin piece of pie!

1. Which word best tells about how much food Kim cooked?
   sliver amazed (surplus)
2. Which word best tells about what Kim did with the forks and plates?
   (rearrange) tremendous palate
3. Which word best tells how much pie May ate?
   tremendous surplus (sliver)

Teacher: Have children read the story independently. Ask a volunteer to read each question aloud. Then read the word choices to children and have them circle the best answer. Ask children why they chose the words they did.

46

sliver Tell children that you will describe different things and if they think a sliver is being described, they should say “sliver.” If not, they should say nothing.

- Dad cut the loaf of bread in half.
- Melissa cut a thin piece off of the chocolate bar.
- Ari cut the apple into several thin pieces.

Word Chat

Student Book, page 46

Guide children as they complete the Student Book activity. Then use children’s responses and the prompts below to discuss each word.

surplus Tell children that you will describe a situation and if they think it describes a time when there is a surplus, they should open their arms wide and say “surplus.” If not, they should say nothing.

- We only had three cookies, so George did not get one.
- There were nine pairs of scissors left over on the supply table.
- After dinner half of the meatloaf was left on the platter.

rearrange Tell children that you will describe a situation and if they think something is being rearranged, they should move their hands back and forth and say “rearranged.” If not, they should say nothing.

- Molly didn’t touch anything on Lee’s desk.
- Mom moved the cups to a lower shelf so we could reach them.
- We all traded seats.

3 Using the Vocabulary

Word Chat

Student Book, page 47

Guide children as they complete the Student Book activity. Then use children's responses and the prompts below to discuss each word.

For each vocabulary word, provide children with the first part of a sentence that includes the vocabulary word. Have children provide an ending that shows they know what the new word means.

amazed I was amazed when I stepped outside because....

tremendous The tremendous ice cream sundae was....

palate Kate only eats foods that please her palate such as....

Continue the discussion with the remaining words from the lesson.

surplus Mom and Dad are preparing a surplus of food because....

rearrange Jason wants to rearrange his closet because....

sliver Jen took only a sliver of cheese because....

WORD CHALLENGE

Explain to children that the word *palate* has more than one meaning. They have already learned that it means "someone's choice of what foods and drinks they like." Tell children that another meaning is "the roof of the mouth" and point to that part of the mouth. Then provide the following prompts and ask children which meaning *palate* has in each of these sentences.

- Sometimes when I eat pizza or soup that is very hot, I burn my **palate**. (the roof of the mouth)
- Vanilla is the ice cream flavor that pleases my **palate**. (someone's choice of foods)

4 Using the Vocabulary

Word Organizers

Help your class complete the graphic organizers below. You may draw them on the board or on chart paper, or use the organizers in the back of this book to make transparencies.

Write the vocabulary word in the last blue box. Then write the word tiny *in the first box.*

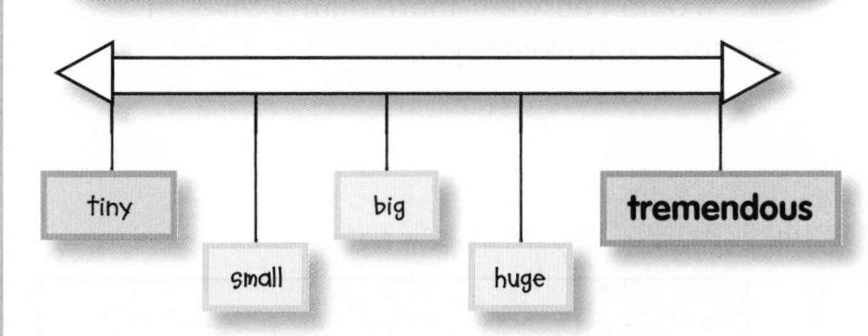

Tell children that you wrote tremendous *at one end and* tiny *at the other end because both are words you might use to describe the size of something. Invite children to think of other words that tell what size something is. Help children think of words that build from* tiny *to* tremendous. *Ask children where each of the words should go on the chart and why. Record their answers, modeling the differences in meaning where needed.*

Write the vocabulary word in the center.

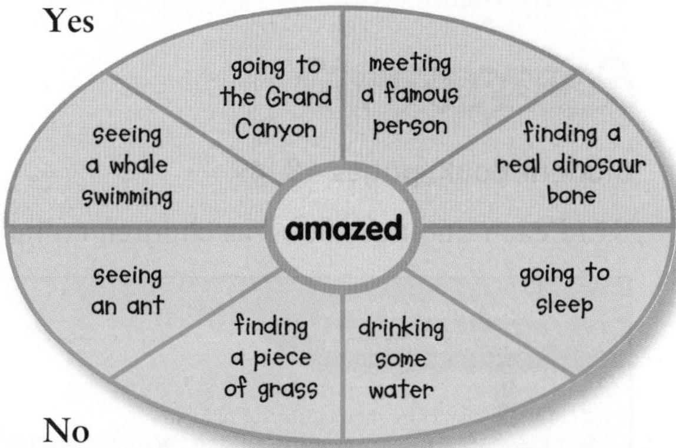

Ask children to name some things or places that might amaze them. As needed, call out sample answers and ask the question, "Would that amaze you?" Record appropriate answers in the top of the circle.

Ask children to name things that are not at all amazing. Model sample answers as needed and record appropriate answers in the bottom of the circle.

Ask children to explain how they decide if something would or would not amaze them.

Your Turn to Write

Encourage children to relate the words to their own experiences. Discuss a few of the prompts below to prepare children for writing. Have children write about one of the prompts in their journals or on a separate piece of paper.

tremendous Is it easy to climb a tremendous mountain? What other tremendous things can be found outdoors? Can you name some animals that are tremendous?

amazed Who do you know that amazes you? Why? Are there animals that amaze you? Are there machines that amaze you?

rearrange Would you like to rearrange our classroom? How would you change things? Is there a room at home you would like to rearrange?

sliver Do you ever have a sliver of cake or pie? Why might you only want a sliver of something? What other things can be cut into slivers?

palate Do a lot of foods please your palate? What are some of the foods that please your palate? What are some foods that don't please your palate?

surplus What do we have a surplus of in our classroom? Do you have a surplus of anything at home? If you could have a surplus of anything, what would it be? Why?

5 Assessing the Vocabulary

Review

Blackline Master, page 169

Read the following questions aloud and have children circle *yes* or *no*.

1. If you had a **surplus** of crayons, could you share them? (yes)
2. If a park is **tremendous**, can a lot of people play there? (yes)
3. Would a singing turtle **amaze** you? (yes)
4. Do all foods please your **palate**? (no)
5. Would it be easy to **rearrange** all the books in the library? (no)
6. Would you want more than a **sliver** of a food you liked? (yes)

Assessment

Student Book, pages 48–49

Read each question aloud as children complete the activity.

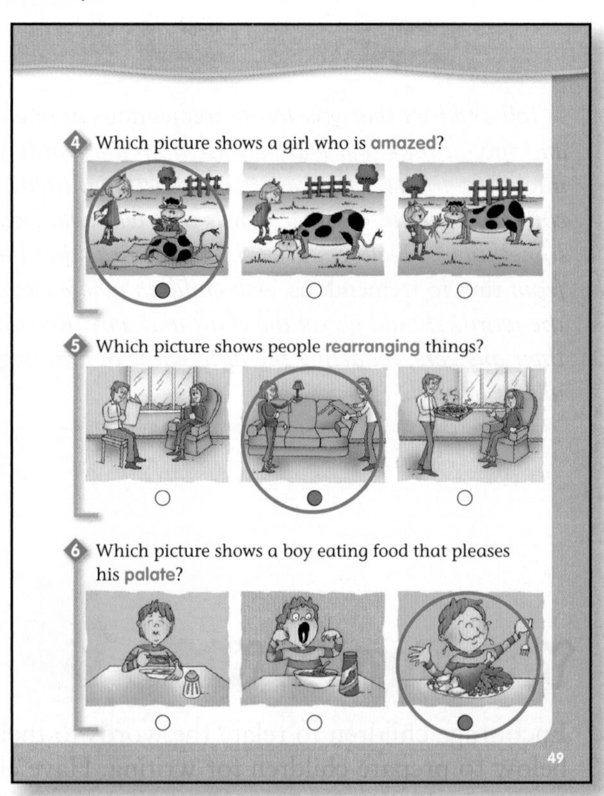

Cumulative Review

Ask the first question and model how you might arrive at an answer. Then have children answer the remaining questions and explain their answers.

Lesson 11	Lesson 12	
preposterous	palate	Is it **preposterous** to eat foods that please your **palate**?
dissolve	surplus	Would you want to **dissolve** a **surplus** of snow?
ghastly	rearrange	Is **rearranging** snakes in boxes a **ghastly** thing to do?
swift	tremendous	Can a **tremendous** animal be **swift**?
caution	sliver	Would you **caution** someone to eat only a **sliver** of cake?
sly	amazed	Could a **sly** person **amaze** you?

Never Trust a SQUIRREL

Vocabulary

dull If you say something is dull, you mean that it is rather boring and not very exciting.

eager If you are eager for something, you want it so much you can hardly wait.

alert If you alert someone, you make them aware of something that is important or dangerous.

petrified If you are petrified, you are so scared that you can hardly move.

adventurous Someone who is adventurous is willing to take risks and to try new things.

rely When you rely on someone, you count on them to do something for you.

At a Glance

STANDARDS

Vocabulary
- Use visual references to build upon word meaning
- Use vocabulary to describe ideas, feelings, and experiences

Comprehension
- Use a variety of strategies to comprehend text

Writing
- Describe connections between personal experiences and written and visual texts

LESSON RESOURCES

Read-Aloud Anthology: pp. 71–77	Word Cards: Lesson 13
Student Book: pp. 50–53	Photo Cards: 5, 32, 35, 39, 73–79, 82

1 Introducing the Vocabulary

Read-Aloud

Read-Aloud Anthology, pages 71–77

In *Never Trust a Squirrel!* a guinea pig named William learns that he can't trust squirrels, but he can always trust his mother.

Bringing the Story to Life

Use pantomime to act out the many physical parts of this story, such as hiding in a drainpipe, trying to climb a tree, and trying to dislodge the hiding guinea pigs. Read the section at the top of page 76 with heightened suspense.

Word Watcher

Word Watcher Chart, Lesson 13 Word Cards

- Tell children that they will learn about these words throughout the week and that each time a child uses one of the words correctly in the classroom, you will place a mark next to the word.
- Distribute the word cards and ask children with cards that begin with *a* to stand. Say their words, use each one in a sentence, and give the words a tally. Continue for the words beginning with *d*, *e*, *p*, and *r*.

Sending the Words Home

Blackline Master—English, page 145; Spanish, page 146

Distribute the activity letter to inform parents of the vocabulary words for this week.

Research Says. . .

"...research strongly points to the need for frequent encounters with new words if they are to become a permanent part of an individual's vocabulary repertoire."

—*Bringing Words to Life,* Isabel L. Beck, *et al.*

2 Using the Vocabulary

Word Snapshots

Photo Cards: 5, 32, 35, 39, 73–79, 82

Hold up the card pairs and ask children the following questions. Discuss which photos best show the vocabulary words.

dull (73 and 35) Which card shows a boy who is having a dull time?

eager (74 and 79) Which of these cards shows an animal who is eager?

alert (75 and 32) Which card shows one person alerting another person?

petrified (76 and 39) Which card shows someone who is petrified?

adventurous (77 and 82) Which card shows children being adventurous?

rely (78 and 5) Which card shows someone relying on a friend?

ELL SUPPORT

Show the photo cards one by one. Say the words and have children repeat them. Read the sentence on the back of each card. Then give children a sentence starter with a vocabulary word and have them complete it. Write children's sentences on the board.

Lesson 13 Listen. Circle.

1 Today is Pam's first day at a new school. Pam is eager to make new friends.

2 Mom is teaching Rob to swim. Rob is petrified of the water!

3 Ben and Jan are watching a show. They think the show is very dull.

Teacher: Read aloud each numbered item as children read along silently. Then have children circle the best picture for each numbered item. Ask children why they chose each picture they did.

50

dull Tell children that you will describe a situation and if they think it describes something dull, they should say "dull." If not, they should say nothing.

- Susan thought the movie was very boring.
- Susan thought the movie was very funny.
- Susan thought the movie was very scary.

Word Chat

Student Book, page 50

Guide children as they complete the Student Book activity. Then use children's responses and the prompts below to discuss each word.

eager Tell children that you will describe a situation and if they think it describes someone who is eager, they should clap their hands, bounce up and down, and happily say "eager." If not, they should say nothing.

- Anna was tired after the long hike.
- Anna was surprised when it started to rain.
- Anna couldn't wait for her grandmother to come for a visit.

petrified Tell children that you will describe a situation and if they think it describes someone who is petrified, they should say "petrified." If not, they should say nothing.

- Jeremy saw a snake in his tent and he was so afraid he couldn't move!
- Jeremy was very scared when he heard the loud thunder.
- Jeremy was very hungry and decided to make a sandwich.

3 Using the Vocabulary

Word Chat

Student Book, page 51

Guide children as they complete the Student Book activity. Then use children's responses and the prompts below to discuss each word.

For each vocabulary word, provide children with the first part of a sentence that includes the vocabulary word. Have children provide an ending for the sentence that shows they know what the new word means.

alert Mom alerted me that....

adventurous Rita is an adventurous person because....

rely Jon relies on his big sister to....

eager I am eager to go....

Continue the discussion with the remaining words from the lesson.

dull Carl thought the game was dull because....

petrified Sara was petrified when....

WORD CHALLENGE

Explain to children that the word *dull* has more than one meaning. They have already learned that it means "boring and not very exciting." Tell them that another meaning is "not sharp or pointed." Then provide the following prompts and ask children which meaning the word *dull* has in each prompt.

- It is hard to cut bread with a knife that is **dull**. (not sharp or pointed)
- Tina returned the book to the library because she thought it was **dull**. (boring and not very exciting)

4 Using the Vocabulary

Word Organizers

Help your class complete the graphic organizers below. You may draw them on the board or on chart paper, or use the organizers in the back of this book to make transparencies.

Write the word in the blue diamond.

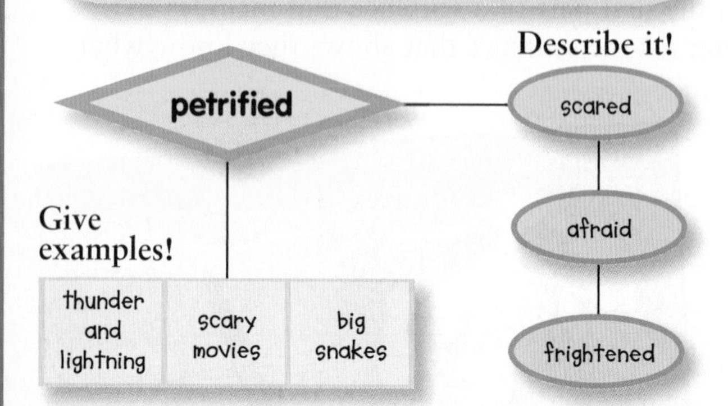

Ask children to think of words that tell what petrified *means. Record their answers in the ovals, modeling sample answers as necessary.*

Ask children to explain why they chose these words.

Invite children to name some things that make them feel petrified. Record their answers in the boxes, providing sample answers if necessary.

Discuss what is petrifying about each of the answers.

Write the vocabulary word in the blue box.

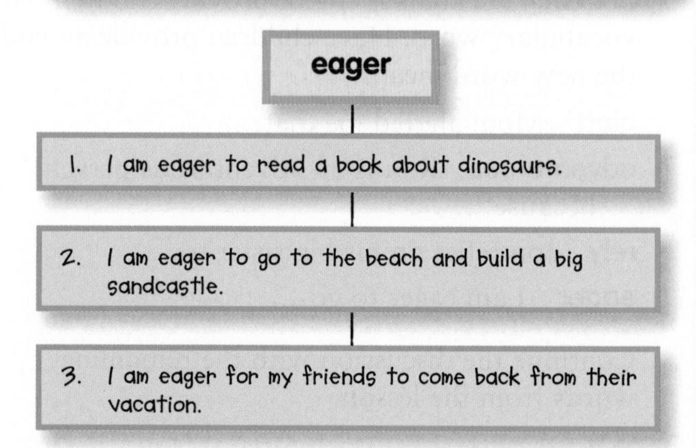

Ask children to create sentences about things they are eager to do. You may want to start them off by modeling a sentence for them. Then record their sentences.

After children generate sentences, have them tell why they are eager to do these things.

Your Turn to Write

Encourage children to relate the words to their own experiences. Discuss a few of the prompts below to prepare children for writing. Have children write about one of the prompts in their journals or on a separate piece of paper.

dull What activity do you think is dull? Why do you think so? How do you feel when you watch a dull movie or TV show?

eager What books are you eager to read? Is there a person that you're eager to see? What are you eager to do today?

alert When should someone alert a police officer or a firefighter? When should someone alert a lifeguard? How does a smoke alarm alert people?

petrified What makes you feel petrified? What do you do when you feel that way? How can you help someone else who feels petrified?

adventurous Who do you know that's adventurous? What do they do? Would you like to be adventurous? What kinds of things would you like to do?

rely Who are the people you rely on? What do they do for you? Does anyone rely on you?

5 Assessing the Vocabulary

Review

Blackline Master, page 169

Read the following questions aloud and have children circle *yes* or *no*.

1. If you were hungry, would you be **eager** to have a meal? (yes)
2. Would an **adventurous** person be afraid to try new things? (no)
3. If the bathtub were leaking, should you **alert** your parents? (yes)
4. Do you **rely** on someone to drive you different places? (yes)
5. If you are **petrified** of spiders, do you like to play with them? (no)
6. If a story is **dull**, do you want to finish reading it? (no)

Assessment

Student Book, pages 52–53

Read each question aloud as children complete the activity.

Show What You Know
Listen. Fill in the bubble.

1. Which picture shows a boy who is **petrified**?
2. Which picture shows people who are **adventurous**?
3. Which picture shows a girl having a **dull** time?

52 Teacher: Read aloud each numbered item and have children fill in the bubble under the best picture.

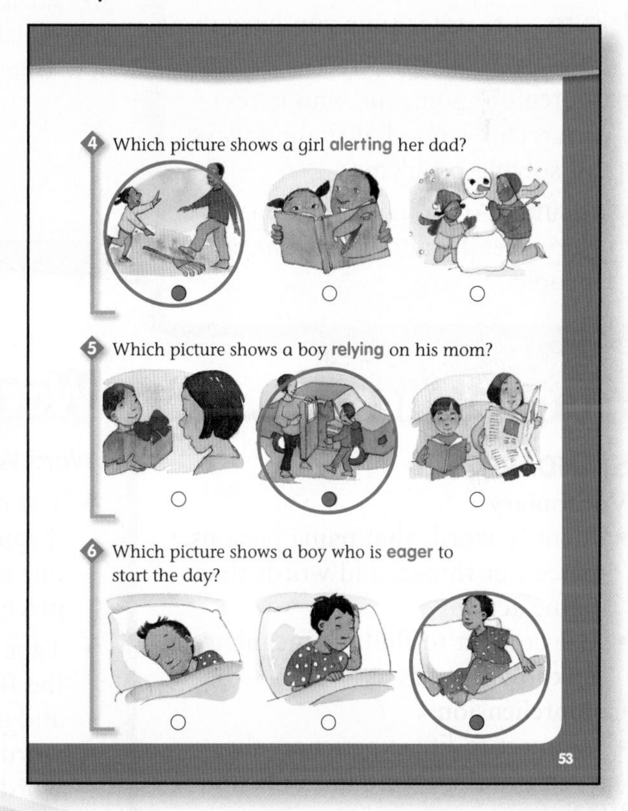
4. Which picture shows a girl **alerting** her dad?
5. Which picture shows a boy **relying** on his mom?
6. Which picture shows a boy who is **eager** to start the day?

53

Cumulative Review

Ask the first question and model how you might arrive at an answer. Then have children answer the remaining questions and explain their answers.

Lesson 12	Lesson 13	
surplus	rely	Do you **rely** on having a **surplus** of food in your refrigerator?
sliver	eager	Are you **eager** to have a **sliver** of blueberry pie?
palate	dull	Is your **palate dull**?
tremendous	petrified	If you saw a **tremendous** spider, would you be **petrified**?
rearrange	alert	Would your teacher **alert** you if he **rearranged** the classroom?
amazed	adventurous	Are you **amazed** by **adventurous** people?

Lesson 14

Vocabulary

relax When you relax, you let go of all your worries and you rest.

appear When someone or something appears, you are suddenly able to see it.

tumble When you tumble, you fall head first and roll over into a ball.

leisure Leisure is time you have to just do what you enjoy.

resourceful Someone who is resourceful is good at finding ways of solving problems.

outgoing An outgoing person is very friendly and likes to meet people.

At a Glance

STANDARDS

Vocabulary
- Identify words that name persons, places, or things, and words that name actions
- Use context to find the meaning of unknown words

Comprehension
- Connect to life experiences the events and information in texts

Writing
- Record or dictate knowledge of a topic in various ways

LESSON RESOURCES

Read-Aloud Anthology: pp. 78–83	Word Cards: Lesson 14
Student Book: pp. 54–57	Photo Cards: 79–84

1 Introducing the Vocabulary

Read-Aloud

Read-Aloud Anthology, pages 78–83

Flip-Flops tells how a girl started with a problem and ended up with a new friend.

Bringing the Story to Life

As you read the story, use a real flip-flop or one made from paper to act out how Penny uses her flip-flop. Then have pairs of children use construction paper to make flip-flops and act out how Meggie and Penny became friends.

Word Watcher

Word Watcher Chart, Lesson 14 Word Cards

- Tell children that they will learn about these words throughout the week and that each time a child uses one of the words correctly in the classroom, you will place a mark next to the word.
- Tape seashell shapes to word cards and scatter them on the floor. Invite children to pretend to walk on the beach and gather shells. As a child hands a shell to you, read the word on it and ask children to repeat the word. Use the word in a sentence and then make a tally for each word on the chart.

Sending the Words Home

Blackline Master—English, page 147; Spanish, page 148

Distribute the activity letter to inform parents of the vocabulary words for this week.

Research Says...

"To be effective word learners and word users, students need...strategies...that help them get meanings from content and...make connections between words they already know."

—Learning First Alliance

2 Using the Vocabulary

Word Snapshots

Photo Cards: 79–84

Have children stand in a circle, facing one another. One at a time, give each photo card to a child in the circle, saying the vocabulary word and the sentence on the back of the card. With all the photos facing the inside of the circle, say one of the vocabulary words and have the children point to the card that shows that word. Continue until all the words have been used. After children identify each card correctly, ask how they knew that was the correct card.

ELL SUPPORT

Hold up the photo cards, one at a time. Say the words and have children repeat after you. Put the cards in a bag and have a child pick one card. Ask the child a yes/no question using the vocabulary word. Continue with the other words.

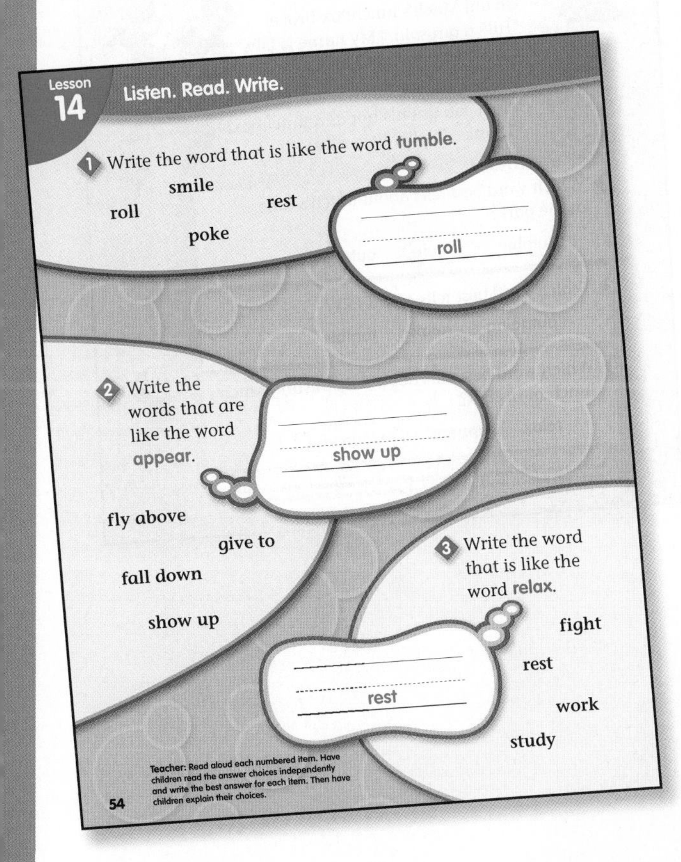

Word Chat

Student Book, page 54

Guide children as they complete the Student Book activity. Then use children's responses and the prompts below to discuss each word.

Divide the class into two groups. Assign the first word to one group and the second word to the other. Explain that you will say a sentence with a missing word, and the group that has the word that fits the sentence should say their word aloud.

tumble/leisure

- A clown dives to the ground to ______ across the floor. (tumble)
- The two girls spent their ______ time at the park. (leisure)
- A cartoon rabbit trips and ______ down some stairs. (tumbles)
- Their ______ time was over; they had to go back to work. (leisure)

appear/resourceful

- Using a telephone book as a footstool is being ______ . (resourceful)
- The sun ______ from behind the cloud. (appeared)
- The stars ______ as soon as the sky got dark. (appeared)
- Jessica made a happy face out of a coat hanger. She is ______ . (resourceful)

relax/outgoing

- The ______ girl made five new friends in less than a minute! (outgoing)
- The new boy was ______ ; he said hello to everyone he met. (outgoing)
- After a hard day of work, it was time to ______ . (relax)
- I like to ______ by reading a book and resting. (relax)

Word Chat

Student Book, page 55

Guide children as they complete the Student Book activity. Then use children's answers and the prompts below to discuss each word.

leisure Would a person with lots of leisure time be happy or upset? Why?

outgoing Would an outgoing person have many friends or few friends? Why is that?

resourceful If a resourceful person had too many books for their bookcase, might they make new shelves out of boxes or pile the books in a corner? Explain.

Continue the discussion with the remaining words from the lesson.

appear What might appear from behind a tree, a squirrel or a giant elephant? Tell why you said that.

tumble Would you rather tumble onto feathers or onto pebbles? Explain why.

relax What would a person be more likely to use to relax, a hammer or a pillow? Explain your answer.

WORD CHALLENGE

Review with children the meaning of the word *outgoing*. Then use the following prompts to help children brainstorm words that mean the opposite.

- The girl in the story was very **outgoing.** She tried to make friends with many people. How would you describe the girl in the story if she were the opposite of **outgoing**? (afraid to talk to strangers) Would she have made friends with Meggie? (probably not)
- Can you think of a word that means the opposite of **outgoing**? *(shy)*

4 Using the Vocabulary

Word Organizers

Help your class complete the graphic organizers below. You may draw them on the board or on chart paper, or use the organizers in the back of this book to make transparencies.

Write the vocabulary word in the blue box.

1. My sister uses an old cup to hold all of her pens and pencils.
2. My dad covered a small hole in the wall with one of my pictures.
3. My teacher used a ruler to get my pencil when it fell between the bookcases.

Ask children to create sentences describing people who are resourceful. You may want to start them off by modeling a sentence for them. Then record their sentences.

After children generate sentences, have them tell whether being resourceful is a good or bad quality and why.

Write the vocabulary word in the center.

Ask children to name things that they do to relax. Record appropriate answers in the top half of the circle, modeling sample answers if needed.

Ask children why these activities are relaxing.

Ask children to name things they do that are not relaxing. These may be things that involve work or things that make them feel upset. Record appropriate answers in the bottom half of the circle.

Ask children why these activities are not relaxing.

Your Turn to Write

Encourage children to relate the words to their own experiences. Discuss a few of the prompts below to prepare children for writing. Have children write about one of the prompts in their journals or on a separate piece of paper.

relax When do you relax? Where do you like to relax? Do you think animals need to relax?

appear What kinds of things have you seen appear? What would you not want to see appear in front of you?

tumble Where would it be fun to tumble? Have you ever tumbled on accident?

leisure When do you have leisure time? What do you like to do during leisure time? Could you ever have too much leisure time?

resourceful Who is the most resourceful person you know? What makes them resourceful? Describe a time when you solved a problem by being resourceful.

outgoing Are you outgoing? Who is the most outgoing person you know? Is being outgoing a good quality?

5 Assessing the Vocabulary

Review

Blackline Master, page 169

Read the following questions aloud and have children circle *yes* or *no*.

1. Could someone **relax** if they thought there was a monster under their bed? (no)
2. Might you want a **resourceful** person to help you unstick the zipper on your jacket? (yes)
3. Would you go to school during your **leisure** time? (no)
4. Would an **outgoing** person like to go to parties? (yes)
5. Might the principal **appear** in your classroom? (yes)
6. Might someone **tumble** down a hill? (yes)

Assessment

Student Book, pages 56–57

Read each question aloud as children complete the activity.

Show What You Know
Listen. Fill in the bubble.

1. Which picture shows a dog **relaxing**?
2. Which picture shows a parade **appearing**?
3. Which picture shows a monkey **tumbling**?

56 Teacher: Read aloud each numbered item and have children fill in the bubble under the best picture.

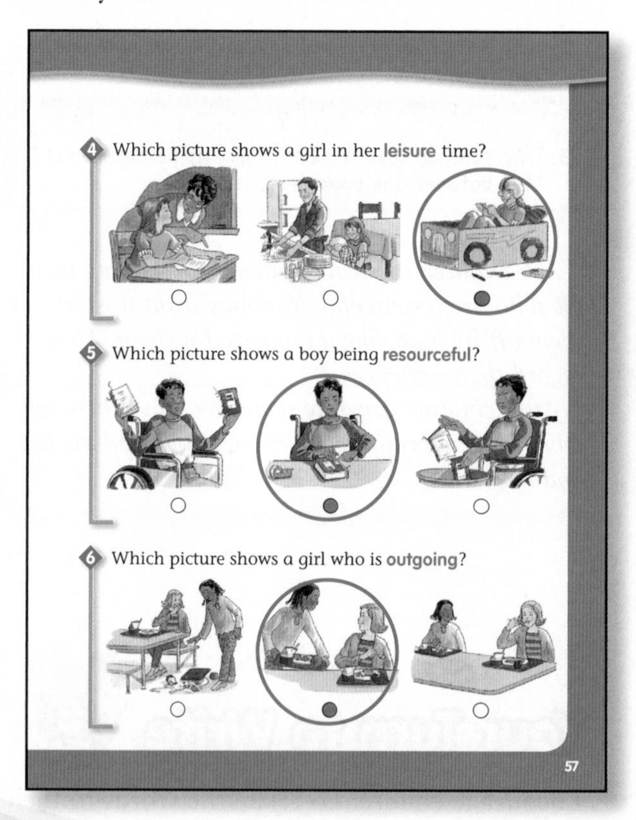

4. Which picture shows a girl in her **leisure** time?
5. Which picture shows a boy being **resourceful**?
6. Which picture shows a girl who is **outgoing**?

57

Cumulative Review

Ask the first question and model how you might arrive at an answer. Then have children answer the remaining questions and explain their answers.

Lesson 13	Lesson 14	
dull	leisure	Is **leisure** time usually **dull**?
alert	relax	Should you **alert** your friends when you plan to **relax**?
eager	appear	Would you be **eager** for bees to **appear** at your picnic?
petrified	tumble	Would you be **petrified** to **tumble** on a grassy lawn?
rely	resourceful	Might you **rely** on a **resourceful** person to fix your bike?
adventurous	outgoing	Might an **outgoing** person be **adventurous**?

Lesson 15

My Building

Vocabulary

glimpse To get a glimpse of something means to get a quick look at it.

pleasant Something pleasant is very nice and it pleases you.

strain To strain means to push, pull, or stretch something in a way that might hurt it.

grand If you say something is grand, you think it is so wonderful that you almost can't believe it is real.

skyscraper A skyscraper is a very tall building in a city.

observant Someone who is observant pays a lot of attention to things.

At a Glance

STANDARDS

Vocabulary
- Use vocabulary to describe ideas, feelings, and experiences
- Develop vocabulary by discussing characters and events from a story

Comprehension
- Retell or act out order of important events in stories

Writing
- Write to discover, develop, and refine ideas

LESSON RESOURCES

Read-Aloud Anthology: pp. 84–88	Word Cards: Lesson 15
Student Book: pp. 58–61	Photo Cards: 8, 22, 28, 56, 85–90, 119, 134

1 Introducing the Vocabulary

Read-Aloud

Read-Aloud Anthology, pages 84–88

The poem "My Building" describes how interesting life can be when you live in a tall building full of people.

Bringing the Poem to Life

As you read this poem, emphasize the rhyming words. Use gestures to act out parts of the poem, such as waving to the children, petting the dogs, and saluting the doorman.

Word Watcher

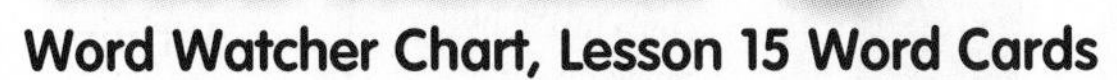

Word Watcher Chart, Lesson 15 Word Cards

- Tell children that they will learn about these words throughout the week and that each time a child uses one of the words correctly in the classroom, you will place a mark next to the word.
- Hide the word cards around the classroom. Then ask volunteers to find each card by giving a clue, for example, *The word card for* skyscraper *is behind the plant.* As each word is found, say the word and have children repeat it. Then use the word in a sentence and give the word its first tally of the week.

Sending the Words Home

Blackline Master—English, page 149; Spanish, page 150

Distribute the activity letter to inform parents of the vocabulary words for this week.

Research Says...

"Reading aloud is...helpful when...after reading, [the reader] engages the child in a conversation about the book."

—Put Reading First

2 Using the Vocabulary

Word Snapshots

Photo Cards: 8, 22, 28, 56, 85–90, 119, 134

Hold up the card pairs and ask children the following questions. Discuss which photos show activities the children enjoy and why.

glimpse (85 and 134) Which card shows someone who is glimpsing?

pleasant (86 and 22) Which card shows someone in a pleasant situation?

strain (87 and 28) Which card shows someone straining?

grand (88 and 56) Which card shows something grand?

skyscraper (89 and 119) Which card shows a skyscraper?

observant (90 and 8) Which card shows someone being observant?

ELL SUPPORT

Hold up the photo cards, one at a time. Read aloud the sentence on the back and have children say each vocabulary word with you. Then line the photo cards along the board ledge. Provide sentence starters for each word and have children complete the sentences.

Word Chat

Student Book, page 58

Guide children as they complete the Student Book activity. Then use children's responses and the prompts below to discuss each word.

Lesson 15

Listen. Circle.

1. Cindi and Mark found a book in the backyard. Cindi is very **observant**. Mark is not.
2. Grandpa opened the big door to his house. Once inside he knew his arm was **strained**.
3. Mom took Pat to visit Ann in the city. Ann works in a **skyscraper**.

Teacher: Read aloud each numbered item as children read along silently. Then have children circle the best picture for each numbered item. Ask children why they chose each picture they did.

58

observant Tell children that you will describe someone and if they think the person is being observant, they should point to their eyes and say "observant." If not, they should say nothing.

- Brittany doesn't see that she has a spider crawling up her arm.
- Jake is jogging and listing to his walkman.
- Travis is writing down all the things he sees at the mall.

strain Tell children that you will describe a situation and if they think you are describing someone who is straining, they should say groan and say "Ugh! Strain." If not, they should say nothing.

- Lisa stretched her arms around the heavy books and lugged them up the stairs.
- Bobby carried a bowl of popcorn into the living room.
- Juan carried the kitten into the vet's office.

skyscraper Tell children that you will describe a building and if they think you are describing a skyscraper, they should look up to the ceiling and say "skyscraper." If not, they should say nothing.

- It has more than 1,000 doors!
- It is shorter than the tree in the yard.
- At night the lights from the windows look like stars in the sky.

3 Using the Vocabulary

Word Chat

Student Book, page 59

Guide children as they complete the Student Book activity. Then use children's responses and the prompts below to discuss each word.

pleasant Would you rather have a pleasant day or an awful day? Explain your answer.

glimpse If you glimpse at something, do you look at it carefully or quickly? Explain your answer.

grand Is a grand trip a wonderful trip or a trip not worth mentioning? Explain your choice.

observant Would an observant person remember who came to the party? Why?

Continue the discussion with the remaining words from the lesson.

strain If you strain your arm, do you hurt the muscle a little bit or do you paint it different colors? Tell why.

skyscraper Might a skyscraper take a long time to build? Why or why not?

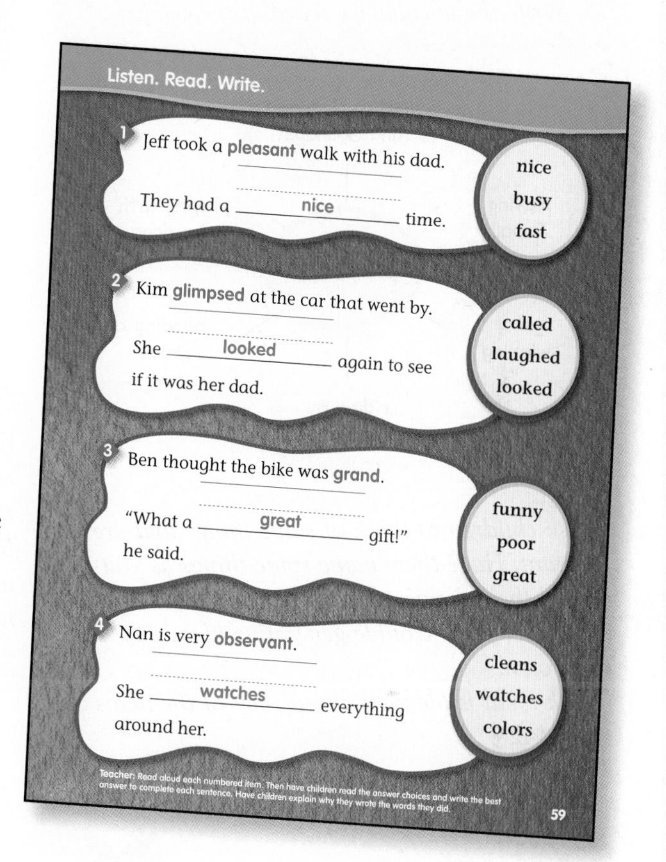

WORD CHALLENGE

Review with children the meaning of the word *grand*. Then use the following prompts to help children brainstorm words that mean the opposite. *(horrible, dreadful, terrible, awful, very bad)*

- James went away on vacation and had a **grand** time. Say the same sentence, but use a word that means the opposite of *grand*.
- Maria bought a dress that was very **grand**! Say the same sentence, but use a word that means the opposite of *grand*.

4 Using the Vocabulary

Word Organizers

Help your class complete the graphic organizers below. You may draw them on the board or on chart paper, or use the organizers in the back of this book to make transparencies.

Write the vocabulary word in the center.

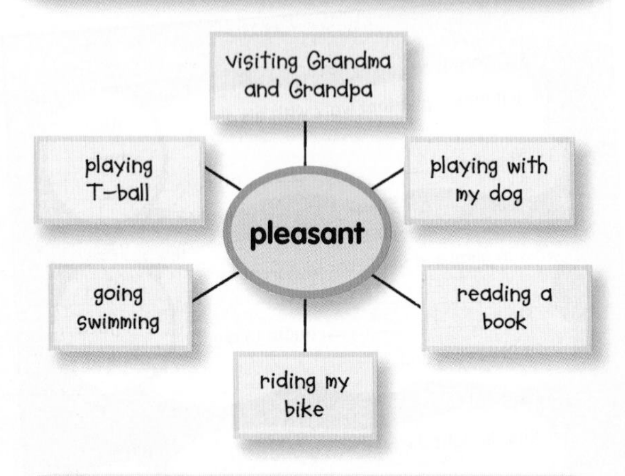

Ask children to think of some things that are pleasant. Have them name some things as you record their answers. Model sample answers if children have trouble generating ideas on their own.

Ask what is pleasant about each of the items recorded.

Write the vocabulary word in the last blue box. Then write the word bad *in the first box.*

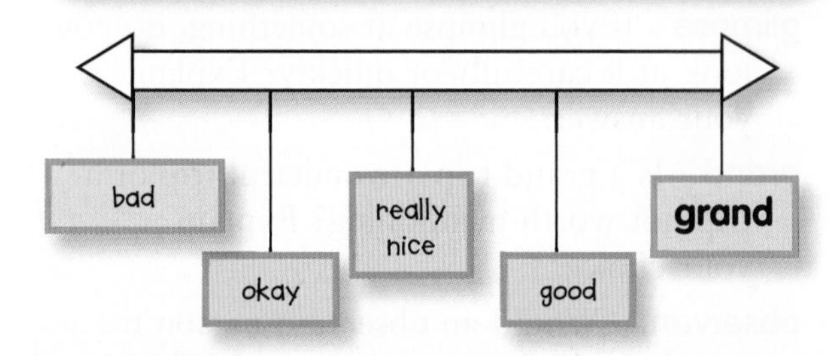

Tell children that you wrote grand *at one end and* bad *at the other end because both are words you might use to describe something. Tell children that there are words that mean something better than* bad, *but not as good as* grand. *Say the words* okay, really nice, *and* good. *Ask children where each of these words should go on the chart. Record their answers, modeling the differences in the meaning where needed.*

Your Turn to Write

Encourage children to relate the words to their own experiences. Discuss a few of the prompts below to prepare children for writing. Have children write about one of the prompts in their journals or on a separate piece of paper.

glimpse When do you glimpse at something rather than take a long look? What might you see if you glimpsed at something and what might you see if you took a careful look?

pleasant Are you having a pleasant day today? Explain why. What do you think is the most pleasant part of the day?

strain How would it feel to hold a leash that a dog is straining? Have you ever strained your arms or your legs?

grand What might be a grand present for you? Can you think of a grand time you have had? Where were you?

skyscraper What does a skyscraper look like? Where would you go to see lots of skyscrapers? Would you want to live in a skyscraper?

observant Do you think someone who makes airplanes is observant? Why do you think so? Are you an observant person?

5 Assessing the Vocabulary

Review

Blackline Master, page 169

Read the following questions aloud and have children circle *yes* or *no*.

1. Do you like to spend time with **pleasant** people? (yes)
2. Would **observant** people notice if something in their home was missing? (yes)
3. If you pick up a sandwich, do you **strain** your arms? (no)
4. Is a broken toy **grand**? (no)
5. Do you think many families could live in one **skyscraper**? (yes)
6. When you **glimpse** at something, do you study it for a long time? (no)

Assessment

Student Book, pages 60–61

Read each question aloud as children complete the activity.

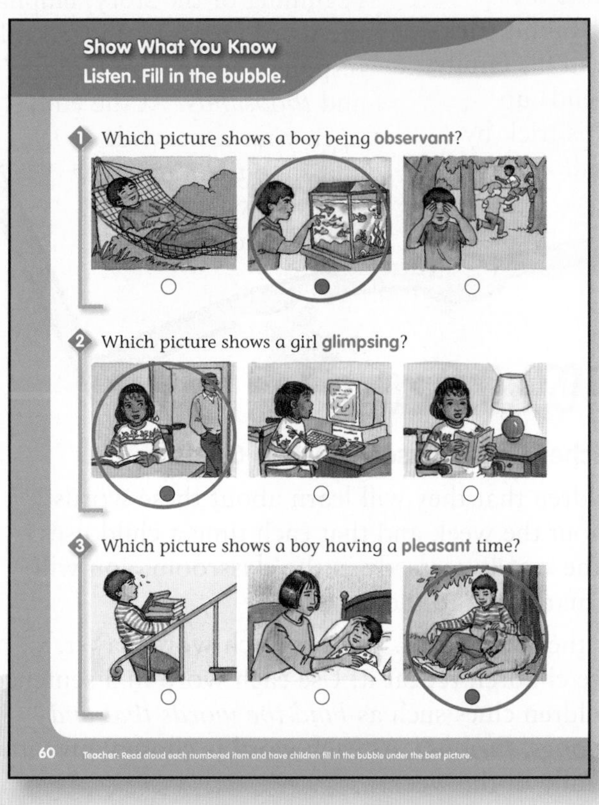

Show What You Know
Listen. Fill in the bubble.

1 Which picture shows a boy being **observant**?

2 Which picture shows a girl **glimpsing**?

3 Which picture shows a boy having a **pleasant** time?

60 Teacher: Read aloud each numbered item and have children fill in the bubble under the best picture.

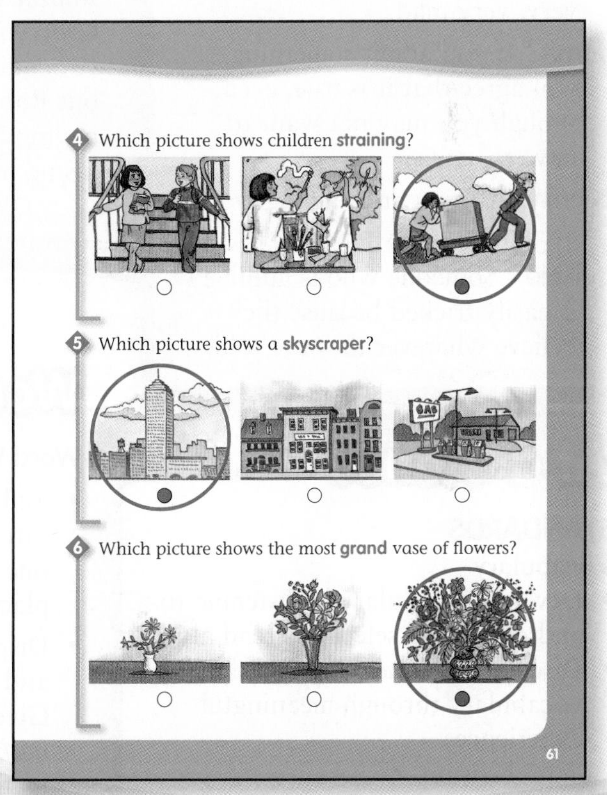

4 Which picture shows children **straining**?

5 Which picture shows a **skyscraper**?

6 Which picture shows the most **grand** vase of flowers?

61

Cumulative Review

Ask the first question and model how you might arrive at an answer. Then have children answer the remaining questions and explain their answers.

Lesson 14	Lesson 15	
tumble	strain	Can you **strain** your back if you **tumble**?
appear	glimpse	If a butterfly **appeared**, would you **glimpse** at it?
leisure	pleasant	Would it be **pleasant** to have lots of **leisure** time?
outgoing	skyscraper	Why might **outgoing** people live in **skyscrapers**?
relax	grand	Would it be **grand** to **relax** on the beach?
resourceful	observant	Can a person be both **observant** and **resourceful**?

Lesson 16

RABBIT COUNTS THE CROCODILES

Vocabulary

longs When someone longs for something, they want it very badly, but think they will never have it.

realize If you realize something, you begin to understand it or figure it out.

furious To be furious is to be very, very mad.

admit If you admit something, you agree that it is true, even though you may not want to have to say it.

cunning If you are cunning, you are able to trick people.

gullible Someone who is gullible is easily tricked because they believe whatever they are told.

At a Glance

STANDARDS

Vocabulary

- Develop vocabulary by listening to and discussing selections read aloud
- Discuss word meaning and develop vocabulary through meaningful experiences

Comprehension

- Use prior knowledge to make sense of texts

Writing

- Write brief descriptions using sensory details

LESSON RESOURCES

Read-Aloud Anthology: pp. 89–94

Student Book: pp. 62–65

Word Cards: Lesson 16

Photo Cards: 32, 43, 71, 86, 91–96, 116, 138

1 Introducing the Vocabulary

Read-Aloud

Read-Aloud Anthology, pages 89–94

In the Japanese legend *Rabbit Counts the Crocodiles*, Rabbit tricks Crocodile and his family, but Rabbit ends up paying for his trick by losing his tail!

Bringing the Story to Life

When Rabbit speaks at the beginning of the story, emphasize the word *hundred*. In Crocodile's response, emphasize *hundreds* and *thousands*. At the end, open your arms wide and snap them together to show what the last crocodile did!

Word Watcher

Word Watcher Chart, Lesson 16 Word Cards

- Tell children that they will learn about these words throughout the week and that each time a child uses one of the words correctly in the classroom, you will place a mark next to the word.
- Display the word cards. Point to each word, say it, and have children repeat it. Use each word in a sentence. Give children clues such as *Find the words that end with* s (*longs, furious*). As each word is chosen, give it its first tally of the week.

Sending the Words Home

Blackline Master—English, page 151; Spanish, page 152

Distribute the activity letter to inform parents of the vocabulary words for this week.

Research Says...

"Word meanings are not learned from a single context or single encounter. More typically, they are learned from repeated encounters and incorporated into a working vocabulary as they are used."

—Learning First Alliance

2 Using the Vocabulary

Word Snapshots

Photo Cards: 32, 43, 71, 86, 91–96, 116, 138

Hold up the card pairs and ask children the following questions. Discuss which photos show experiences the children can relate to.

longs (91 and 116) Which of these cards shows someone who longs for something?

realize (92 and 71) Which card shows a person who realizes something?

furious (93 and 138) Which card shows a boy looking furious?

admit (94 and 32) Which card shows someone admitting something?

cunning (95 and 86) Which card shows a girl being cunning?

gullible (96 and 43) Which of these cards shows someone being gullible?

ELL SUPPORT

Show children the photo cards, one at a time. Pronounce each word and then ask children to pronounce each word. Then hold up each card and read the sentence on the back of that card. Have children talk about how each photo shows what the word means.

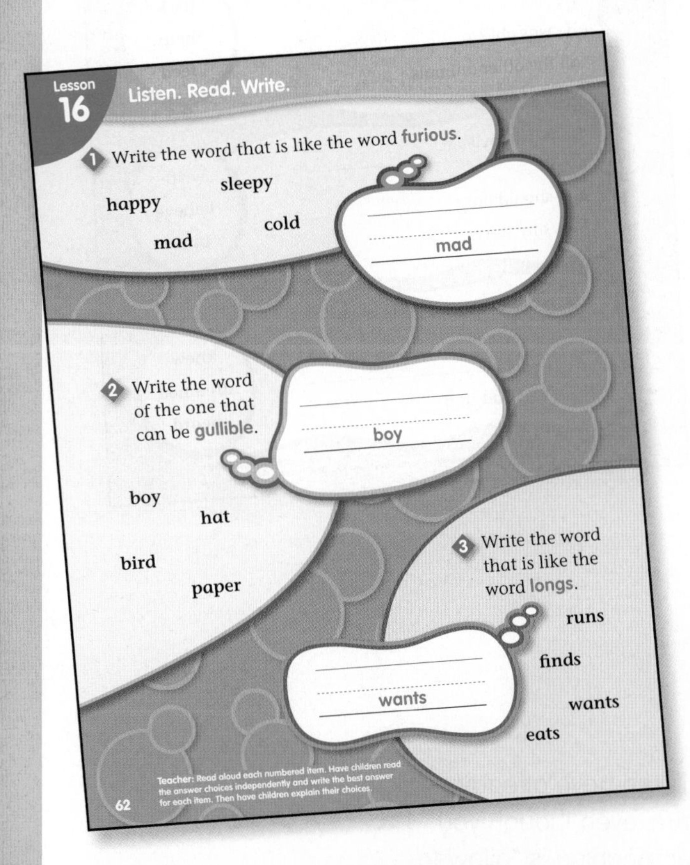

longs Tell children that you will describe a situation and if they think you are describing someone who longs for something, they should say "longs." If not, they should say nothing.

- James must take his puppy to the vet.
- Carla hopes that Dad will get her a puppy.
- Kim thinks her puppy is very smart.

Word Chat

Student Book, page 62

Guide children as they complete the Student Book activity. Then use children's responses and the prompts below to discuss each word.

furious Tell children that you will describe a situation and if they think you are describing a person who is furious, they should growl angrily and say "Grrrr....furious!" If not, they should say nothing.

- Pat was very surprised when her brother bought her a new sweater.
- Pat was very sad when she found out her brother had to go to the hospital.
- Pat was very angry with her brother for taking her favorite book.

gullible Tell children that you will describe a situation and if they think someone in that situation is being gullible, they should say "gullible." If not, they should say nothing.

- I tricked John and told him he had a spider in his hair, and he screamed!
- Juanita didn't believe my story, so she asked someone else if it was true.
- Susan believed me when I told her that her face was blue with orange polka dots!

3 Using the Vocabulary

Word Chat

Student Book, page 63

Guide children as they complete the Student Book activity. Then use children's responses and the prompts below to discuss each word.

admit Which is harder to do, admit something or laugh at something? Why?

cunning Who would you rather have as a friend, a cunning person or a kind person? Tell me why.

gullible Does *gullible* mean that someone believes nothing they are told or everything they are told? Explain what you mean.

realize Does *realize* mean that you really like something or that you begin to understand something? Explain your answer.

Continue the discussion with the remaining words from the lesson.

longs If you long for something, does it mean you don't care for it or you want to have it very badly? Explain why.

furious If you are furious does it mean that you are very mad or very surprised?

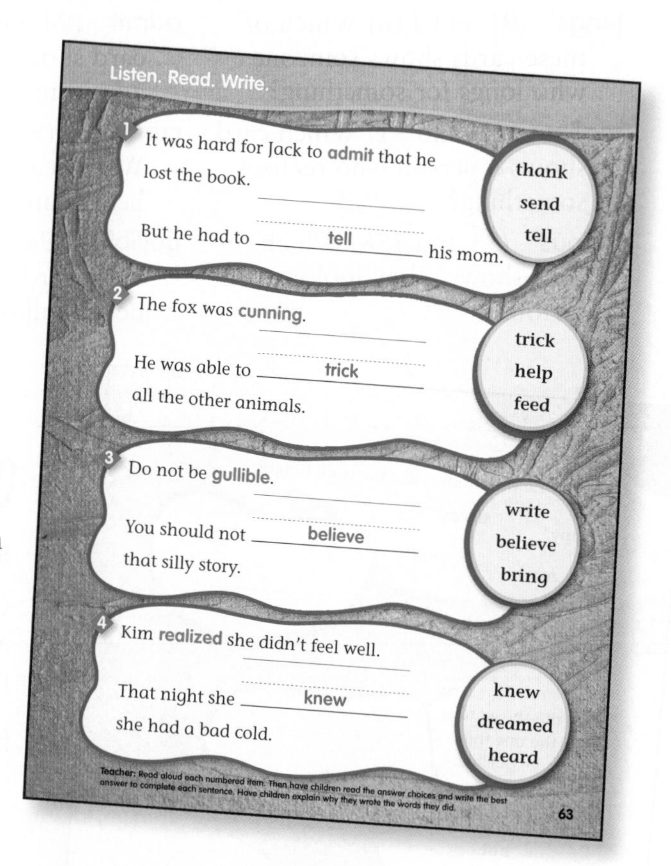

WORD CHALLENGE

Explain that the word *admit* has two meanings. Children have already learned that it means to "agree that something is true, even though you may not want to have to say it." Explain that another meaning is "allow to enter." Then provide the following prompts and have children tell which meaning *admit* has in each prompt.

- You have to pay before you can be **admitted** to the movie theater. (allow to enter)
- I **admitted** that I forgot to do my homework. (agree that something is true)

4 Using the Vocabulary

Word Organizers

Help your class complete the graphic organizers below. You may draw them on the board or on chart paper, or use the organizers in the back of this book to make transparencies.

Write the vocabulary word in the last box. Then write the word happy *in the first box.*

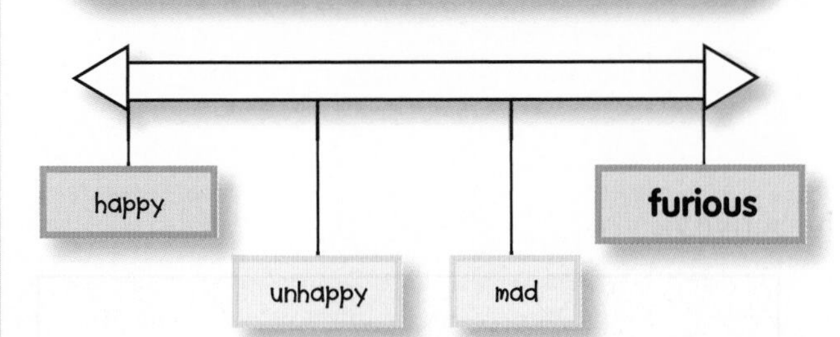

Tell children that furious *means to be very, very mad and that* happy *means the opposite of* furious. *Ask children to think of words that build from* happy *to* furious. *Record their answers, modeling the differences in meaning as appropriate.*

As children suggest words, ask questions such as, "Should I write the word mad *before or after the word* unhappy?*"*

Write the vocabulary word in the center.

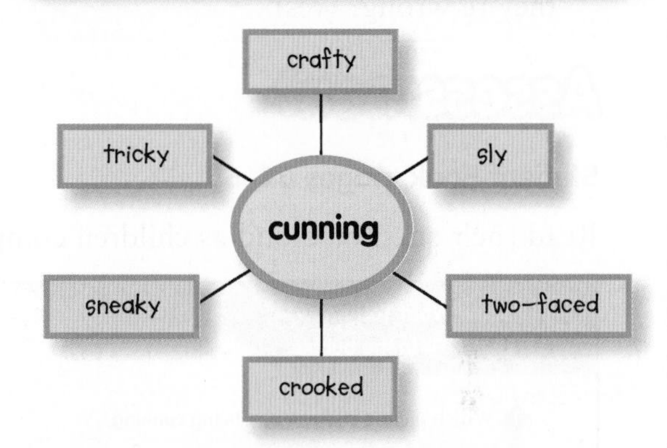

Ask children to think of words that mean the same or almost the same thing as cunning. *Ask them to think of different ways to describe a cunning person. Record their answers, providing sample answers as needed.*

Encourage children to talk about characters in stories who can be described as cunning.

Your Turn to Write

Encourage children to relate the words to their own experiences. Discuss a few of the prompts below to prepare children for writing. Have children write about one of the prompts in their journals or on a separate piece of paper.

longs Is there something that you long for? What is it? Do you think you will get it?

realize When you realize something, how does that make you feel? What do you realize now that you didn't know when you were younger?

furious Have you ever been furious? What did you do to feel better? Describe how you look and act when you are furious.

admit Have you ever had to admit something? Was it hard to do? How did you feel afterwards?

cunning Describe something a cunning person might do. Would you want to be friends with someone who was cunning? Why or why not?

gullible Do you know any gullible people? How do they act? Have you ever been gullible?

5 Assessing the Vocabulary

Review

Blackline Master, page 169

Read the following questions aloud and have children circle *yes* or *no*.

1. Is it hard for some people to **admit** when they're wrong? (yes)
2. Could someone **long** for a kitten? (yes)
3. Is it easy to fool a **gullible** person? (yes)
4. Might someone **realize** they are lost? (yes)
5. Is a **furious** person having fun? (no)
6. Is a **cunning** person sneaky? (yes)

Assessment

Student Book, pages 64–65

Read each question aloud as children complete the activity.

Show What You Know
Listen. Fill in the bubble.

1 Which picture shows a boy being **cunning**?

2 Which picture shows a girl who **longs** for something?

3 Which picture shows a girl who just **realized** something?

64 Teacher: Read aloud each numbered item and have children fill in the bubble under the best picture.

4 Which picture shows a girl being **gullible**?

5 Which picture shows a woman who is **furious**?

6 Which picture shows a boy who is **admitting** something?

65

Cumulative Review

Ask the first question and model how you might arrive at an answer. Then have children answer the remaining questions and explain their answers.

Lesson 15	Lesson 16	
strain	furious	Would you be **furious** if you **strained** your back?
skyscraper	longs	Do you **long** to live in a **skyscraper**?
pleasant	realize	Would it be nice to **realize** that something was **pleasant**?
observant	gullible	Do you think a **gullible** person is **observant**?
grand	cunning	Might a **cunning** person have a **grand** plan?
glimpse	admit	If you **glimpsed** at a surprise present, would you **admit** it?

MICKEY MOUSE SPEAKS!

Vocabulary

romp When children or animals romp, they play happily.

fad If something is a fad, it is popular for a very short time.

gather When you gather things, you collect them all into a group.

household Your household is your home, all of the people who live there, and all of the things that are a part of it.

entertain To entertain means to do something like sing, dance, or play an instrument to please an audience.

creative A creative person is someone who is always thinking up new and interesting ideas.

At a Glance

STANDARDS

Vocabulary
- Use context to find the meaning of unknown words
- Develop vocabulary by discussing characters and events from a story

Comprehension
- Establish purpose for reading or listening (to be informed)

Writing
- Record or dictate knowledge of a topic in various ways

LESSON RESOURCES

Read-Aloud Anthology: pp. 95–100
Student Book: pp. 66–69
Word Cards: Lesson 17
Photo Cards: 97–102

1 Introducing the Vocabulary

Read-Aloud

Read-Aloud Anthology, pages 95–100

People all over the world know Mickey Mouse, but do you know how the cartoon Mickey began? *Mickey Mouse Speaks!* is a true story about the first Mickey Mouse cartoons.

Bringing the Story to Life

Use your voice to sound like a radio announcer as you read the opening newspaper article. Read the rest of the selection in a conversational tone, pausing to give emphasis to the title of each new section.

Word Watcher

Word Watcher Chart, Lesson 17 Word Cards

- Tell children that they will learn about these words throughout the week and that each time a child uses one of the words correctly in the classroom, you will place a mark next to the word.
- Put the cards in a bag or large hat. Have children take turns drawing out cards. Say each word and have children repeat it. Then use each word in a sentence and give the word its first tally of the week.

Sending the Words Home

Blackline Master—English, page 153; Spanish, page 154

Distribute the activity letter to inform parents of the vocabulary words for this week.

Research Says...

"The development of a reading vocabulary that is both extensive and accurate is a necessary phase of good comprehension."

—*How to Increase Reading Ability*, A. J. Harris and E. R. Sipay

2 Using the Vocabulary

Word Snapshots

Photo Cards: 97–102

Hold up each card and read the sentence on the back of the card. Then ask the following questions.

romp How can you tell these animals are romping?

fad What things do you see in this picture that are fads? Do you like these fads?

gather What is the boy in this picture gathering?

household What parts of this picture are part of a household? Why is that?

entertain Who in this picture is entertaining? How can you tell?

creative What makes the girl in this picture creative?

ELL SUPPORT

Discuss the photo cards and how each picture relates to each vocabulary word. Place the photo cards facedown on the floor and have a child flip over a card. Then ask a yes/no question using the vocabulary word. For example, for *fad* you could say, *Does only one person follow a fad?* Continue with the other cards.

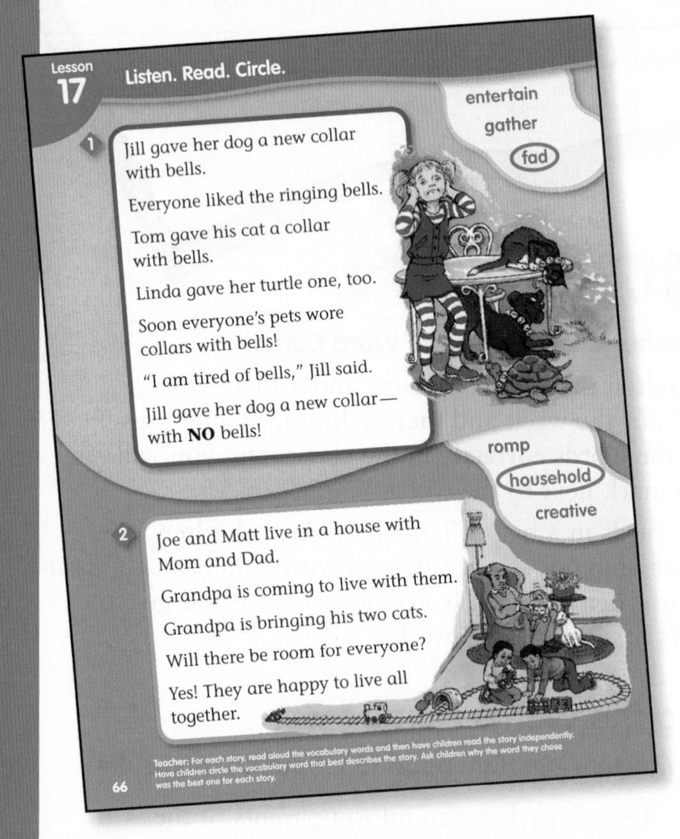

Lesson 17

Listen. Read. Circle.

1

Jill gave her dog a new collar with bells.

Everyone liked the ringing bells.

Tom gave his cat a collar with bells.

Linda gave her turtle one, too.

Soon everyone's pets wore collars with bells!

"I am tired of bells," Jill said.

Jill gave her dog a new collar—with **NO** bells!

entertain

gather

fad

2

Joe and Matt live in a house with Mom and Dad.

Grandpa is coming to live with them.

Grandpa is bringing his two cats.

Will there be room for everyone?

Yes! They are happy to live all together.

romp

household

creative

Teacher: For each story, read aloud the vocabulary words and then have children read the story independently. Have children circle the vocabulary word that best describes the story. Ask children why the word they chose was the best one for each story.

66

Word Chat

Student Book, page 66

Guide children as they complete the Student Book activity. Then use children's responses and the prompts below to discuss each word.

fad Tell children that you will describe some things and if children think these things could be a fad, they should say "fad." If not, they should say nothing.

- rainbow-colored sunglasses
- writing with a pencil
- a shirt with buttons that squeak when you push them

household Tell children that you are going to describe some people and if children think these people are part of your household, they should shout "Household! Home, Sweet Home!" If not, they should say nothing.

- your best friend who comes over to eat dinner with you
- your sister who shares a bedroom with you
- the letter carrier who brings your mail

creative Tell children that you will name some activities and if they think an activity is creative, they should tap their foreheads and say "creative." If not, they should say nothing.

- make a duck out of clay
- build a sand castle
- eat a big dinner

Word Chat

Student Book, page 67

Guide children as they complete the Student Book activity. Then use children's responses and the prompts below to discuss each word.

Display the vocabulary words and review each word's meaning. Then write the following rhymes on the board for each word. Read each rhyme aloud, pausing at the end for children to say the vocabulary word that completes the rhyme.

There's no reason to frown or stomp.
You should run and jump and
______ . **(romp)**

We found some coins!
Which would you rather—
Leave them there
Or stop and ______ ? **(gather)**

It's boring flying on this plane,
But they show a movie to ______ . **(entertain)**

My mother draws flowers
On the walls where we live.
She has many ideas.
She is so ______ . **(creative)**

Continue the activity with the remaining words from the lesson.

Fred likes socks. Fred is glad.
Red socks are the latest ______ . **(fad)**

Behind that fence, I am told,
Lives a very nice ______ . **(household)**

WORD CHALLENGE

Point out that many of the words in this story talk about how Walt Disney was very **creative**. Encourage children to think about how things would be different if he did not have new and interesting ideas about how to make his cartoons better. (His cartoons would be all the same and would never change.) Use the following prompts to help children brainstorm words that mean the opposite of some of the words found in the story.

- Walt Disney wanted his cartoons to **entertain** people. If the cartoons were not fun to watch, they would ______ the audience. (bore)
- People **gathered** at movie theaters to see Mickey Mouse cartoons. When the cartoons were over, people ______ and went home. (left)

4 Using the Vocabulary

Word Organizers

Help your class complete the graphic organizers below. You may draw them on the board or on chart paper, or use the organizers in the back of this book to make transparencies.

Write the vocabulary word in the diamond.

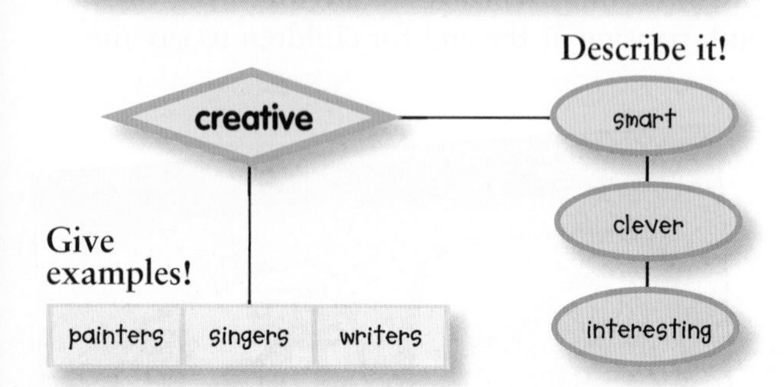

Encourage children to think of ways to describe people who are creative. Record their answers, modeling sample answers as needed.
Ask children why they think creative people are each of these things.

Invite children to think of examples of types of people who are creative. Provide sample answers if needed, and record appropriate answers.
Ask children to explain how each of these types of people are creative.

Write the vocabulary word in the blue box.

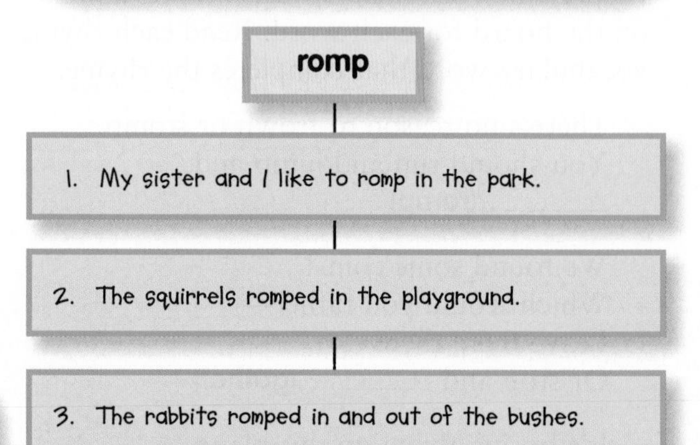

Ask children to create sentences about things that might romp. You may want to start them off by modeling a sentence for them. Then record their sentences.
After children generate sentences, have them tell why people or animals might romp.

Your Turn to Write

Encourage children to relate the words to their own experiences. Discuss a few of the prompts below to prepare children for writing. Have children write about one of the prompts in their journals or on a separate piece of paper.

romp What is your favorite place to romp? What is your favorite time to romp? Are there times when you would not want to romp?

fad What kinds of things become fads? Would you like to start a fad? Can you think up a toy that could become a fad?

gather Do you like to gather with friends? Are there objects that you like to gather, like shells, leaves, stones, or flowers? Tell about what you like to gather.

household How big is your household? How many people are in it? Who is the youngest? Who is the oldest?

entertain Do you like to be entertained? Who entertains you best? Do you like to entertain people? Tell an entertaining story.

creative What are some creative things you like to do? What makes something creative? Is it fun to be creative?

5 Assessing the Vocabulary

Review

Blackline Master, page 169

Read the following questions aloud and have children circle *yes* or *no.*

1. Would you **romp** with someone you don't like? (no)
2. Could shoes that light up be a **fad**? (yes)
3. Might a teacher **gather** books? (yes)
4. Do children live in **households**? (yes)
5. Do you think a broken television could **entertain** people? (no)
6. Might a person who plants a garden be **creative**? (yes)

Assessment

Student Book, pages 68–69

Read each question aloud as children complete the activity.

Show What You Know
Listen. Fill in the bubble.

1. Which picture shows horses **romping**?
2. Which picture shows a girl following a **fad**?
3. Which picture shows a squirrel **gathering** something?

68 Teacher: Read aloud each numbered item and have children fill in the bubble under the best picture.

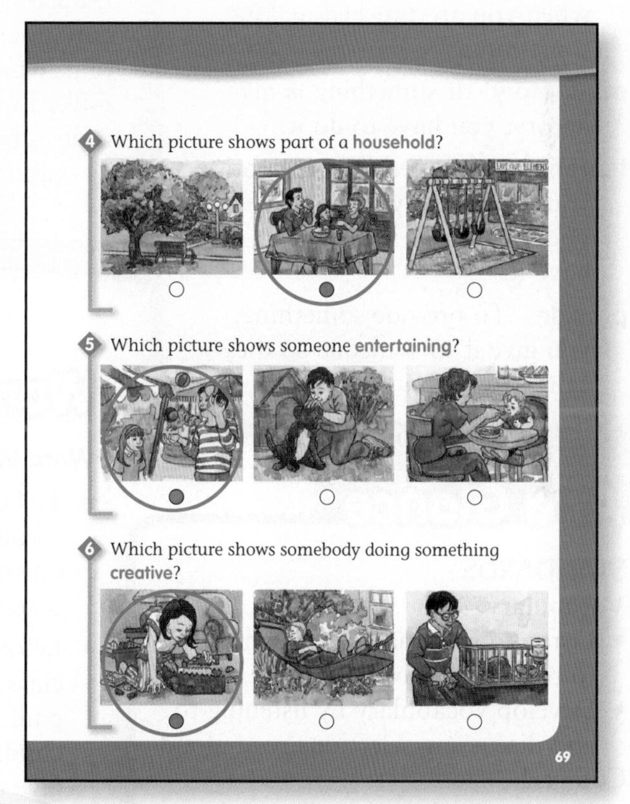

4. Which picture shows part of a **household**?
5. Which picture shows someone **entertaining**?
6. Which picture shows somebody doing something **creative**?

69

Cumulative Review

Ask the first question and model how you might arrive at an answer. Then have children answer the remaining questions and explain their answers.

Lesson 16	Lesson 17	
longs	romp	Do children **long** to **romp** all summer?
gullible	fad	Are you **gullible** if you follow a **fad**?
furious	gather	Would you be **furious** if someone **gathered** all your toys?
admit	household	Would you **admit** being wrong to anyone in your **household**?
realize	entertain	Do you **realize** that it takes talent to **entertain** people?
cunning	creative	Might a **cunning** person also be **creative**?

Lesson 18

Kiss the Cow!

Vocabulary

pasture A pasture is a field of grass or other plants that animals such as cows and horses like to eat.

velvet Velvet is a kind of soft, fuzzy cloth.

scrap A scrap is a little piece of something that is left over when you are finished making something.

mandatory If something is mandatory, you have to do it.

tempting If something is tempting, you want it very much, even if you know you should not have it.

provide To provide something, you give it to someone so they can use it.

At a Glance

STANDARDS

Vocabulary
- Listen to imaginative texts in order to respond to vivid language
- Develop vocabulary by listening to and discussing selections read aloud

Comprehension
- Use a variety of strategies to comprehend text

Writing
- Write in different forms for different purposes

LESSON RESOURCES

Read-Aloud Anthology: pp. 101–107	Word Cards: Lesson 18
Student Book: pp. 70–73	Photo Cards: 103–108

1 Introducing the Vocabulary

Read-Aloud

Read-Aloud Anthology, pages 101–107

In the fantasy story *Kiss the Cow!* Mama May's cow, Luella, stops giving milk when young Annalisa milks Luella and then refuses to kiss the cow as required.

Bringing the Story to Life

Give distinctive voices to Mama May and Annalisa. Make Mama May's voice soft and lyrical and Annalisa's sassy and loud. Encourage children to chime in on the last lines of each verse of Mama May's song.

Word Watcher

Word Watcher Chart, Lesson 18 Word Cards

- Tell children that they will learn about these words throughout the week and that each time a child uses one of the words correctly in the classroom, you will place a mark next to the word.
- Before class begins, put all of the cards into a pail. When class begins, call on volunteers to pick a card from the pail. After each card is withdrawn, say the word and have children repeat it. Then use the word in a sentence, and give the card its first tally of the week.

Sending the Words Home

Blackline Master—English, page 155; Spanish, page 156

Distribute the activity letter to inform parents of the vocabulary words for this week.

Research Says…

"…reading is built on a foundation of oral language competence—in other words, not just on phonology but also on vocabulary, grammar, and so on."

—*Reading Improvement,* Marlow Ediger

2 Using the Vocabulary

Word Snapshots

Photo Cards: 103–108

Read the sentence on the back of each card as you give photo cards to six children. Then say the sentences below, which use the word in a different context. For each sentence, have the child with that card hold it up and repeat the word.

pasture The barn was located in the pasture.

velvet The woman wore a velvet dress.

scrap We gave the scraps of food to the dog.

mandatory It is mandatory to wear your seatbelt.

tempting The chocolate chip cookies are very tempting.

provide My parents provide clothes for me to wear.

ELL SUPPORT

Hold up each photo card, one at a time. Discuss the words and how they relate to the story. Then have children take turns role-playing the different characters in the story. They can use the vocabulary words to describe the character they are playing in the story. For example, a child acting out the role of the cow Luella could say, *I have a velvety nose and I live in the pasture.*

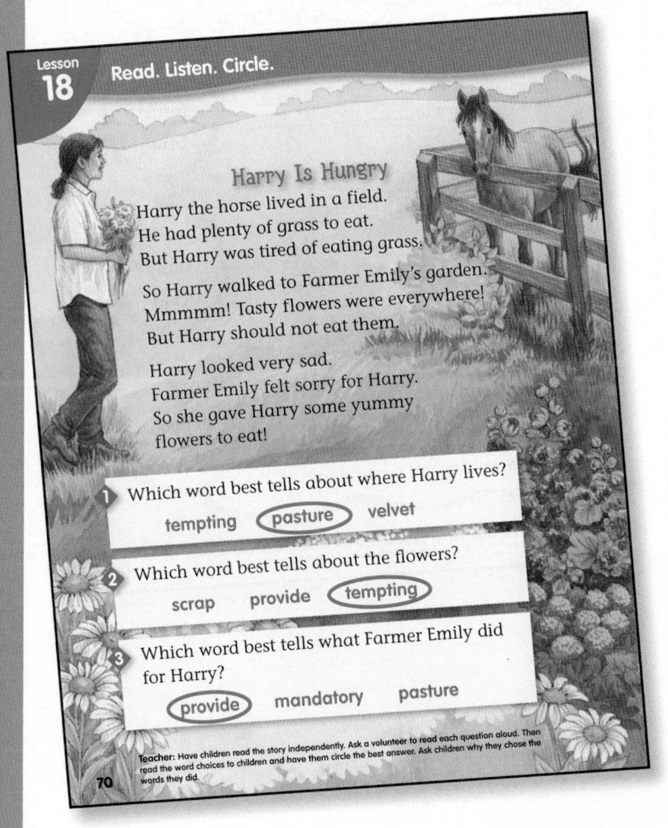
Lesson 18 Read. Listen. Circle.

Harry Is Hungry

Harry the horse lived in a field.
He had plenty of grass to eat.
But Harry was tired of eating grass.

So Harry walked to Farmer Emily's garden.
Mmmmm! Tasty flowers were everywhere!
But Harry should not eat them.

Harry looked very sad.
Farmer Emily felt sorry for Harry.
So she gave Harry some yummy flowers to eat!

1. Which word best tells about where Harry lives?
   tempting (pasture) velvet
2. Which word best tells about the flowers?
   scrap provide (tempting)
3. Which word best tells what Farmer Emily did for Harry?
   (provide) mandatory pasture

Teacher: Have children read the story independently. Ask a volunteer to read each question aloud. Then read the word choices to children and have them circle the best answer. Ask children why they chose the words they did.

70

Word Chat

Student Book, page 70

Guide children as they complete the Student Book activity. Then use children's responses and the prompts below to discuss each word.

Divide the class into two groups. Assign the first word to one group and the second word to the other. Explain that you will say a sentence with a missing word, and the group that has the word that fits the sentence should say their word aloud.

pasture/velvet

- The goat ate a daisy in the ______ . (pasture)
- The beautiful curtains were made out of ______ . (velvet)
- Her skin was so soft it felt like ______ . (velvet)
- I painted a picture of sheep in the ______ . (pasture)

provide/scrap

- Kim brought the tennis rackets, and I ______ the ball. (provided)
- Our teacher ______ paper so we could take the test. (provided)
- There were lots of ______ of paper left over from our craft project. (scraps)
- After peeling potatoes, we threw away the ______ . (scraps)

tempting/mandatory

- My mom says it's ______ that I clean up my room. (mandatory)
- Fried mosquitoes with mud ketchup are not very ______ . (tempting)
- I wish it wasn't ______ that we go to school. (mandatory)
- On a hot, sunny day, it is very ______ to jump in my neighbor's pool. (tempting)

3 Using the Vocabulary

Word Chat

Student Book, page 71

Guide children as they complete the Student Book activity. Then use children's responses and the prompts below to discuss each word.

For each vocabulary word, provide children with the first part of a sentence that includes the vocabulary word. Have children provide an ending for the sentence that shows they know what the new word means.

mandatory Wearing seatbelts is mandatory because....

provide We hope Mom will provide us with....

velvet Mary used velvet to make....

scrap After dinner we gathered some scraps of....

Continue the discussion with the remaining words from the lesson.

tempting An ice cream sundae is tempting to eat because....

pasture We took our horse to the pasture because....

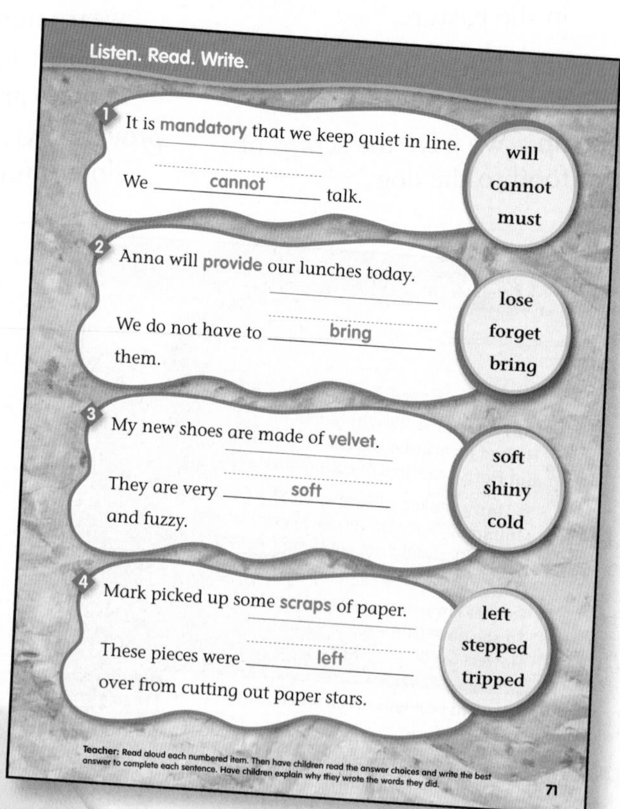

WORD CHALLENGE

Remind children that Luella the cow lived in a **pasture**. Encourage them to think of another word that means about the same as the word *pasture. (field, meadow, prairie, park)* Encourage them to think of some words that mean about the same as other vocabulary words from the lesson.

- What other words could you use for **scraps**? *(bits, pieces, crumbs)*
- What words mean about the same as **provide**? *(give, supply, pass out)*

Word Organizers

Help your class complete the graphic organizers below. You may draw them on the board or on chart paper, or use the organizers in the back of this book to make transparencies.

Write the vocabulary word in the blue box.

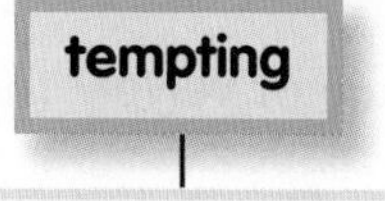

1. It is tempting to play with Mom's computer.

2. The chocolate cake smelled very tempting.

3. A hamburger with extra fries is tempting.

Ask children to think about things that are tempting to themselves or others. Help children use their ideas to compose sentences. You may want to start by modeling a sentence for them. Then record their sentences.

Write the vocabulary word in the center.

Yes

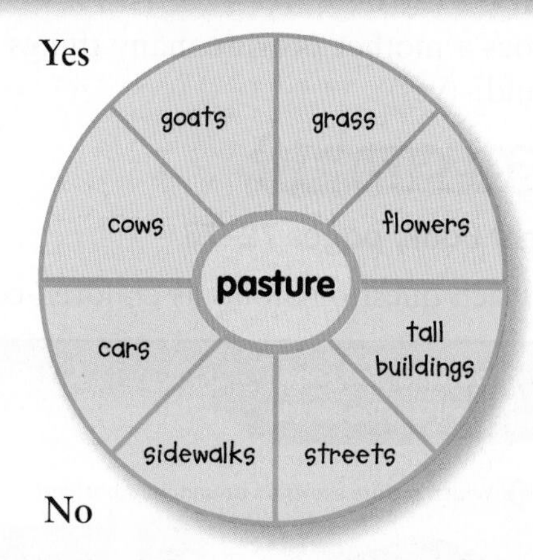

No

Ask children to name some things that they would expect to see in a pasture. As needed, call out sample answers and ask, "Would you see that in a pasture?" Record appropriate answers.

Ask children to name some things that they would not expect to see in a pasture. Model sample answers as needed and record appropriate answers.

Ask children to explain how they decide if something might be found in a pasture or not.

Your Turn to Write

Encourage children to relate the words to their own experiences. Discuss a few of the prompts below to prepare children for writing. Have children write about one of the prompts in their journals or on a separate piece of paper.

pasture Have you ever been in a pasture? Would you like to go to a pasture? Why or why not?

velvet What are some things people make from velvet? Would you like to sleep on a bed with a velvet cover and pillow? Explain your reasons.

scrap What kinds of scraps do people throw out? What kinds of scraps might people keep? Why?

mandatory What are some things that are mandatory? What is mandatory at school?

tempting What are some things that are tempting for you? Have you ever gotten any of them?

provide What are some things you could provide to your parents? Have you ever provided your friends with anything? What do you like best, providing things for other people or having things provided for you?

5 Assessing the Vocabulary

Review

Blackline Master, page 169

Read the following questions aloud and have children circle *yes* or *no*.

1. Might you see a skyscraper in the middle of a **pasture**? (no)
2. Does a mother **provide** many things to her child? (yes)
3. Would you ever throw **scraps** in a garbage bag? (yes)
4. Is it **mandatory** to wear purple shirts every day of the week? (no)
5. Is a warm cake **tempting** to a hungry boy? (yes)
6. Are houses made of **velvet**? (no)

Assessment

Student Book, pages 72–73

Read each question aloud as children complete the activity.

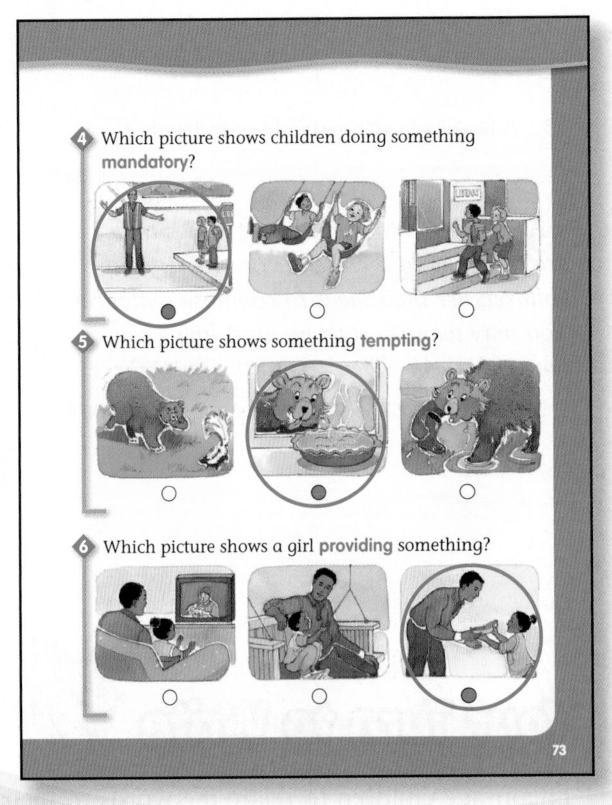

Cumulative Review

Ask the first question and model how you might arrive at an answer. Then have children answer the remaining questions and explain their answers.

Lesson 17	Lesson 18	
creative	pasture	Might you do some **creative** things in a **pasture**?
fad	velvet	Could **velvet** pants become a **fad**?
gather	scrap	Might you **gather** some **scraps** of cloth to make a quilt?
romp	mandatory	Should it be **mandatory** to **romp** on a playground?
entertain	tempting	Is it **tempting** to **entertain** your friends?
household	provide	Do **households** and schools **provide** many things for children?

Coyote and the Stars

Vocabulary

delicate Something that is delicate is small and light and easily broken.

vast If something is vast, it is so large that it seems like it has no end.

investigate When you investigate something, you try to find out what it is all about.

variety A variety is many different kinds of something.

enhance When you enhance something, you make it better.

accomplish When you accomplish something, you complete something that was very hard to do.

At a Glance

STANDARDS

Vocabulary
- Use visual references to build upon word meaning
- Speak to express the mood of a story by using a variety of words

Comprehension
- Make and explain inferences

Writing
- Compose original texts

LESSON RESOURCES

Read-Aloud Anthology: pp. 108–113

Student Book: pp. 74–77

Word Cards: Lesson 19

Photo Cards: 109–114

1 Introducing the Vocabulary

Read-Aloud

Read-Aloud Anthology, pages 108–113

Coyote and the Stars is a Native American legend that tells how the desert, including its nighttime sky, was decorated by the animals that live there.

Bringing the Story to Life

Tape up a large piece of white paper. As you tell the story, add simple, colorful illustrations to match the animals' actions so children can better visualize the progress as the animals "create" the desert scenery. Use glitter to make the stars!

Word Watcher

Word Watcher Chart, Lesson 19 Word Cards

- Tell children that they will learn about these words throughout the week and that each time a child uses one of the words correctly in the classroom, you will place a mark next to the word.
- Display the word cards along the board ledge. Have a volunteer select a card. Say the word and ask children to repeat it with you. Use the word in a sentence and make the appropriate tally mark. Repeat with the remaining cards.

Sending the Words Home

Blackline Master—English, page 157; Spanish, page 158

Distribute the activity letter to inform parents of the vocabulary words for this week.

Research Says...

"Good vocabulary instruction helps students gain ownership of words, instead of just learning them well enough to pass a test."

—*Word Power*, Steven A. Stahl and Barbara Kapinus

2 Using the Vocabulary

Word Snapshots

Photo Cards: 109–114

Display the photo cards and ask children to work in pairs to make up a short story about a card. Provide the following story starters.

delicate Snowflakes are delicate and do not last very long. Tell us more.

vast The desert is so vast that it seems to go on forever. What happened there?

investigate Lindsey and Emma investigated bees and pollen. Tell what they found.

variety I have never seen such a variety of goldfish! Tell us more.

enhance Sally uses flowers and icing to enhance cakes. Tell how.

accomplish When you graduate to another grade, you have accomplished something very special. Tell us more.

ELL SUPPORT

Discuss how each card relates to *Coyote and the Stars*. Then place the cards in a paper bag so they cannot be seen. Say each word and have a child choose a card from the bag to see if it matches the word that was said. If it is a match, have children say the word aloud with you.

Lesson 19 Read. Listen. Circle.

Flutter's Flight

Flutter is a tiny butterfly.
Her wings are light and thin.
One day, she flew over a field.

Flutter flew and flew.
The other side of the field
was very far away.
She stopped to rest on a rock.

Flutter saw a beautiful flower.
She wanted to find out about the flower.
She flew close and looked at it carefully.

1. Which word best tells about Flutter?
vast (delicate) accomplish

2. Which word best tells about the size of the field?
enhance investigate (vast)

3. Which word best tells what Flutter did when she saw the flower?
(investigate) variety delicate

Teacher: Have children read the story independently. Ask a volunteer to read each question aloud. Then read the word choices to children and have them circle the best answer. Ask children why they chose the words they did.

74

investigate Tell children that you will describe a situation and if they think something is being investigated, they should say "A-ha! Investigate!" If not, they should say nothing.

- A man drops some money.
- A scientist digs up dinosaur bones and studies them closely.
- A girl follows some footprints to see where they lead.

Word Chat

Student Book, page 74

Guide children as they complete the Student Book activity. Then use children's responses and the prompts below to discuss each word.

delicate Tell children that you will describe some things and if they think you are describing something delicate, they should cup their hands and quietly whisper "delicate." If not, they should say nothing.

- a spider's web
- a bike helmet
- a tiny glass vase

vast Tell children that you will describe a place and if they think the place is vast, they should spread their arms wide and roar, "VAST!" If not, they should say nothing.

- the distance from Earth to the moon
- the ocean
- the classroom

3 Using the Vocabulary

Word Chat

Student Book, page 75

Guide children as they complete the Student Book activity. Then use children's responses and the prompts below to discuss each word.

variety Would you be likely to get bored if you had a variety of games to play? Why or why not?

vast Would you want to row across a vast lake? Explain.

enhance Would you be happy or unhappy if someone enhanced your bedroom. Why?

accomplished Would you feel proud or embarrassed if you accomplished something? Explain.

Continue the discussion with the remaining words from the lesson.

investigate Would it be fun to investigate a smelly trash can? Why or why not?

delicate Would you toss something delicate up in the air or would you hold it gently in your hands? Explain your answer.

WORD CHALLENGE

Discuss "opposites" with children. Explain that sometimes words mean the opposite or nearly the opposite, like *fast* and *slow*. Divide the children into two groups. Assign one group **delicate** and the other group **vast**. Have the groups take turns suggesting words that mean the opposite or nearly the opposite of their assigned word, such as *strong, sturdy, hard, tough,* and *unbreakable*; and *tiny, small, little, short,* and *teeny*.

Then ask children if they can think of words that mean the opposite or almost the opposite of **investigate** *(ignore)*, **variety** *(same)*, **enhance** *(damage, spoil, ruin)*, and **accomplish** *(fail, quit)*.

4 Using the Vocabulary

Word Organizers

Help your class complete the graphic organizers below. You may draw them on the board or on chart paper, or use the organizers in the back of this book to make transparencies.

Write the words shown in blue boxes to begin.

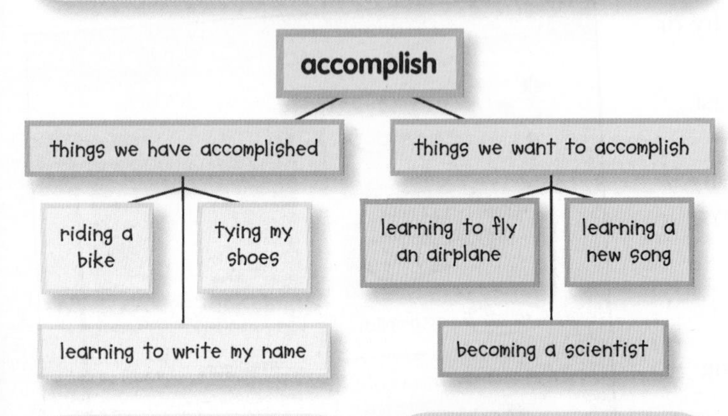

Ask children to name some things they have accomplished and record their answers. Model sample answers as needed.

Ask children to explain how difficult it was or was not to accomplish these things.

Ask children to name some things they want to accomplish. Encourage children to think of things they want to accomplish in both the near and distant future. Record their answers, modeling sample answers as needed.

Write the vocabulary word in the center.

enhance

hang curtains

paint walls

put flowers out

hang a picture on the wall

put up wallpaper

get new furniture

Ask children what things can be done to enhance a room. Record their answers, modeling answers whenever necessary.

Ask children if they have made any enhancements to their own rooms.

Your Turn to Write

Encourage children to relate the words to their own experiences. Discuss a few of the prompts below to prepare children for writing. Have children write about one of the prompts in their journals or on a separate piece of paper.

delicate Do you own any things that are delicate? Have you ever broken something that was delicate? Could you fix it?

vast Have you ever traveled a vast distance? Where did you go? Would it be fun to eat a vast amount of ice cream?

investigate Have you ever investigated anything? What sorts of things would you be interested in investigating?

variety Do you like to eat a variety of foods? What are a variety of kinds of books that you like to read?

enhance What things would you add to your desk to enhance it? If you wanted to enhance your shoes, what could make them better? Have you ever enhanced anything at home?

accomplish What is the thing you have accomplished that makes you most proud? What was the hardest thing you ever had to accomplish? Was it worth it when you finished?

5 Assessing the Vocabulary

Review

Blackline Master, page 169

Read the following questions aloud and have children circle *yes* or *no*.

1. Would a **delicate** statue break if you dropped it? (yes)
2. Could you walk across a **vast** field in just a couple of seconds? (no)
3. If you **investigate** something, do you ignore it? (no)
4. Can you buy a **variety** of foods in a large grocery store? (yes)
5. If you lose something, do you **enhance** it? (no)
6. Might you be proud of yourself if you **accomplished** something? (yes)

Assessment

Student Book, pages 76–77

Read each question aloud as children complete the activity.

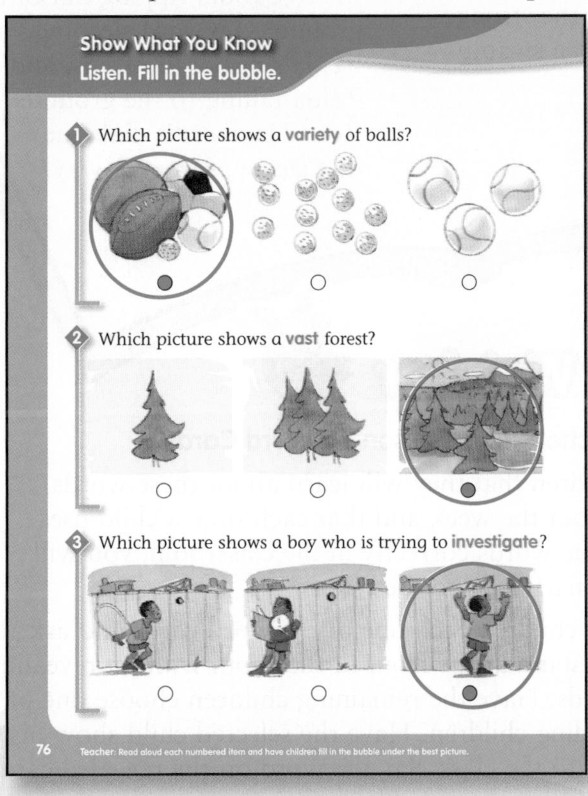

Cumulative Review

Ask the first question and model how you might arrive at an answer. Then have children answer the remaining questions and explain their answers.

Lesson 18	Lesson 19	
tempting	delicate	Is it **tempting** to eat a **delicate** frosting flower off of a fancy cake?
pasture	vast	Would a large **pasture** seem **vast** to a small mouse?
scrap	investigate	Might you **investigate** a mysterious **scrap** of shiny paper?
provide	variety	Does a good restaurant **provide** a **variety** of foods for dinner?
velvet	enhance	Could you **enhance** a dress by adding **velvet** to it?
mandatory	accomplish	Is it **mandatory** to **accomplish** something great in your life?

Lesson 20

STRONG ENOUGH

Vocabulary

boast When you boast about something, you talk about it in a way that is so proud that it is like showing off.

mighty When something is mighty, it is very large and strong.

flatter When you flatter someone, you tell them nice things about themselves to make them feel good.

frighten To frighten someone is to scare them very badly.

enormous If something is enormous, it is almost larger than you can imagine.

humble If someone is humble, they do not look for a lot of attention.

At a Glance

STANDARDS

Vocabulary
- Use vocabulary to describe ideas, feelings, and experiences
- Develop vocabulary by discussing characters and events from a story

Comprehension
- Retell or act out order of important events in stories

Writing
- Describe connections between personal experiences and written and visual texts

LESSON RESOURCES

Read-Aloud Anthology: pp. 114–120
Student Book: pp. 78–81
Word Cards: Lesson 20
Photo Cards: 22, 56, 70, 76, 84, 86, 115–120

1 Introducing the Vocabulary

Read-Aloud

Read-Aloud Anthology, pages 114–120

In *Strong Enough* an alligator learns not to brag about being the strongest alligator in the swamp.

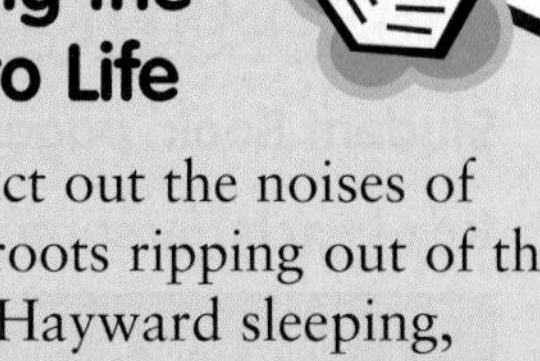

Bringing the Story to Life

Loudly act out the noises of the tree roots ripping out of the ground, Hayward sleeping, Zelda's heavy footsteps, and Zelda falling to the ground. Read Hayward's dialogue in a sleepy, sarcastic way.

Word Watcher

Word Watcher Chart, Lesson 20 Word Cards

- Tell children that they will learn about these words throughout the week and that each time a child uses one of the words correctly in the classroom, you will place a mark next to the word.
- Give six children each one of the word cards and ask them to stand at the front of the room without revealing their cards. Have the remaining children choose one of the standing children. Have the selected child show his or her card to the class. Say the word on the revealed card, have children repeat it, then use it in a sentence and make the appropriate tally mark.

Sending the Words Home

Blackline Master—English, page 159; Spanish, page 160

Distribute the activity letter to inform parents of the vocabulary words for this week.

Research Says...

"Talk with students about new vocabulary and concepts and help them relate the words to their prior knowledge and experiences."

—Put Reading First

2 Using the Vocabulary

Word Snapshots

Photo Cards: 22, 56, 70, 76, 84, 86, 115–120

Hold up the card pairs and ask children the following questions. Discuss which photos best show the vocabulary words.

boast (115 and 76) Which card shows someone who is boasting?

mighty (116 and 56) Which card shows something that is mighty?

flatter (117 and 22) Which card shows someone being flattered?

frighten (118 and 86) Which card shows someone who looks frightened?

enormous (119 and 70) Which card shows something that is enormous?

humble (120 and 84) Which card shows someone looking humble?

ELL SUPPORT

Discuss the vocabulary words with children. Pronounce each word and have them repeat after you. Then line the cards along the board ledge. Tell children a sentence using a vocabulary word. Have a child find the appropriate card to match your sentence. Then read part of the sentence on the back of each photo card as a sentence starter. Have children complete each sentence.

mighty Tell children that you will describe some things and if they think you are describing someone or something that is mighty, they should make a muscle with their arm and yell, "MIGHTY!" If not, they should say nothing.

- a tiny chicken resting in the hay
- a strong woman lifting up a tiger
- a big river that floods nearby homes

Word Chat

Student Book, page 78

Guide children as they complete the Student Book activity. Then use children's responses and the prompts below to discuss each word.

humble Tell children that you will describe a person and if they think you are describing someone humble, they should bow and say "humble." If not, they should say nothing.

- A rich woman always wears fancy clothes.
- The winner of a race tells the loser that the loser ran a very good race.
- A man says he is the best dancer in the state.

flatter Tell children that you will describe some things and if they think they would be flattered to hear these things, they should pretend to blush and say "flatter." If not, they should say nothing.

- You sang that song so well.
- Your hair looks very messy today.
- You always help other people.

3 Using the Vocabulary

Word Chat

Student Book, page 79

Guide children as they complete the Student Book activity. Use children's responses and the prompts below to discuss each word.

enormous Is a mountain enormous? Explain what you mean.

frighten Does *frighten* mean that you make someone feel better? Why or why not?

boast Does *boast* mean that someone brags and shows off? Why or why not?

Continue the discussion with the remaining words from the lesson.

mighty Does *mighty* mean that something is small and afraid? Explain your answer.

flatter Would you flatter someone if you said nice things about them? Explain what you mean.

humble Does a humble person like a lot of attention? Why or why not?

WORD CHALLENGE

Discuss with children the relationship among **flatter, boast,** and **humble**. Remind children that *flatter* is when you say good things about someone. Explain that *boast* and *humble* can be used to describe the way people act about the good things people say about them.

Group children in pairs. Have half of the children create and perform brief skits in which one child flatters the other, who then reacts in a humble way. Have the other half of the children create and perform brief skits in which one child flatters the other, who then reacts by boasting about himself or herself. Have the children watching each skit yell out "boast!" or "humble!" once they have figured out which action is being performed.

4 Using the Vocabulary

Word Organizers

Help your class complete the graphic organizers below. You may draw them on the board or on chart paper, or use the organizers in the back of this book to make transparencies.

Write the vocabulary word in the center.

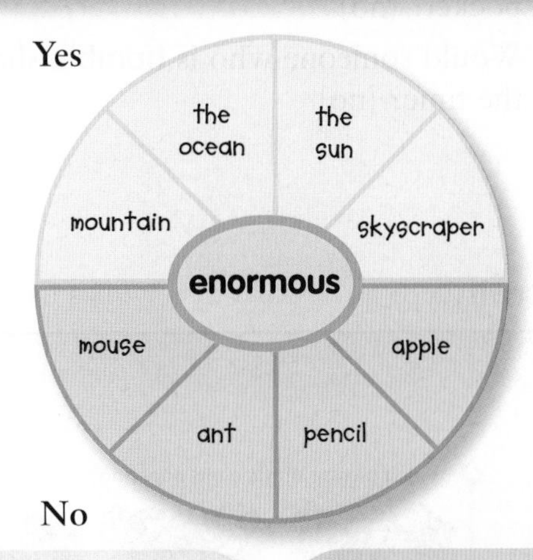

Ask children to name some of the most enormous things they can think of. As needed, call out sample answers and ask the question, "Is that enormous?" Record appropriate answers.

Ask children to name things that are not at all enormous. Model sample answers as needed and record appropriate answers.

Ask children to explain how they decide if something is enormous or not.

Write the vocabulary word in the blue box.

frighten

1. A giant monster under my bed would frighten me.
2. I frighten my sister when I pretend to be a hungry bear.
3. Loud noises can frighten a baby.

Ask children to think of sentences about things that are frightening to themselves or others. You may want to start them off by modeling a sentence for them. Then record appropriate sentences.

After children generate sentences, have them tell what might make something frightening. For example, unknown or dangerous things can be frightening.

Your Turn to Write

Encourage children to relate the words to their own experiences. Discuss a few of the prompts below to prepare children for writing. Have children write about one of the prompts in their journals or on a separate piece of paper.

boast What kinds of things might someone boast about? Have you ever boasted? What did you boast about and why?

mighty Have you ever seen a mighty animal? Where did you see it? If you could be a mighty animal, which one would you be?

flatter Has anyone ever flattered you? How does it feel to be flattered? What are some things you can say that would flatter someone you know?

frighten What are some things that frighten you? What do you do when you are frightened? How can you make someone else feel better when they are frightened?

enormous What is the most enormous thing you have ever seen? How did you feel when you saw it? Have you ever been inside an enormous building?

humble Do you know someone who is humble? Do you know someone who is not humble?

5 Assessing the Vocabulary

Review

Blackline Master, page 169

Read the following questions aloud and have children circle *yes* or *no*.

1. Do shy people often **boast** about themselves? (no)
2. Would a **mighty** king be afraid of a mouse? (no)
3. Would you **flatter** your mother if you told her she is smart? (yes)
4. Could a scary movie **frighten** you? (yes)
5. Can you put something **enormous** in your pocket? (no)
6. Would someone who is **humble** show off all the time? (no)

Assessment

Student Book, pages 80–81

Read each question aloud as children complete the activity.

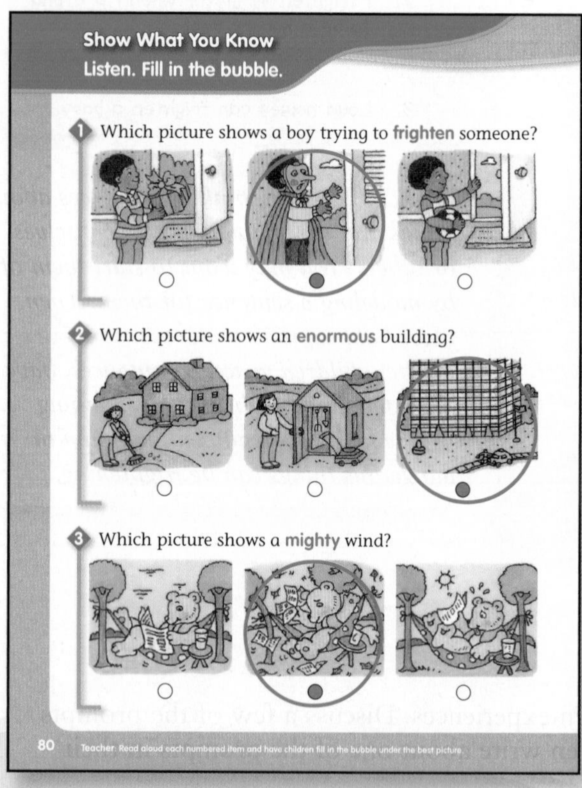

Cumulative Review

Ask the first question and model how you might arrive at an answer. Then have children answer the remaining questions and explain their answers.

Lesson 19	Lesson 20	
variety	boast	Might someone **boast** about having a **variety** of talents?
vast	mighty	Do **mighty** eagles soar in a **vast** blue sky?
enhance	flatter	Might you **flatter** people who **enhance** the world in some way?
delicate	frighten	Could a **delicate** butterfly **frighten** you?
investigate	enormous	Would you want to **investigate** an **enormous** hidden cave?
accomplish	humble	Are some people **humble** about the great things they **accomplish**?

Lesson 21

The Tortoise and the Baboon

Vocabulary

determined If you are determined to do something, you have decided to do it and nothing will stop you.

savory Savory food tastes good because it is salty or spicy, not sweet.

scamper When people or animals scamper, they move quickly with small, light steps.

frantic If someone is frantic, they are behaving in a wild way because they are scared, worried, or in a hurry.

stunned If you are stunned by something, you are so shocked or surprised by it that you can hardly speak or move.

shrewd Shrewd people are able to use all that they know to make things turn out well for themselves.

At a Glance

STANDARDS

Vocabulary
- Discuss word meaning and develop vocabulary through meaningful experiences
- Identify words that name persons, places, or things, and words that name actions

Comprehension
- Connect to life experiences the events and information in texts

Writing
- Write to record ideas and reflections

LESSON RESOURCES

Read-Aloud Anthology: pp. 121–126
Student Book: pp. 82–85
Word Cards: Lesson 21
Photo Cards: 121–126

1 Introducing the Vocabulary

Read-Aloud

Read-Aloud Anthology, pages 121–126

In the African folk tale *The Tortoise and the Baboon*, when Baboon plays a trick on Tortoise, Tortoise pays Baboon back by teaching him a lesson.

Bringing the Story to Life

Add animation to the dialogue by using different voices for Tortoise and Baboon. Adjust the pace as well, speaking slowly and deliberately for Tortoise and using a quick and lively pace for Baboon.

Word Watcher

Word Watcher Chart, Lesson 21 Word Cards

- Tell children that they will learn about these words throughout the week and that each time a child uses one of the words correctly in the classroom, you will place a mark next to the word.
- Display the word cards. Have a child select a card and hand it to you. Read the word aloud and have children repeat it. Use the word in a sentence and give it its first tally of the week. Continue with the remaining words.

Sending the Words Home

Blackline Master—English, page 161; Spanish, page 162

Distribute the activity letter to inform parents of the vocabulary words for this week.

Research Says...

"Discussion adds an important dimension to vocabulary instruction...[c]hildren who enter a vocabulary lesson without any knowledge of a target word seem to learn a great deal from their peers...."

—*Vocabulary Development,* Steven A. Stahl

2 Using the Vocabulary

Word Snapshots

Photo Cards: 121–126

Hold up each card and read the sentence on the back of the card. Then ask the following questions.

determined How can you tell this man is determined?

savory What things in this picture are savory? How do you know?

scamper How can you tell that this squirrel is scampering?

frantic What makes this man look frantic?

stunned Which girl is stunned? How do you know?

shrewd Who in this picture looks shrewd? What makes him look shrewd?

ELL SUPPORT

Discuss how each photo card relates to the story. Then place the photo cards down on the floor so that the photos cannot be seen. Say each word and have children repeat after you. Then have a child flip a card over to see if it matches the word that was said. Once the match is found, provide a sentence starter using the word and have the child complete the sentence.

Word Chat

Student Book, page 82

Guide children as they complete the Student Book activity. Then use children's responses and the prompts below to discuss each word.

scamper Tell children that you will describe a situation and if they think you are describing an animal that is scampering, they should say "scamper." If not, they should say nothing.

- The mouse ran away from the cat.
- The mouse raced away with the cheese.
- The mouse walked slowly toward the crumbs and sniffed them.

shrewd Tell children that you will describe a person and if they think the person is being shrewd, they should say "shrewd." If not, they should say nothing.

- Carla's money fell out of a hole in her pocket.
- Carla planned how she would save enough money to buy a new bike.
- Carla spent all her money on a broken skateboard.

frantic Tell children that you will describe a situation and if they think someone is frantic, they should say "frantic." If not, they should say nothing.

- Max was in such a hurry that he packed three left shoes in his suitcase!
- Max had plenty of time to pack.
- The suitcase broke, and Max rushed to stuff his things into a big, plastic bag.

3 Using the Vocabulary

Word Chat

Student Book, page 83

Guide children as they complete the Student Book activity. Then use children's responses and the prompts below to discuss each word.

frantic Would a frantic person be calm or worried? Why?

savory Is a savory dish spicy or sweet? Explain.

determined Does *determined* mean that you've decided to do something or that you're still thinking about whether to do it? Explain your answer.

stunned Would a person who is stunned be sleepy or shocked? Why is that?

Continue the discussion with the remaining words from the lesson.

scamper When an animal scampers, does it move quickly or slowly? Why?

shrewd Is a shrewd person silly or clever? Explain your answer.

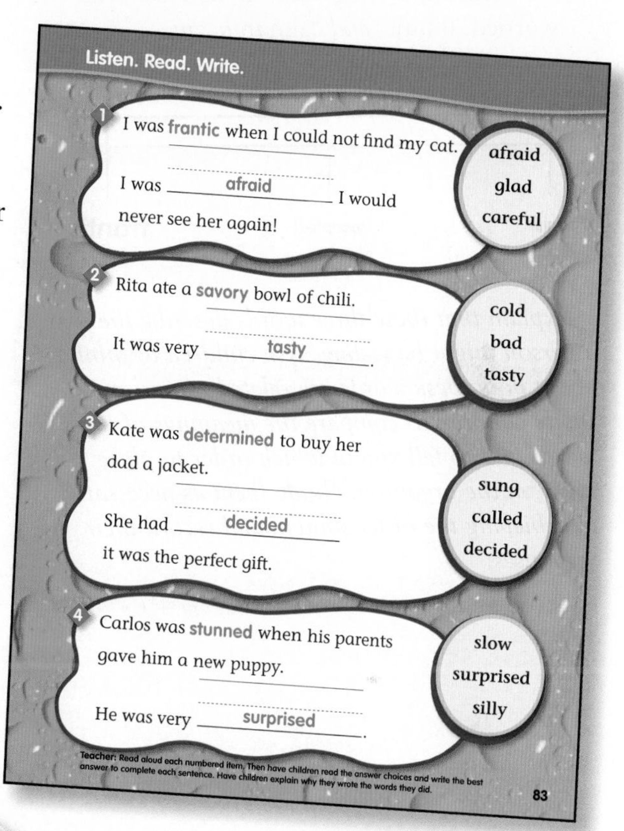
Listen. Read. Write.

1 I was **frantic** when I could not find my cat.
I was ___afraid___ I would never see her again!
afraid / glad / careful

2 Rita ate a **savory** bowl of chili.
It was very ___tasty___.
cold / bad / tasty

3 Kate was **determined** to buy her dad a jacket.
She had ___decided___ it was the perfect gift.
sung / called / decided

4 Carlos was **stunned** when his parents gave him a new puppy.
He was very ___surprised___.
slow / surprised / silly

Teacher: Read aloud each numbered item. Then have children read the answer choices and write the best answer to complete each sentence. Have children explain why they wrote the words they did.

83

WORD CHALLENGE

Review the meanings of the words *stunned* and *savory* with children. Then use the following prompts to help children brainstorm words that mean the same or almost the same thing.

- In the story Baboon was **stunned** when he realized that Tortoise was teaching him a lesson. Can you think of any words that mean the same or almost the same thing as *stunned*? *(surprised, shocked, astonished)*
- In the story Tortoise wanted to eat the **savory** leaves. Can you think of any words that mean the same or almost the same thing as *savory*? *(salty, spicy, tasty, yummy)*

Word Organizers

Help your class complete the graphic organizers below. You may draw them on the board or on chart paper, or use the organizers in the back of this book to make transparencies.

Outside of the organizer, write the words worried, frantic, *and* calm *to begin.*

Explain that these three words describe the way a person might be feeling. Ask children to think about how these words are related to one another. Invite children to compare the meanings of these words and to tell you in which order to place them on the organizer. Guide them as necessary in achieving the order shown, and record their responses.

Write the words shown in blue boxes to begin.

Tell children that some foods can be described as sweet, while other foods can be described as savory. Ask children to name some foods that are sweet. Record appropriate answers.

Ask children to name some foods that are savory. Model sample answers as needed. Record appropriate answers.

Ask children to explain the difference between sweet and savory foods. Ask which they like better and why.

Your Turn to Write

Encourage children to relate the words to their own experiences. Discuss a few of the prompts below to prepare children for writing. Have children write about one of the prompts in their journals or on a separate piece of paper.

determined What is something that you are determined to do in school? What is something that you are determined to do at home? How can you be sure that you will do it?

savory What is your favorite savory food? Why do you like it? Would you rather have something sweet or something savory for dinner?

scamper What are some animals that scamper? Can a hippopotamus scamper? Why or why not?

frantic Have you ever been frantic? How does someone who is frantic act? What are some things that might make a person frantic?

stunned What was a time when you were stunned? What happened to make you feel that way? If a famous person walked into the classroom, would you be stunned?

shrewd Who do you think is shrewd? What makes you think so? Are you a shrewd person? Can you think of story characters who are shrewd?

5 Assessing the Vocabulary

Review

Blackline Master, page 169

Read the following questions aloud and have children circle *yes* or *no*.

1. Is a **shrewd** person a fool? (no)
2. Can you be **determined** to finish the book you're reading? (yes)
3. Might deer **scamper** away if they see a bear? (yes)
4. Might you be **frantic** if your pet were missing? (yes)
5. Might you be **stunned** if you saw someone who looked just like you? (yes)
6. Is chocolate cake **savory**? (no)

Assessment

Student Book, pages 84–85

Read each question aloud as children complete the activity.

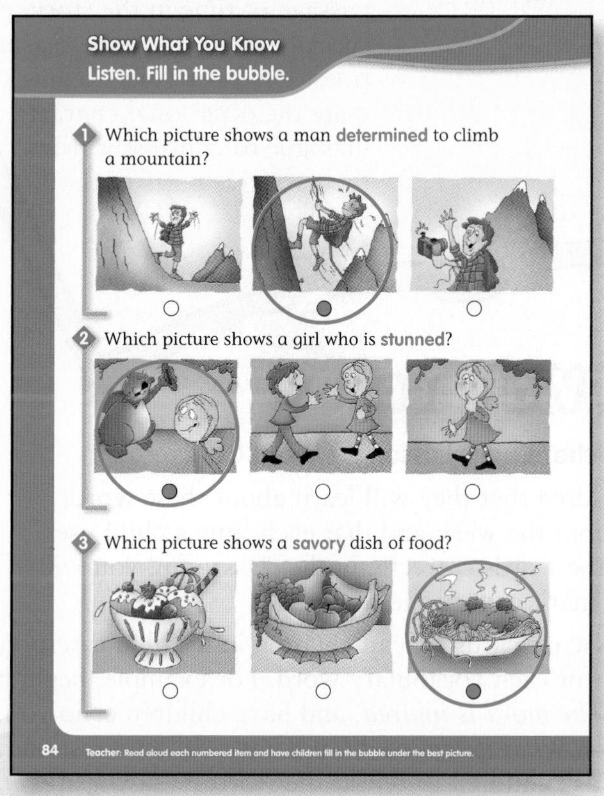

Cumulative Review

Ask the first question and model how you might arrive at an answer. Then have children answer the remaining questions and explain their answers.

Lesson 20	Lesson 21	
boast	determined	If you are **determined** to do something, would you **boast** about it?
frighten	frantic	If you **frighten** someone, might the person be **frantic**?
enormous	scamper	Could an **enormous** animal **scamper** away?
flatter	savory	If you **flatter** someone, might he cook a **savory** meal for you?
humble	stunned	Would a **humble** person be **stunned** if her friends gave her a party?
mighty	shrewd	Can a **mighty** person also be **shrewd**?

Lesson 22

Seal Surfer

Vocabulary

injured A person or animal that is injured has hurt some part of its body.

bask To bask in the sunshine is to lie back and enjoy how warm it feels.

haul When you haul something, you move something heavy by pulling it.

elated To be elated is to feel completely happy about something.

seasonal If something is seasonal, it happens every year at the same time.

contemplate When you contemplate something, you think about it very deeply.

At a Glance

STANDARDS

Vocabulary
- Use context to find the meaning of unknown words
- Use visual references to build upon word meaning

Comprehension
- Use specific details and information from a text to answer literal questions

Writing
- Write to discover, develop, and refine ideas

LESSON RESOURCES

Read-Aloud Anthology: pp. 127–134

Student Book: pp. 86–89

Word Cards: Lesson 22

Photo Cards: 4, 22, 31, 38, 47, 71, 127–132

1 Introducing the Vocabulary

Read-Aloud

Read-Aloud Anthology, pages 127–134

In *Seal Surfer* a boy learns about life by watching a seal pup change and grow through the seasons.

Bringing the Story to Life

To help children understand the passage of time in the story, put special emphasis on the season titles. Use your voice to animate the occasional character dialogue to contrast it from the narrative parts of the story.

Word Watcher

Word Watcher Chart, Lesson 22 Word Cards

- Tell children that they will learn about these words throughout the week and that each time a child uses one of the words correctly in the classroom, you will place a mark next to the word.
- Use the word cards to lead children in a call-and-response activity for each vocabulary word. For example, begin by saying *The word is injured*, and have children echo you. Then ask *What is the word?* and have children respond. Finally ask children to repeat the word by saying *Again, three times?* After the call-and-response activity, use each word in a sentence and give it its first tally of the week.

Sending the Words Home

Blackline Master—English, page 163; Spanish, page 164

Distribute the activity letter to inform parents of the vocabulary words for this week.

Research Says...

"It takes many encounters with a word in meaningful contexts for students to acquire it."

—"What Elementary Teachers Need To Know About Language," Lily Wong Fillmore and Catherine Snow

2 Using the Vocabulary

Word Snapshots

Photo Cards: 4, 22, 31, 38, 47, 71, 127–132

Hold up card pairs and ask children the following questions. Discuss which photos best show the vocabulary words.

injured (127 and 47) Which card shows an injured boy?

bask (128 and 38) Which card shows an animal basking?

haul (129 and 71) Which card shows someone hauling something?

elated (130 and 22) Which card shows someone who is being elated?

seasonal (131 and 31) Which card shows something seasonal?

contemplate (132 and 4) Which card shows a boy contemplating something?

ELL SUPPORT

Hold up the photo card for each vocabulary word as you say that word and provide a facial expression or pantomime clue. Then say each word again in random order. Have children repeat the word and provide the facial expression or pantomime connected with the word's meaning.

Lesson 22

Listen. Read. Circle.

injured
contemplate
elated

1. Sue saw a beautiful bird fly past her window.
She went outside to see the bird again.
She looked and looked for the bird.
Then she spotted it in a tree.
She was so happy to see the beautiful bird!

seasonal
bask
haul

2. Matt had a bag of dirty clothes in the bathroom.
Matt's mom asked him to move the bag.
Matt picked up the bag.
But it was very heavy.
He had to pull it behind him.

Teacher: For each story, read aloud the vocabulary words and then have children read the story independently. Have children circle the vocabulary word that best describes the story. Ask children why the word they chose was the best one for each story.

86

injured Tell children that you will describe some situations and if they think someone is injured, they should grab their heads in pain and groan "injured." If not, they should say nothing.

- A girl puts a bandage on her knee.
- A boy gets a very bad sunburn.
- A woman ties a scarf around her neck.

Word Chat

Student Book, page 86

Guide children as they complete the Student Book activity. Then use children's responses and the prompts below to discuss each word.

elated Tell children that you will say some things and if a thing would make them feel elated, they should smile widely and say "elated." If not, they should say nothing.

- Your best friend moves away.
- You find ten dollars on the sidewalk.
- Your favorite sports star visits your school.

haul Tell children that you will describe some situations and if they think something is being hauled, they should make pulling motions with their hands and grunt, "haul." If not, they should say nothing.

- A heavy rock is dragged up a hill.
- A person holding a tray of pies falls down the stairs.
- A truck pulls a big boat behind it.

3 Using the Vocabulary

Word Chat

Student Book, page 87

Guide children as they complete the Student Book activity. Then use children's responses and the prompts below to discuss each word.

bask Does bask mean that someone dances in the rain? Why or why not?

seasonal Does seasonal mean that something happens every week? Explain your answer.

contemplate Does contemplate mean that someone thinks very hard about something important? Why do you think so?

injured Does injured mean that someone feels really great? Explain.

Continue the discussion with the remaining words from the lesson.

haul Does haul mean that someone is pulling something heavy? Why?

elated Does elated mean that someone is very angry? Why or why not?

WORD CHALLENGE

Review with children the meanings of the words *injured* and *elated*. Then use the following prompts to help children brainstorm words that mean the opposite.

- In the story Ben thought the seal was **injured**. What could the seal be that would be the opposite of *injured*? (healthy, well, mended)
- In the story Ben was **elated** to see that the seal was alive. What would be the opposite of *elated*? (upset, sad, unhappy)

Word Organizers

Help your class complete the graphic organizers below. You may draw them on the board or on chart paper, or use the organizers in the back of this book to make transparencies.

Write the vocabulary word in the center.

Ask children to think about things that are seasonal. As needed, call out sample answers and ask the question, "Is that seasonal?" Record appropriate answers.

Ask children to list some other activities that they do every day or at many different times of the year. Model sample answers as needed and record appropriate answers.

Ask children to explain how they decide if something is seasonal or not.

Write the vocabulary word in the diamond.

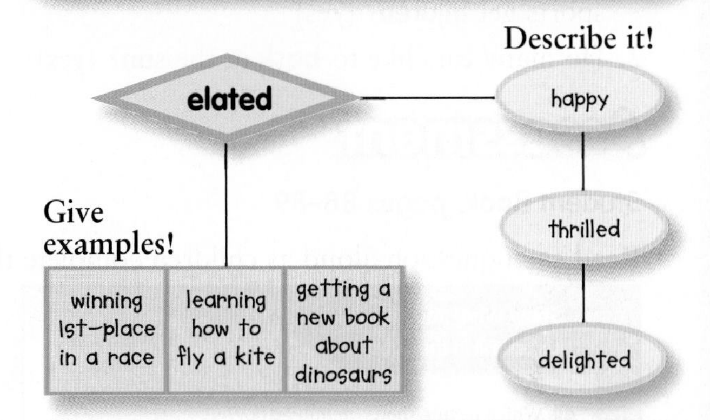

Ask children to describe how they are feeling if they are elated. Record their answers, modeling sample answers as needed.

Ask children to explain why they chose these words.

Ask children to name some examples of things that might make them feel elated. Record appropriate answers.

Have children describe a time when they were elated about something.

Your Turn to Write

Encourage children to relate the words to their own experiences. Discuss a few of the prompts below to prepare children for writing. Have children write about one of the prompts in their journals or on a separate piece of paper.

injured Tell about a time when you were injured. Describe how it felt. Who took care of you?

bask What kind of animals bask in the sun? How do they look? Do you like to bask in the sun?

haul What are some things that people often haul from one place to another? What is the heaviest thing you ever had to haul?

elated At this moment, what could happen to make you feel elated? What would make you feel elated rather than just happy?

seasonal What is your favorite seasonal activity? What makes it special?

contemplate What is one question that you often contemplate? Why do you think about it? How is contemplating different from just thinking about something?

5 Assessing the Vocabulary

Review

Blackline Master, page 169

Read the following questions aloud and have children circle *yes* or *no*.

1. Might people who take part in dangerous sports get **injured**? (yes)
2. Do many cats like to **bask** in the sun? (yes)
3. Is it a good idea to **haul** something heavier than you are in a backpack? (no)
4. Would losing your homework on the day it is due make you feel **elated**? (no)
5. Is seeing a movie a **seasonal** activity? (no)
6. Do some people **contemplate** what kind of job they should get? (yes)

Assessment

Student Book, pages 88–89

Read each question aloud as children complete the activity.

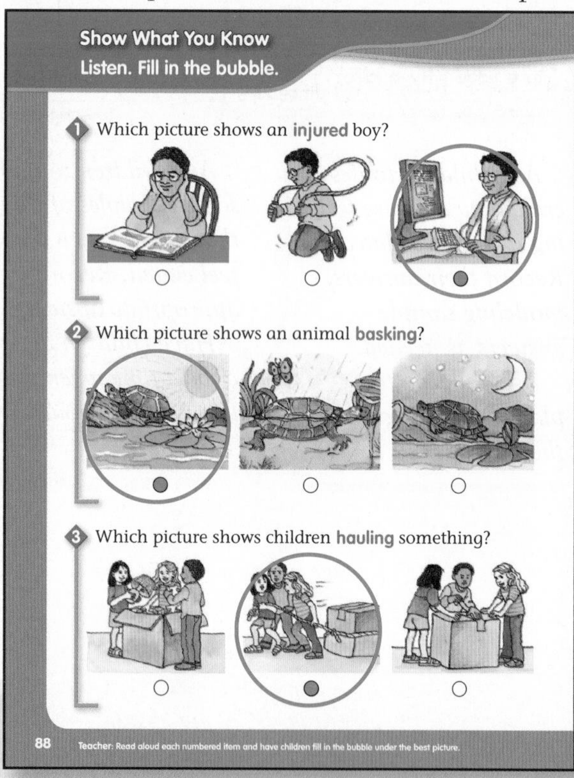
Show What You Know
Listen. Fill in the bubble.

1 Which picture shows an injured boy?

2 Which picture shows an animal basking?

3 Which picture shows children hauling something?

88 Teacher: Read aloud each numbered item and have children fill in the bubble under the best picture.

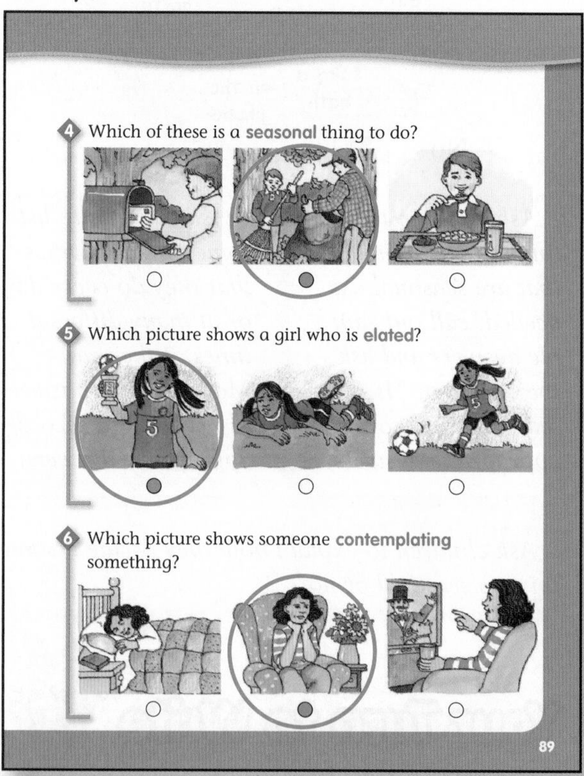
4 Which of these is a seasonal thing to do?

5 Which picture shows a girl who is elated?

6 Which picture shows someone contemplating something?

89

Cumulative Review

Ask the first question and model how you might arrive at an answer. Then have children answer the remaining questions and explain their answers.

Lesson 21	Lesson 22	
frantic	injured	Might an **injured** animal become **frantic**?
shrewd	contemplate	Would you expect **shrewd** people to **contemplate** what to do next?
savory	seasonal	Are **savory** foods often part of **seasonal** celebrations?
scamper	bask	Might you see a squirrel **scamper** and a lizard **bask** in the same park?
determined	haul	Might you be **determined** to **haul** something somewhere?
stunned	elated	Would you be **stunned** to find yourself **elated** about something?

Jamaica and the Substitute Teacher

Vocabulary

memorize When you memorize something, you make sure that you know it without having to look back at it.

stare When you stare, you look straight at something for a long time.

exchange When you exchange something, you give something to someone and they give you something, too.

relief Relief is what you feel when you get rid of something that has been bothering you or when you finish something that was difficult.

regret When you regret something, you wish you had not done it.

anxious If you feel anxious about something, you are worried about what might happen.

At a Glance

STANDARDS

Vocabulary
- Develop vocabulary by listening to and discussing selections read aloud
- Speak to express the mood of a story by using a variety of words

Comprehension
- Make and explain inferences

Writing
- Compose original texts

LESSON RESOURCES

Read-Aloud Anthology: pp. 135–142

Student Book: pp. 90–93

Word Cards: Lesson 23

Photo Cards: 133–138

1 Introducing the Vocabulary

Read-Aloud

Read-Aloud Anthology, pages 135–142

In *Jamaica and the Substitute Teacher*, a girl learns that all students are special to the substitute teacher.

Bringing the Story to Life

To help children identify with Jamaica's desire to impress the substitute teacher, create a character voice for Mrs. Duval that is very soothing and inviting. Use facial expression to help convey Jamaica's variety of emotions.

Word Watcher

Word Watcher Chart, Lesson 23 Word Cards

- Tell children that they will learn about these words throughout the week and that each time a child uses one of the words correctly in the classroom, you will place a mark next to the word.
- Before class begins, hide the six word cards in different places around the classroom. Just like the substitute teacher in the story, ask the children to look for the word cards hidden in the room. As children find each word, say the word and have children repeat it. Then use the word in a sentence and give the word its first tally of the week.

Sending the Words Home

Blackline Master—English, page 165; Spanish, page 166

Distribute the activity letter to inform parents of the vocabulary words for this week.

Research Says...

"Conversations about books help children to learn new words and concepts and to relate them to their prior knowledge and experience."

—Put Reading First

2 Using the Vocabulary

Word Snapshots

Photo Cards: 133–138

Discuss each photo card from this lesson individually. Read the sentence on the back of the card and ask children to share personal experiences similar to those depicted in the cards. Then display the cards in the groups indicated below and have children tell a story using all three cards in a group.

Group 1	Group 2
memorize	**stare**
exchange	**regret**
relief	**anxious**

ELL SUPPORT

Display and name the photo cards and have children repeat after you. Temporarily mount the cards on a large poster board with room to write under each card. Help children brainstorm examples of the vocabulary words and write them under each card. For example, for *memorize* an example could be a home address.

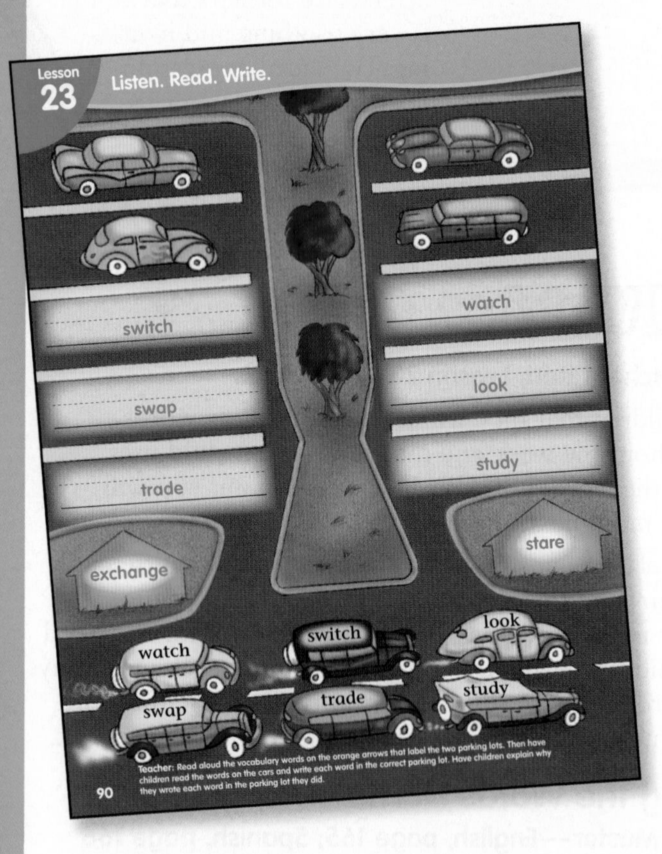

Word Chat

Student Book, page 90

Guide children as they complete the Student Book activity. Then use children's responses and the prompts below to discuss each word.

exchange Tell children that you will describe some situations and if they think things are being exchanged, they should say "exchange." If not, they should say nothing.

- I didn't like my sandwich so I gave it to Tim, and he gave me his sandwich to eat.
- I gave my mother a present.
- I paid a man ten dollars and he sold me a new hat.

stare Tell children that you will describe some people and if children think the people are staring at something, they should open their eyes really wide and say "stare." If not, they should say nothing.

- The girl flipped quickly through the books.
- The boy watched the whole television show without blinking once!
- The boy's new haircut was so terrible that he couldn't look away from the mirror.

anxious Tell children that you will describe some situations and if they think these situations would make them anxious, they should look worried and say "anxious." If not, they should say nothing.

- walking a hungry lion on a leash
- checking out a book from the library
- going to a new school where you don't know anyone

3 Using the Vocabulary

Word Chat

Student Book, page 91

Guide children as they complete the Student Book activity. Then use children's responses and the prompts below to discuss each word.

relief Who would more likely feel relief, someone who was just beginning to dig a hole or someone who had just finished digging a hole? Why?

memorize If you memorize a knock-knock joke, do you have to read it out of a book or can you just tell it to someone? Explain your answer.

anxious Who would be more likely to feel anxious, a singer on a stage or the people listening in the audience? Why?

regret Which would you regret, buying a new pair of shoes or walking through a mud puddle in a new pair of shoes? Why is that?

Continue the discussion with the remaining words from the lesson.

exchange Why might you exchange a shirt at the store, because you want another shirt that is exactly the same as yours or because you need a shirt that is a size bigger to fit you? Explain your answer.

stare Would you be more likely to stare at something you see every day or something you have never seen before? Why?

WORD CHALLENGE

Explain that some words in this lesson are used to describe Jamaica's feelings. If Jamaica had not copied on her test, her feelings would have been the opposite of what they were. Encourage children to think about what words mean the opposite of each of these vocabulary words.

- How could you describe someone who was the opposite of **anxious**? (relaxed, calm, peaceful)
- What is the opposite of feeling **regret**? (feeling pride, feeling happy)

Word Organizers

Help your class complete the graphic organizers below. You may draw them on the board or on chart paper, or use the organizers in the back of this book to make transparencies.

Write the vocabulary word in the center.

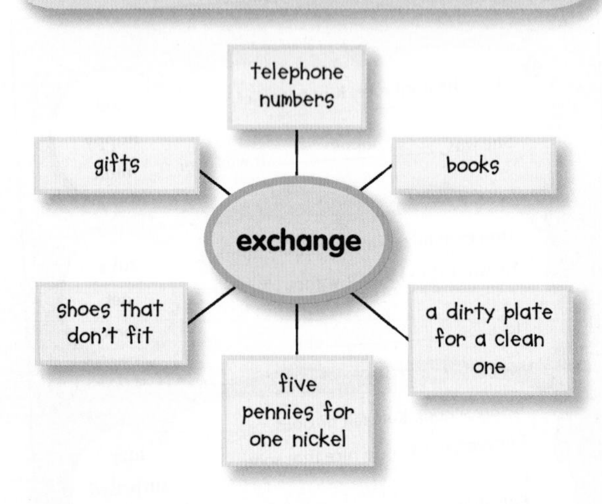

Ask children to name things that could be exchanged. Record their responses, modeling answers whenever necessary.
Ask children to tell about a time that they exchanged something.

Outside of the organizer, write the following phrases and words to begin: not see at all, look at for a second, *and* stare.

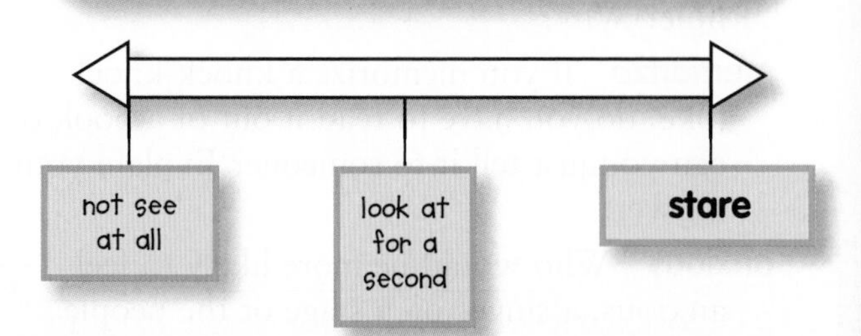

Explain that the three items you have written describe the way a person might look at something. Ask children to think about how these things are related to one another. Invite children to tell you in which order to place these items on the organizer. Guide them as necessary in achieving the order shown, and record their responses.

Your Turn to Write

Encourage children to relate the words to their own experiences. Discuss a few of the prompts below to prepare children for writing. Have children write about one of the prompts in their journals or on a separate piece of paper.

memorize What are some things that are important to memorize? Tell about some things that you have memorized. How do you go about memorizing something?

stare Describe what someone looks like when they stare at something. When or why might someone stare at something?

exchange Is there something you have that you would like to exchange for something else? Can you make an exchange that is unfair?

relief Tell about a time when you felt a great sense of relief. Describe how it felt when you realized that you didn't have to worry or that the situation was over.

regret What are some reasons that you might feel regret? Tell about a time when you felt regret. How was it different from feeling proud of what you had done?

anxious How can you tell when you are feeling anxious? What happens in your body? How is feeling anxious different from feeling calm?

5 Assessing the Vocabulary

Review

Blackline Master, page 169

Read the following questions aloud and have children circle *yes* or *no*.

1. Might you **memorize** a person's name? (yes)
2. Might people **stare** at a map? (yes)
3. Could you **exchange** pants that don't fit for ones that do fit? (yes)
4. Would you feel **relief** if you had to take a test you hadn't studied for? (no)
5. Are most people **anxious** about playing their favorite game? (no)
6. Is coming to school on time something you should **regret**? (no)

Assessment

Student Book, pages 92–93

Read each question aloud as children complete the activity.

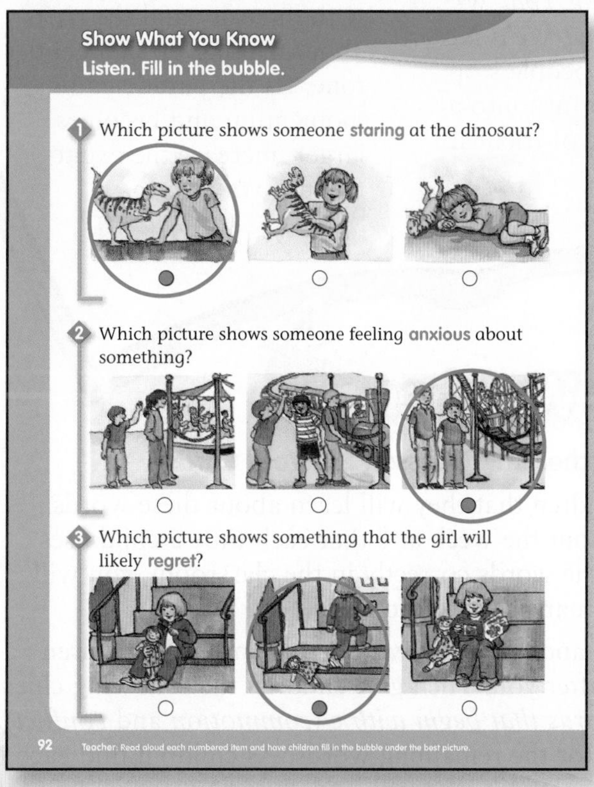

Show What You Know
Listen. Fill in the bubble.

1. Which picture shows someone **staring** at the dinosaur?
2. Which picture shows someone feeling **anxious** about something?
3. Which picture shows something that the girl will likely **regret**?

92 Teacher: Read aloud each numbered item and have children fill in the bubble under the best picture.

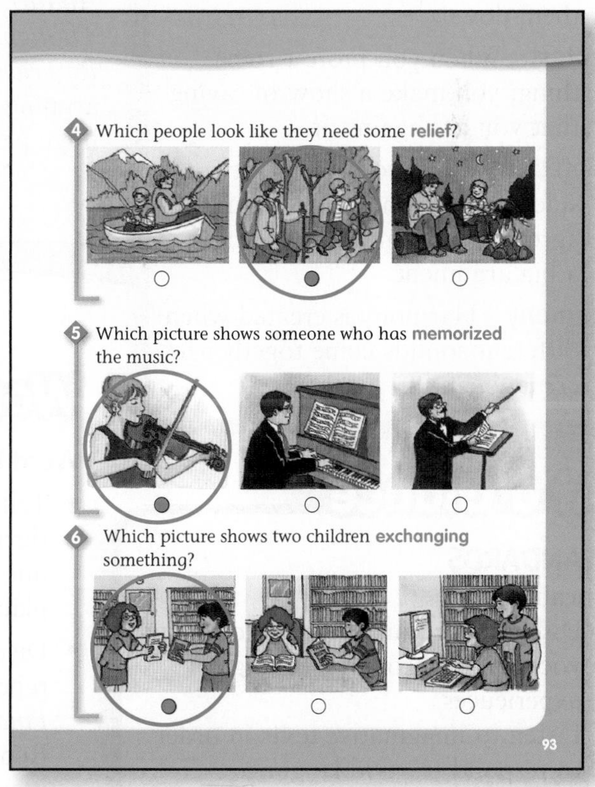

4. Which people look like they need some **relief**?
5. Which picture shows someone who has **memorized** the music?
6. Which picture shows two children **exchanging** something?

93

Cumulative Review

Ask the first question and model how you might arrive at an answer. Then have children answer the remaining questions and explain their answers.

Lesson 22	Lesson 23	
injured	regret	Might you **regret** getting **injured**?
bask	stare	Would you **stare** at a cat who was **basking** in the sun?
seasonal	anxious	Are there any **seasonal** changes that would make you feel **anxious**?
contemplate	exchange	Might you **contemplate exchanging** lunches with your friend?
haul	relief	How might you get **relief** after **hauling** wood to the fireplace?
elated	memorize	Would you be **elated** if you **memorized** when your favorite television programs come on?

Lesson 24

And to Think That We Thought That We'd Never Be Friends

Vocabulary

commotion A commotion is a lot of noise and people moving around.

fret When you fret about something, you look and act as if you are worried about it.

soothe When you soothe someone who is angry or upset, you calm them down.

protest When you protest something, you make a show of saying that you are against it.

conflict When two people or two sides have a conflict, they can't agree about something and have a big argument.

harmony Harmony is created when different sounds come together to create beautiful music.

At a Glance

STANDARDS

Vocabulary
- Discuss word meaning and develop vocabulary through meaningful experiences
- Listen to imaginative texts in order to respond to vivid language

Comprehension
- Connect to life experiences the events and information in texts

Writing
- Write in different forms for different purposes

LESSON RESOURCES

Read-Aloud Anthology: pp. 143–150

Student Book: pp. 94–97

Word Cards: Lesson 24

Photo Cards: 139–144

1 Introducing the Vocabulary

Read-Aloud

Read-Aloud Anthology, pages 143–150

In the story in rhyme *And to Think That We Thought That We'd Never Be Friends*, people stop arguing and turn into a huge parade of friends!

Bringing the Story to Life

Read the parts about fighting with intensity and the parts about making up in a gentler tone. As the parade gains momentum and becomes larger, increase the excitement in your voice.

Word Watcher

Word Watcher Chart, Lesson 24 Word Cards

- Tell children that they will learn about these words throughout the week and that each time a child uses one of the words correctly in the classroom, you will place a mark next to the word.
- Display and name the word cards and have children repeat after you. Then give children the following clue: *Find words that begin with* c (*commotion* and *conflict*). Repeat for the remaining words. As children find each word, use it in a sentence, and give the word its first tally of the week.

Sending the Words Home

Blackline Master—English, page 167; Spanish, page 168

Distribute the activity letter to inform parents of the vocabulary words for this week.

Research Says...

"'Knowing' a word is to understand its core meaning and that meaning may alter in different contexts."

—*Basic Education*, Jean H. Osborn and Bonnie B. Armbruster

2 Using the Vocabulary

Word Snapshots

Photo Cards: 139–144

Display the photo cards and ask children to work in pairs to make up a short story about a card. Provide the following story starters.

commotion The noise from the marching bands and crowds created quite a commotion. Tell us more.

fret Crystal began to fret about how much the shot would hurt. Tell why.

soothe Gwen's father soothed her after she had hurt her knee. What happened then?

protest People often protest when they want to stop something from happening. Tell us more.

conflict We saw two elk in a conflict. What happened then?

harmony Mrs. Blevins and the choir practice singing in harmony. Tell how and why.

ELL SUPPORT

Discuss the photo cards and brainstorm ways to pantomime the vocabulary words. Then provide a specific situation such as *The lunchroom was so noisy today that I couldn't hear.* Ask children to respond by showing the pantomime that relates to that situation (commotion). Continue with the other words.

Word Chat

Student Book, page 94

Guide children as they complete the Student Book activity. Then use children's responses and the prompts below to discuss each word.

Divide the class into two groups. Assign the first word to one group and the second word to the other. Explain that you will say a sentence with a missing word, and the group that has the word that fits the sentence should say their word aloud.

protest/commotion

- Bob wrote a letter to ______ the library's closing. (protest)
- Bonnie wanted to ______ the new rules. (protest)
- In all the ______ I didn't hear the directions and got lost! (commotion)
- Steve couldn't hear because of the ______ outside. (commotion)

fret/conflict

- Susan and her brother had a ______ about what movie to watch. (conflict)
- Dan will ______ about jumping off the high diving board. (fret)
- I ______ about reaching my hand into that dark bag. (fret)
- By taking turns we solved the ______ . (conflict)

Word Chat

Student Book, page 95

Guide children as they complete the Student Book activity. Then use children's responses and the prompts below to discuss each word.

For each vocabulary word, provide children with the first part of a sentence that includes the vocabulary word. Have children provide an ending for the sentence that shows they know what the new word means.

commotion There was a big commotion outside when....

soothe Mom soothed me by....

harmony The audience enjoyed the harmony of....

Continue the discussion with the remaining words from the lesson.

protest People protested when the mayor wanted to....

fret I fretted when it started to rain because....

conflict The two neighbors were having a conflict about....

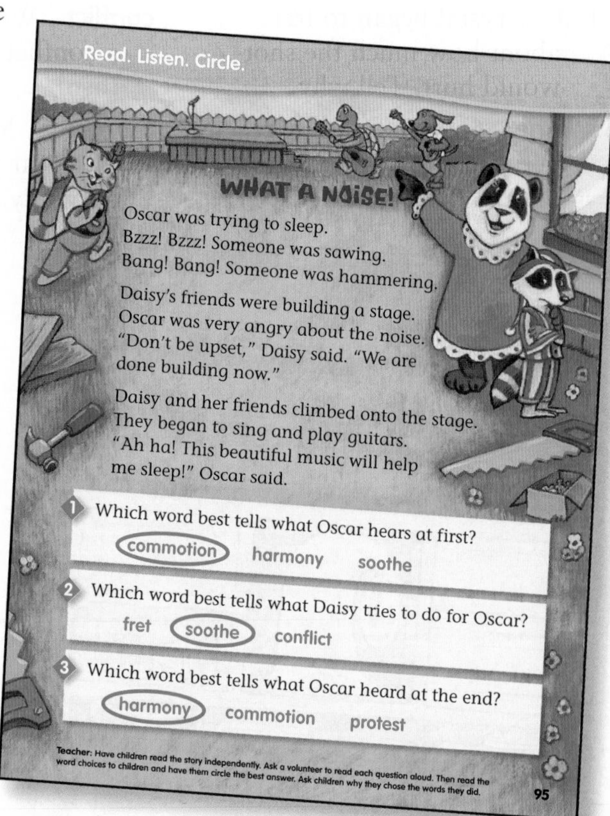

Read. Listen. Circle.

WHAT A NOISE!

Oscar was trying to sleep.
Bzzz! Bzzz! Someone was sawing.
Bang! Bang! Someone was hammering.

Daisy's friends were building a stage.
Oscar was very angry about the noise.
"Don't be upset," Daisy said. "We are done building now."

Daisy and her friends climbed onto the stage.
They began to sing and play guitars.
"Ah ha! This beautiful music will help me sleep!" Oscar said.

1 Which word best tells what Oscar hears at first?
commotion (circled) harmony soothe

2 Which word best tells what Daisy tries to do for Oscar?
fret soothe (circled) conflict

3 Which word best tells what Oscar heard at the end?
harmony (circled) commotion protest

Teacher: Have children read the story independently. Ask a volunteer to read each question aloud. Then read the word choices to children and have them circle the best answer. Ask children why they chose the words they did.

95

WORD CHALLENGE

Explain to children that the word *harmony* has more than one meaning. They have already learned that it means "different sounds coming together to create beautiful music." Tell children that another meaning is "getting along well together." Ask children if they can see why this same word might be used for these two meanings. Then provide the following prompts and ask children which meaning *harmony* has in each prompt.

- The people in my neighborhood live and work in **harmony**. (getting along well together)
- The members of the chorus sang in perfect **harmony**. (different sounds coming together to create beautiful music)

4 Using the Vocabulary

Word Organizers

Help your class complete the graphic organizers below. You may draw them on the board or on chart paper, or use the organizers in the back of this book to make transparencies.

Write the vocabulary word in the diamond.

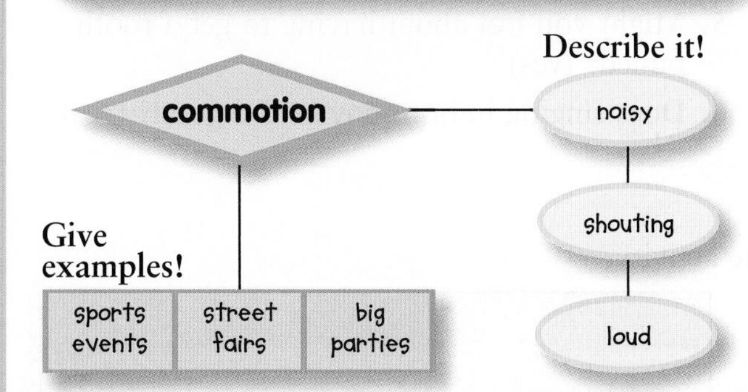

Write the vocabulary word in the blue box.

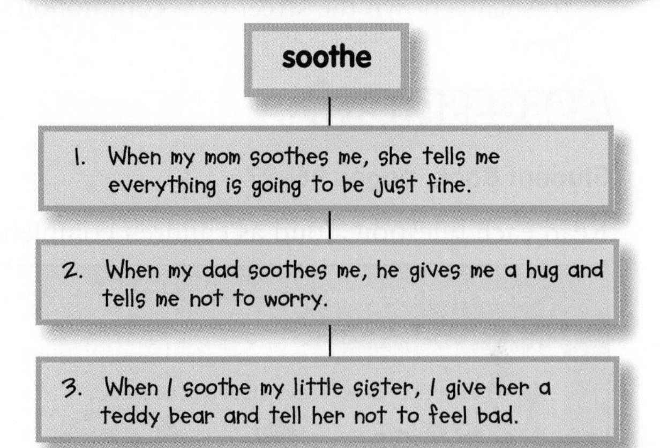

Encourage children to think of words that describe what a commotion sounds like. Record their answers, providing sample answers as necessary.

Ask children why each of these words might describe a commotion.

Invite children to think of examples of places where they might hear a commotion. Record their suggestions, modeling sample answers if needed.

Ask children to explain why they might hear a commotion at these places.

Ask children to think of sentences about ways that people can soothe each other. Help children use their ideas to compose sentences. You may want to start by modeling a sentence for them. Then record their sentences.

Your Turn to Write

Encourage children to relate the words to their own experiences. Discuss a few of the prompts below to prepare children for writing. Have children write about one of the prompts in their journals or on a separate piece of paper.

commotion What kinds of things might cause a commotion? What are some commotions that you have heard? Do you think a commotion is fun?

fret What things do you fret about? When you fret about something, how do you feel? What do you do to help you stop fretting?

soothe Who soothes you when you're upset or angry? What do they say or do to help you feel better? Do you ever soothe someone else?

protest What kinds of things do people protest? Is there something you would like to protest? How would you protest this thing?

conflict Have you ever had a conflict? What was the conflict about? How do you feel when you have a conflict? How do you feel when you make up?

harmony What do you like best about hearing people sing or play musical instruments in harmony? Have you created harmony with other people?

5 Assessing the Vocabulary

Review

Blackline Master, page 169

Read the following questions aloud and have children circle *yes* or *no*.

1. Would a group of people yelling and rolling trashcans down the street be a **commotion**? (yes)
2. Does a person **protesting** something like that thing very much? (no)
3. Would you have a **conflict** with someone you always agreed with? (no)
4. If you **soothe** someone, might you give them a hug? (yes)
5. Might you **fret** about having to get a tooth pulled? (yes)
6. Does singing in **harmony** sound good? (yes)

Assessment

Student Book, pages 96–97

Read each question aloud as children complete the activity.

Show What You Know
Listen. Fill in the bubble.

1. Which picture shows a group that is in **harmony**?
2. Which picture shows a boy and girl in a **conflict**?
3. Which picture shows a **commotion**?

96 Teacher: Read aloud each numbered item and have children fill in the bubble under the best picture.

4. Which picture shows a boy who is **fretting**?
5. Which picture shows people who are **protesting**?

6. Which picture shows someone who is **soothing** another person?

97

Cumulative Review

Ask the first question and model how you might arrive at an answer. Then have children answer the remaining questions and explain their answers.

Lesson 23	Lesson 24	
relief	soothe	When someone **soothes** you, do you feel **relief**?
anxious	conflict	Do you feel **anxious** when you have a **conflict** with a friend?
memorize	harmony	Can you **memorize** a song to create **harmony** when you sing it?
stare	protest	Do you **stare** at people who are **protesting**?
regret	commotion	If you caused a **commotion**, would you **regret** it?
exchange	fret	Do you **fret** about **exchanging** gifts with a friend?

Fun with New Words

Dear Family,

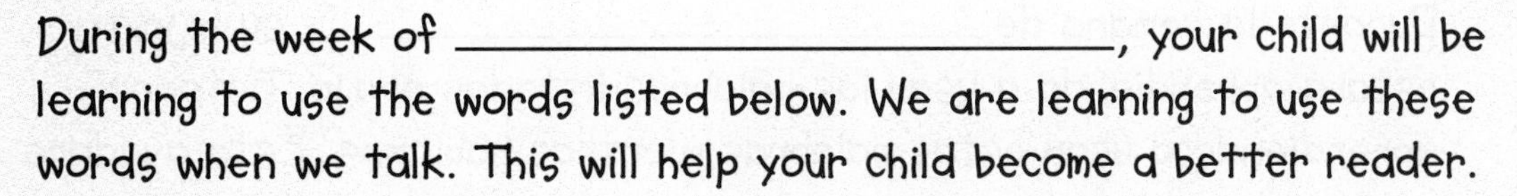

During the week of ______________________, your child will be learning to use the words listed below. We are learning to use these words when we talk. This will help your child become a better reader.

This week please try to use these words as often as you can. You may wish to do the activities, too, so your child can get extra practice with the words. Have fun using these words!

Teacher ______________________

comforting

Something comforting makes you feel better when you are sad or afraid.

Ask your child to describe something that they think is comforting.

expression

Your expression is the look on your face that shows what you are feeling.

With your child take turns making expressions and guessing what they are (angry, sad, happy, etc.).

fleet

A person or animal that is fleet moves fast.

Have your child name an animal that is fleet.

lively

Someone or something that is lively is full of life.

Invite your child to act out how someone who is lively and someone who is not lively would get ready in the morning.

versatile

If someone or something is versatile, it can do many different things.

Help your child make a list of the many things he or she can do.

glimmer

To glimmer is to shine or twinkle softly.

Ask your child to draw a picture of something that glimmers.

Go to http://www.elementsofreading.com/parentplace for fun, educational activities that you can do at home with your child.

Diversión con palabras nuevas

Estimada Familia,

Durante la semana de ______________________, su hijo/a estará aprendiendo a usar las palabras listadas abajo. Estamos aprendiendo a usar estas palabras mientras hablamos. Ésto ayudará que su hijo/a llegue a ser un lector mejor.

Esta semana, haga el favor de tratar de usar estas palabras tanto como pueda. A lo mejor, desea hacer las actividades también, para que su hijo/a tenga más práctica con las palabras. ¡Diviértase usando estas palabras!

Maestro/a ______________________

comforting

Es algo que se le hace sentir tranquilo a alguien cuando está triste o cuando tiene miedo.

Pídale a su hijo/a contarle cosas que le resulta comforting.

expression

Es la mirada en la cara que demuestra lo que se siente uno.

Junto con su hijo/a haga turnos haciendo expressions *y adivinando qué son (enojada, triste, feliz, etc.).*

fleet

Se dice de la persona o del animal que se mueve con rapidez.

Haga que su hijo/a nombre un animal fleet.

lively

Ser uno lleno de vida.

Anime a su hijo/a comportarse cómo se levantaría por la mañana alguien lively *y alguien no* lively.

glimmer

Brillar levemente con luz suave y vacilante.

Haga que su hijo/a dibuje algo que glimmers.

versatile

Una persona o una cosa *versatile* es capaz de hacer muchas cosas.

Ayude a su hijo/a hacer una lista de las muchas cosas que puede hacer.

Fun with New Words

Dear Family,

During the week of ____________________, your child will be learning to use the words listed below. We are learning to use these words when we talk. This will help your child become a better reader.

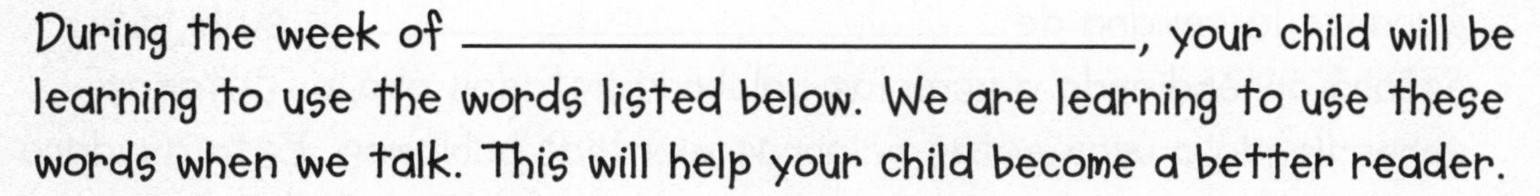

This week please try to use these words as often as you can. You may wish to do the activities, too, so your child can get extra practice with the words. Have fun using these words!

Teacher ____________________

delightful

If you say someone or something is delightful, you mean that it is very pleasant.

Ask your child to plan a delightful activity for you to share.

fierce

A fierce animal or person behaves in a mean way and often looks for a fight.

Ask your child to draw a picture of a fierce animal.

clumsy

A clumsy person has trouble moving or handling things and often trips over or breaks them.

Ask your child to tell about a time when he or she was clumsy in your home.

rescue

When you rescue someone, you save them from something bad happening.

Ask your child to tell how Big Al rescued the little fish in the story they recently heard.

suspense

Suspense is the feeling you get when you know something is about to happen very soon.

Ask your child to tell you a story that will keep you in suspense until the end.

capture

If you capture someone or something, you catch it and keep it from getting away.

Ask your child about how the fish were captured in the story Big Al.

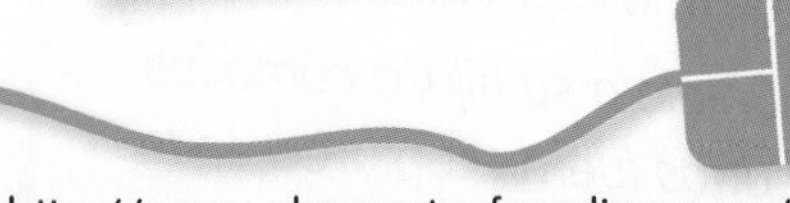

Go to http://www.elementsofreading.com/parentplace for fun, educational activities that you can do at home with your child.

Diversión con palabras nuevas

Estimada Familia,

Durante la semana de ______________________, su hijo/a estará aprendiendo a usar las palabras listadas abajo. Estamos aprendiendo a usar estas palabras mientras hablamos. Ésto ayudará que su hijo/a llegue a ser un lector mejor.

Esta semana, haga el favor de tratar de usar estas palabras tanto como pueda. A lo mejor, desea hacer las actividades también, para que su hijo/a tenga más práctica con las palabras. ¡Diviértase usando estas palabras!

Maestro/a ______________________

delightful

Se dice para describir algo o alguien agradable que da gusto.

Pídale a su hijo/a organizar una actividad delightful *para compartir juntos.*

fierce

Se dice para describir comportamiento salvaje y antipático de una persona o un animal.

Pídale a su hijo/a dibujar un animal fierce.

clumsy

Se dice de una persona torpe que se mueve con dificultad, y que muchas veces se cae, o que rompe las cosas.

Pídale a su hijo/a contar alguna vez en que se sentía clumsy *en casa.*

rescue

Librar a una persona de una situación desagradable.

Pregúntele a su hijo/a cómo Big Al rescued *el pescadito en el cuento que escuchó hace poco tiempo.*

capture

Tomar algo o alguien en posesión y no dejarle escapar.

Pregúntele a su hijo/a cómo los pescados fueron captured *en la historia Big Al.*

suspense

Es la sensación que pronto algo va a pasar.

Pídale a su hijo/a contar una historia en la que mantenga la suspense *hasta el final.*

Fun with New Words

Dear Family,

During the week of ______________________, your child will be learning to use the words listed below. We are learning to use these words when we talk. This will help your child become a better reader.

This week please try to use these words as often as you can. You may wish to do the activities, too, so your child can get extra practice with the words. Have fun using these words!

Teacher ______________________

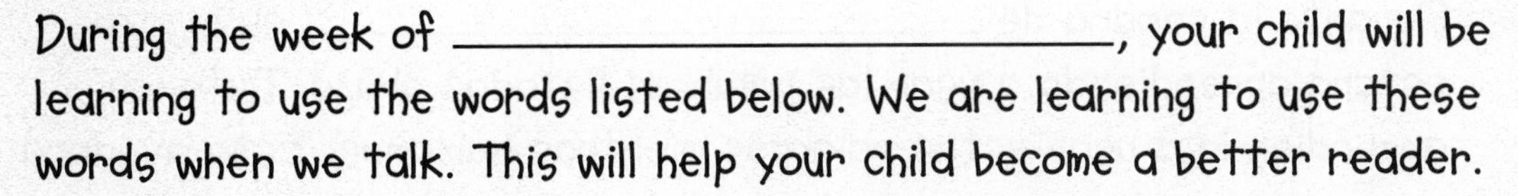

deserve

If you deserve something, you should get it because of what you have done.

Ask your child to describe something he or she deserves to have and explain why.

plead

If you plead with someone, you beg them to do something for you that will help you out.

Ask your child to draw a picture of something he or she would plead for. Then have your child tell you why he or she would plead for it.

deceive

If you deceive someone, you make them believe something that is not true.

Ask your child to tell how the coyote deceived the snake in the story One Good Turn Deserves Another.

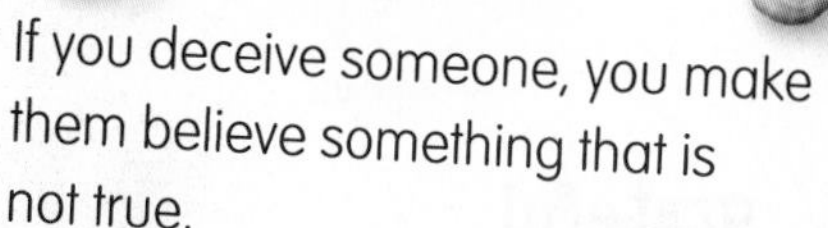

grateful

If you are grateful for something that someone has given you or done for you, you are pleased and wish to thank the person.

Ask your child to point out three things at home he or she is grateful for.

challenge

If you challenge someone, you ask them to do something that is difficult or that you think they cannot do.

Challenge your child to do something, such as recite the alphabet in less than 30 seconds.

amble

When you amble somewhere, you walk there slowly and in a restful way.

When you are walking in a store or to your home, ask your child to show you how to amble.

Go to http://www.elementsofreading.com/parentplace for fun, educational activities that you can do at home with your child.

Diversión con palabras nuevas

Estimada Familia,

Durante la semana de ______________________, su hijo/a estará aprendiendo a usar las palabras listadas abajo. Estamos aprendiendo a usar estas palabras mientras hablamos. Ésto ayudará que su hijo/a llegue a ser un lector mejor.

Esta semana, haga el favor de tratar de usar estas palabras tanto como pueda. A lo mejor, desea hacer las actividades también, para que su hijo/a tenga más práctica con las palabras. ¡Diviértase usando estas palabras!

Maestro/a ______________________

deserve

Ser digno de una cosa por haber hecho algo.

Pregúntele a su hijo/a qué es lo que deserves *y que explique por qué.*

plead

Suplicar a una persona que ayude con algo.

Haga que su hijo/a dibuje algo que estaría dispuesto/a to plead, *y pregúntele por qué.*

grateful

Querer dar las gracias por un beneficio recibido.

Haga que su hijo/a nombre tres cosas que tiene en casa por estar grateful.

deceive

Hacerle creer a alguien algo que no es cierto.

Pregúntele a su hijo/a cómo el coyote deceived *a la serpiente en la historia* One Good Turn Deserves Another.

amble

Caminar de una manera tranquila.

Cuando está caminando con su hijo/a hacía su casa o a comprar, pídale demostrar como to amble.

challenge

Pedir que otra persona haga algo difícil o que no la cree capaz de hacer.

Challenge *a su hijo/a hacer una cosa, como recitar el alfabeto en menos de 30 segundos.*

Fun with New Words

Dear Family,

During the week of ______________________, your child will be learning to use the words listed below. We are learning to use these words when we talk. This will help your child become a better reader.

This week please try to use these words as often as you can. You may wish to do the activities, too, so your child can get extra practice with the words. Have fun using these words!

Teacher ______________________

scrunched

If something is scrunched, it gets pushed together and squeezed.

Ask your child to point out something in your home that is scrunched.

dreadful

If something is dreadful, it is so terrible that it could not be much worse.

Ask your child to name a food that he or she thinks tastes dreadful.

complain

Complain means to talk about how the things that are happening are bad or unfair.

Ask your child to recall a time at home when he or she complained about something.

invisible

If something is invisible, you can't see it.

Ask your child to show you how he or she would shake hands with an invisible friend.

exaggerate

Exaggerate means to make things seem much better or much worse than they really are.

Ask your child to exaggerate about how tall the ceilings in your home are.

scold

If you scold someone, you say angry things to them about something they have done.

Ask your child to describe a time at home when he or she was scolded.

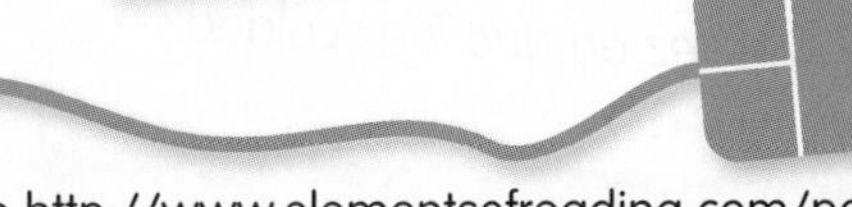

Go to http://www.elementsofreading.com/parentplace for fun, educational activities that you can do at home with your child.

Diversión con palabras nuevas

Estimada Familia,

Durante la semana de ______________________________, su hijo/a estará aprendiendo a usar las palabras listadas abajo. Estamos aprendiendo a usar estas palabras mientras hablamos. Ésto ayudará que su hijo/a llegue a ser un lector mejor.

Esta semana, haga el favor de tratar de usar estas palabras tanto como pueda. A lo mejor, desea hacer las actividades también, para que su hijo/a tenga más práctica con las palabras. ¡Diviértase usando estas palabras!

Maestro/a ______________________________

scrunched

Estar arrugado, apretado, o doblado varias veces.

Pídale a su hijo/a indicar una cosa en su casa que está scrunched.

dreadful

Es algo tan terrible que no podría ser mucho peor.

Pregúntele a su hijo/a qué comida, segun él/ella, tiene un sabor dreadful.

invisible

Es algo que no se puede ver.

Pídale a su hijo/a demostrar cómo le ofrecería la mano a un amigo invisible.

complain

Hacer una expresión de dolor, de pena, de descontento, o de enfado.

Pídale a su hijo/a recordar una vez que él/ella complained *de algo.*

scold

Expresar severamente a una persona la desaprobación por lo que ha hecho.

Pregúntele a su hijo/a describir alguna vez en que fue scolded.

exaggerate

Hacer que algo parezca mucho mejor o mucho peor de lo que realmente es.

Pídale a su hijo/a to exagerrate *la altura del techo de su casa.*

Fun with New Words

Dear Family,

During the week of ______________________, your child will be learning to use the words listed below. We are learning to use these words when we talk. This will help your child become a better reader.

This week please try to use these words as often as you can. You may wish to do the activities, too, so your child can get extra practice with the words. Have fun using these words!

Teacher ______________________

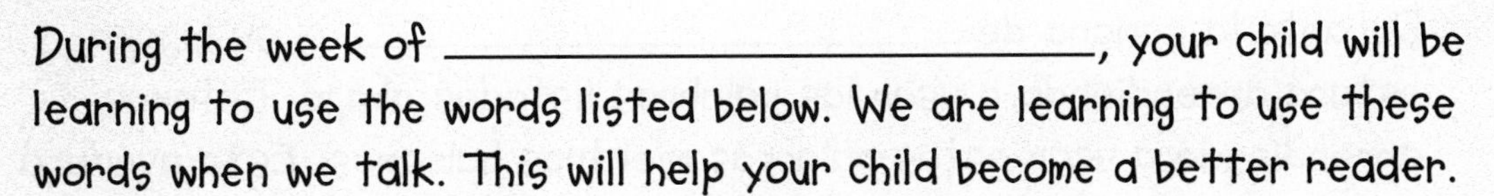

suspend

When you suspend something, you hold it up or hang it up off the ground.

Have your child show you things around your home that are suspended.

pride

Pride is the feeling you get when you have done something well.

Ask your child to tell you about something he or she has done that fills him or her with pride.

ridiculous

Something ridiculous is very foolish and makes no sense.

Have your child show you how to sit on a chair in a ridiculous way.

serenade

If you serenade someone, you sing or play a song for them on a musical instrument.

Ask your child to serenade you with a favorite song.

perform

When you perform, you do something like sing, dance, play an instrument, or speak in front of a group.

Make up a dance or a song with your child that you and your child can perform for other family members.

spangled

Something that is spangled is covered with small, shiny things.

Use glue and sparkly glitter or pieces of tinfoil to help your child create a spangled design on a piece of paper.

Go to http://www.elementsofreading.com/parentplace for fun, educational activities that you can do at home with your child.

Diversión con palabras nuevas

Estimada Familia,

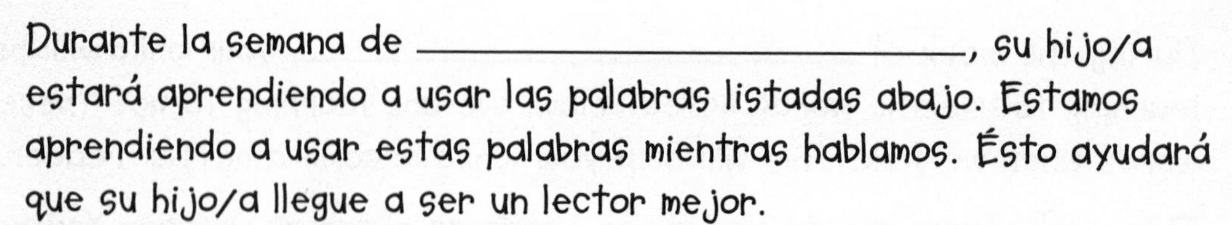

Durante la semana de ______________________, su hijo/a estará aprendiendo a usar las palabras listadas abajo. Estamos aprendiendo a usar estas palabras mientras hablamos. Ésto ayudará que su hijo/a llegue a ser un lector mejor.

Esta semana, haga el favor de tratar de usar estas palabras tanto como pueda. A lo mejor, desea hacer las actividades también, para que su hijo/a tenga más práctica con las palabras. ¡Diviértase usando estas palabras!

Maestro/a ______________________

suspend

Colgar algo en alto para que se quede aguantado desde arriba por algún punto.

Haga que su hijo/a le enseñe cosas por la casa que estén suspended.

pride

La sensación de haber hecho algo bien.

Pídale a su hijo/a contarle a Ud. algo que ha hecho su hijo/a que le llene con pride.

serenade

Cantarle a una persona o tocarle una canción con un instrumento musical.

Pídale a su hijo/a to serenade *a Ud. con una canción favorita.*

ridiculous

Se dice para describir una tontería que no tiene sentido.

Haga que su hijo/a demuestre cómo sentarse en una silla de una manera ridiculous.

spangled

Se dice para describir algo cubierto por pequeñas cosas brillantes.

Use pegamento, pedacitos de papel de aluminio, y otras cositas brillantes sobre una hoja de papel para ayudarle a su hijo/a crear un diseño spangled.

perform

Hacer una actuación, como cantar, bailar, tocar un instrumento musical, o hablar en frente de un público.

Invente con su hijo/a un baile o una canción para que luego lo perform *los dos para la familia.*

Fun with New Words

Dear Family,

During the week of ______________________, your child will be learning to use the words listed below. We are learning to use these words when we talk. This will help your child become a better reader.

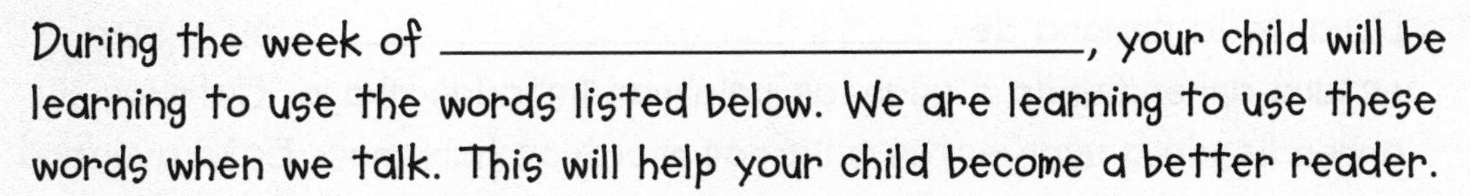

This week please try to use these words as often as you can. You may wish to do the activities, too, so your child can get extra practice with the words. Have fun using these words!

Teacher ______________________

tidy

Something that is tidy is very neat and clean.

Ask your child to help make a room in your home look tidy.

chuckle

When you chuckle, you laugh quietly.

Ask your child to talk about something that recently happened that made him or her chuckle.

astonished

If you are astonished, something has surprised you so much that you feel shocked.

Ask your child to make an astonished face with you on the count of three.

irk

If you irk someone, you make them a little bit angry.

Ask your child what things at home irk him or her and how he or she can help fix these things.

coincidence

A coincidence is when two things just happen but seem like they go together.

Tell your child a family story that involves a coincidence.

admire

When you admire someone, you look up to them and want to be like them. When you admire something, you like looking at it.

Ask your child to tell about a family member he or she admires.

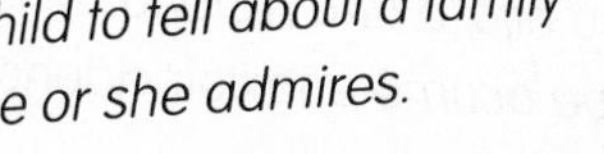

Go to http://www.elementsofreading.com/parentplace for fun, educational activities that you can do at home with your child.

Diversión con palabras nuevas

Estimada Familia,

Durante la semana de ______________________, su hijo/a estará aprendiendo a usar las palabras listadas abajo. Estamos aprendiendo a usar estas palabras mientras hablamos. Ésto ayudará que su hijo/a llegue a ser un lector mejor.

Esta semana, haga el favor de tratar de usar estas palabras tanto como pueda. A lo mejor, desea hacer las actividades también, para que su hijo/a tenga más práctica con las palabras. ¡Diviértase usando estas palabras!

Maestro/a ______________________

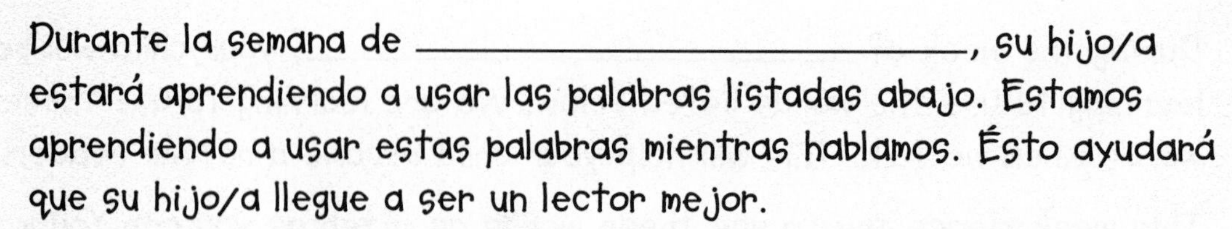

tidy

Estar muy ordenado y limpio.

Pídale a su hijo/a ayudar a hacer tidy *una habitación de su casa.*

chuckle

Reír entre dientes.

Pregúntele a su hijo/a algo que pasó hace poco que le hizo chuckle.

irk

Molestar a otra persona.

Pregúntele a su hijo/a cuáles cosas en casa le irk *y cómo puede ayudar a arreglarlas.*

astonished

Estar tan sorprendido hasta quedarse asombrado.

Pídale a su hijo/a hacer una cara de astonished *después de contar a tres.*

admire

Tener en gran estima una persona por lo extraordinario de sus cualidades y tener deseo ser como la persona. Cuando admira algo, resulta agradable mirarlo.

Pídale a su hijo/a que hable de un miembro de la familia que admires.

coincidence

Cuando pasan a la vez dos o más cosas no relacionadas, pero parece que vayan juntos.

Cuéntele a su hijo/a una historia de la familia en que ocurrió una coincidence.

Fun with New Words

Dear Family,

During the week of ______________________________, your child will be learning to use the words listed below. We are learning to use these words when we talk. This will help your child become a better reader.

This week please try to use these words as often as you can. You may wish to do the activities, too, so your child can get extra practice with the words. Have fun using these words!

Teacher ______________________________

survive

To survive is to continue to live, even through difficult times and events.

Ask your child to tell you about some of the things he or she needs to survive.

destroy

To destroy something is to break or hurt it so badly that it can't be fixed.

Find a food carton or broken object that was going to be thrown out anyway. Give it to your child and ask them to demonstrate for you how to destroy something.

shelter

To shelter something is to keep it from getting hurt by the sun or the weather.

Use newspapers, towels, cardboard boxes, crayons, and other supplies to construct with your child a fun shelter for a favorite toy.

observe

To observe something is to watch it very closely.

Ask your child to tell you about what the author of One Small Garden *observed when a raccoon family walked into her garden.*

dwell

If you dwell somewhere, you live there.

Discuss with your child places where you have dwelled in the past. Have them tell you about places they have seen where other people dwell.

disturb

When you disturb someone or something, you bother or upset it in some way.

Invite your child to act out some things that would disturb someone who was trying to sleep.

Go to http://www.elementsofreading.com/parentplace for fun, educational activities that you can do at home with your child.

Diversión con palabras nuevas

Estimada Familia,

Durante la semana de ______________________, su hijo/a estará aprendiendo a usar las palabras listadas abajo. Estamos aprendiendo a usar estas palabras mientras hablamos. Ésto ayudará que su hijo/a llegue a ser un lector mejor.

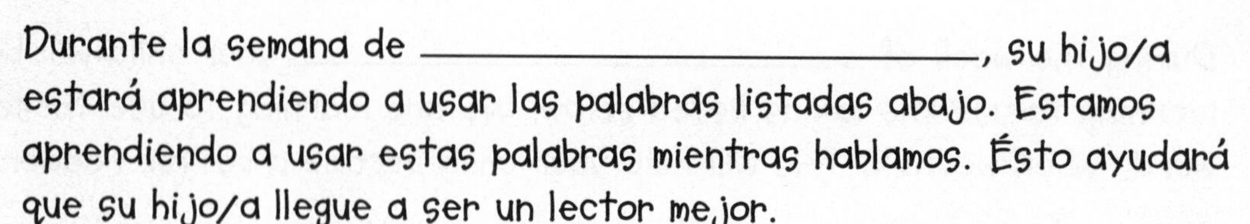

Esta semana, haga el favor de tratar de usar estas palabras tanto como pueda. A lo mejor, desea hacer las actividades también, para que su hijo/a tenga más práctica con las palabras. ¡Diviértase usando estas palabras!

Maestro/a ______________________

survive

Seguir viviendo, a pesar de momentos malos.

Haga que su hijo/a le cuente algunas de las cosas que se necesita para poder survive.

destroy

Romper una cosa para que sea inútil.

Consiga una caja de cartón u otra cosa que iba a tirar a la basura. Désela a su hijo/a y haga que demuestre cómo to destroy *la cosa.*

shelter

Proteger algo del sol o del tiempo para que no le haga daño.

Use periódicos, toallas, cajas de cartón, creyones, y otras provisiones para construir con su hijo/a un shelter *divertido para su juguete favorito.*

observe

Mirar algo con mucha atención.

Pídale a su hijo/a contarle a Ud. qué observed *el autor de* One Small Garden *cuando una familia de mapaches entró en su jardín.*

dwell

Habitar un sitio.

Hable con su hijo/a de los sitios en que Ud. ha dwelled *en el pasado. Haga que su hijo/a le cuente a Ud. algunos sitios en que la gente* dwell.

disturb

Molestar una cosa o a una persona.

Haga que su hijo/a se porte de una manera que puede disturb *a una persona que está tratando de dormir.*

Fun with New Words

Dear Family,

During the week of ______________________, your child will be learning to use the words listed below. We are learning to use these words when we talk. This will help your child become a better reader.

This week please try to use these words as often as you can. You may wish to do the activities, too, so your child can get extra practice with the words. Have fun using these words!

Teacher ______________________

certain

If you are certain about something, you strongly believe that it is true.

Ask your child to name an item that they are certain can be found in your kitchen.

disguise

A disguise is something you wear to make you look like someone or something else.

Ask your child to think of things in your home that could be used to make a disguise.

quiver

To quiver means to shake a tiny bit.

Ask your child to find something in your home that can quiver.

scrumptious

Something scrumptious is so delicious that you don't want to stop eating it.

Ask your child to name three foods that he or she thinks are scrumptious.

convince

If you convince someone, you talk them into believing something or doing something.

Ask your child to convince you to read a story to him or her.

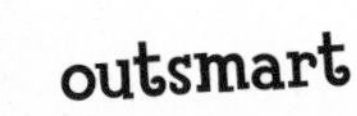

outsmart

When you outsmart someone, you trick them or beat them by doing something clever.

Ask your child to recall a time when he or she outsmarted someone.

Go to http://www.elementsofreading.com/parentplace for fun, educational activities that you can do at home with your child.

Diversión con palabras nuevas

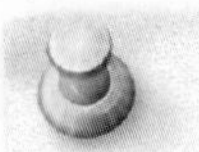

Estimada Familia,

Durante la semana de ______________________, su hijo/a estará aprendiendo a usar las palabras listadas abajo. Estamos aprendiendo a usar estas palabras mientras hablamos. Ésto ayudará que su hijo/a llegue a ser un lector mejor.

Esta semana, haga el favor de tratar de usar estas palabras tanto como pueda. A lo mejor, desea hacer las actividades también, para que su hijo/a tenga más práctica con las palabras. ¡Diviértase usando estas palabras!

Maestro/a ______________________

certain

Es cuando se cree que algo es verdad.

Pídale a su hijo/a nombrar una cosa que él/ella está certain *está en la cocina.*

disguise

Es algo que se pone una persona para esconder su identidad.

Pregúntele a su hijo/a cuáles cosas en la casa se puede utilizar para hacer un disguise.

quiver

Temblar un poco.

Pídale a su hijo/a encontrar algo en la casa que puede quiver.

scrumptious

Algo que tiene un sabor tan rico que no quiere uno dejar de comerlo.

Haga que su hijo/a nombre tres comidas scrumptious.

outsmart

Engañar a otra persona, siendo más listo que ella.

Pregúntele a su hijo/a sobre alguna vez que outsmarted *a otra persona.*

convince

Conseguir que una persona haga o crea algo.

Pídale a su hijo/a que le convince *a Ud. leerle un cuento.*

Fun with New Words

Dear Family,

During the week of ______________________, your child will be learning to use the words listed below. We are learning to use these words when we talk. This will help your child become a better reader.

This week please try to use these words as often as you can. You may wish to do the activities, too, so your child can get extra practice with the words. Have fun using these words!

Teacher ______________________

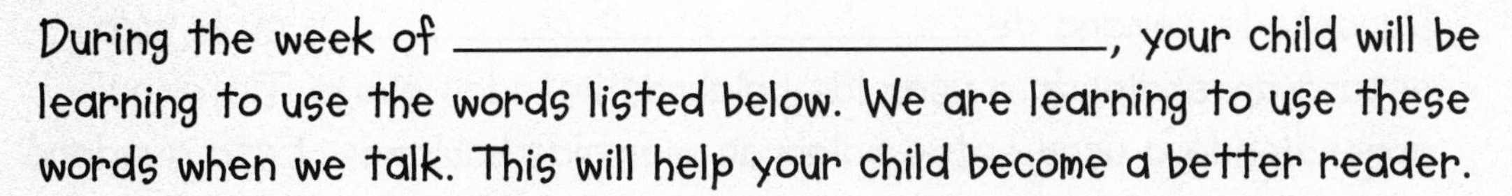

sprinkle

When you sprinkle something, you scatter tiny pieces of it over something else.

Have your child pick some items from your kitchen and demonstrate how to sprinkle them.

gobble

When you gobble food, you eat it quickly and greedily.

Discuss with your child what foods he or she likes to gobble and why.

sloppy

If something is sloppy, it is messy and careless.

Ask your child whether he or she thinks any room in the house is sloppy.

mound

A mound of something is a big, round pile.

Help your child build a mound of pillows and blankets.

tribute

A tribute is something you say or do to show how important you think something or someone is.

Help your child plan a tribute for a family member or friend.

squiggle

A squiggle is a line that bends and curves.

Have the family walk in squiggles for one whole evening.

Go to http://www.elementsofreading.com/parentplace for fun, educational activities that you can do at home with your child.

Diversión con palabras nuevas

Estimada Familia,

Durante la semana de ______________________, su hijo/a estará aprendiendo a usar las palabras listadas abajo. Estamos aprendiendo a usar estas palabras mientras hablamos. Ésto ayudará que su hijo/a llegue a ser un lector mejor.

Esta semana, haga el favor de tratar de usar estas palabras tanto como pueda. A lo mejor, desea hacer las actividades también, para que su hijo/a tenga más práctica con las palabras. ¡Diviértase usando estas palabras!

Maestro/a ______________________

sprinkle

Dejar caer pedacitos de algo sobre otra cosa.

Haga que su hijo/a escoja unas cosas de la cocina y demostrar cómo las puede sprinkle.

gobble

Tragar comida con rapidez sin apenas masticar.

Hable con su hijo/a de las comidas a las que su hijo/a le gusta to gobble *y por qué.*

mound

Es un conjunto de cosas en forma redonda.

Ayude a su hijo/a construir un mound *de almohadas y mantas.*

sloppy

Se dice para describir algo descuidado y desordenado.

Pregúntele a su hijo/a si piensa si está sloppy *alguna habitación de la casa.*

squiggle

Es una línea que dobla y hace curvas.

Haga que la familia camine haciendo squiggles *durante una tarde.*

tribute

Es una muestra de reconocimiento hacía una cosa o una persona.

Ayude a su hijo/a preparar un tribute *para un familiar o un amigo.*

Fun with New Words

Dear Family,

During the week of ______________________________, your child will be learning to use the words listed below. We are learning to use these words when we talk. This will help your child become a better reader.

This week please try to use these words as often as you can. You may wish to do the activities, too, so your child can get extra practice with the words. Have fun using these words!

Teacher ______________________________

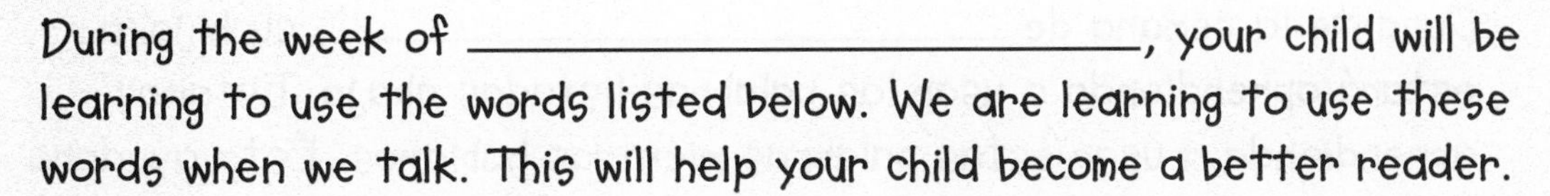

wander

When you wander, you walk around as if you had no special place to go.

Take a walk through your neighborhood with your child and ask him or her to show you how to wander.

artistic

When someone is artistic, they are very good at drawing, painting, or making beautiful things.

Ask your child to make or draw something to show you how artistic he or she is.

nibble

When you nibble food, you eat it in tiny bites.

Ask your child to show you how to nibble an apple, a cracker, or another type of food.

inquire

When you inquire about something, you ask questions about it.

Ask your child to note each time someone in your family inquires about something.

patient

When you are patient, you stay calm while you wait for something to happen.

Ask your child to recall a time when he or she had to be patient.

crouch

When you crouch, you bend your knees and get down very low to the ground.

Use the word crouch *when asking your child to pick something up from the ground.*

Go to http://www.elementsofreading.com/parentplace for fun, educational activities that you can do at home with your child.

Diversión con palabras nuevas

Estimada Familia,

Durante la semana de ______________________________, su hijo/a estará aprendiendo a usar las palabras listadas abajo. Estamos aprendiendo a usar estas palabras mientras hablamos. Ésto ayudará que su hijo/a llegue a ser un lector mejor.

Esta semana, haga el favor de tratar de usar estas palabras tanto como pueda. A lo mejor, desea hacer las actividades también, para que su hijo/a tenga más práctica con las palabras. ¡Diviértase usando estas palabras!

Maestro/a ______________________________

wander

Caminar sin rumbo fijo.

Váyase de paseo por el barrio con su hijo/a y pídale que le enseñe a Ud. cómo to wander.

artistic

Se dice de la persona que demuestra una habilidad especial con cosas relacionadas con el arte, como el dibujo o la pintura.

Pídale a su hijo/a hacer o dibujar algo para demostrar que es artistic.

nibble

Comer dando mordiscos pequeños.

Pídale a su hijo/a demostrar cómo to nibble *una manzana, una galleta, u otro tipo de comida.*

inquire

Hacer preguntas sobre una cosa.

Pídale a su hijo/a anotar cada vez que alguien de la familia inquires *acerca de algo.*

crouch

Doblar las rodillas para bajar el cuerpo hacía el suelo.

Dígale a su hijo/a to crouch *mientras recoja algo del suelo.*

patient

Quedarse tranquilo mientras espera que ocurra algo.

Pídale a su hijo/a recordar alguna vez en que tuvo que estar patient.

Fun with New Words

Dear Family,

During the week of ____________________, your child will be learning to use the words listed below. We are learning to use these words when we talk. This will help your child become a better reader.

This week please try to use these words as often as you can. You may wish to do the activities, too, so your child can get extra practice with the words. Have fun using these words!

Teacher ____________________

dissolve

When something dissolves, it melts and disappears.

Make a powdered juice drink with your child and watch the powder dissolve.

swift

Something that is swift moves fast.

Go outside and have your child show you how swiftly he or she can turn cartwheels.

preposterous

Something preposterous is so strange that it couldn't possibly be true.

Invite your child to share with you the preposterous story of what happened to Herbert Glerbett.

ghastly

If something is ghastly, it is the scariest thing you can think of.

Ask your child to describe for you a ghastly thing that he or she would not want to find under his or her bed.

caution

When you caution someone, you warn that person of danger.

Have your child point out caution signs that you see during the day (stop signs, wet floor signs, etc.). Identify a place in your home that might be dangerous and make a caution sign with your child to warn others about this danger.

sly

Someone who is sly is wise and might do things in a sneaky way to get what they want.

Have your child act out how someone sly would get an extra dessert for dinner.

Go to http://www.elementsofreading.com/parentplace for fun, educational activities that you can do at home with your child.

Diversión con palabras nuevas

Estimada Familia,

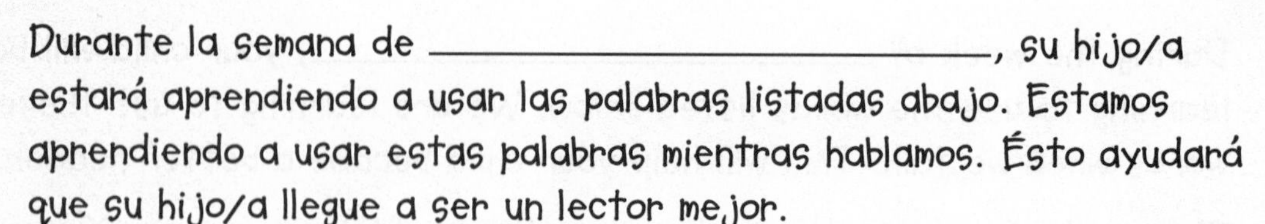

Durante la semana de ______________________________, su hijo/a estará aprendiendo a usar las palabras listadas abajo. Estamos aprendiendo a usar estas palabras mientras hablamos. Ésto ayudará que su hijo/a llegue a ser un lector mejor.

Esta semana, haga el favor de tratar de usar estas palabras tanto como pueda. A lo mejor, desea hacer las actividades también, para que su hijo/a tenga más práctica con las palabras. ¡Diviértase usando estas palabras!

Maestro/a ______________________________

dissolve

Hacer líquida una sustancia y luego desaparecer.

Prepare un jugo en polvo con su hijo/a y observe dissolve *el polvo.*

swift

Se dice para describir algo que se mueve con rapidez.

Salga hacia fuera con su hijo/a y pídale enseñarle a Ud. que swiftly *puede dar unas volteretas laterales.*

ghastly

Se dice para describir algo que da más miedo de lo que se puede imaginar.

Pídale a su hijo/a describir una cosa ghastly *que no le gustaría encontrar debajo de su cama.*

preposterous

Es algo tan extraño que no puede ser verdad.

Haga que su hijo/a comparta con Ud. la historia preposterous *de qué pasó a Herbert Glerbett.*

sly

Se dice de la persona lista que a veces consigue lo que quiere de una manera furtiva.

Haga que su hijo/a actúe cómo una persona sly *conseguiría un postre adicional después de comer.*

caution

Avisarle a alguien que hay peligro.

Haga que su hijo/a indique señales de caution *que se ve a lo largo del día (señales de stop, señales de piso mojado, etc.). Identifique con él/ella un sitio de su lugar que puede ser peligroso y haga una señal de* caution *con su hijo/a para avisar a otros de este peligro.*

Fun with New Words

Dear Family,

During the week of ______________________, your child will be learning to use the words listed below. We are learning to use these words when we talk. This will help your child become a better reader.

This week please try to use these words as often as you can. You may wish to do the activities, too, so your child can get extra practice with the words. Have fun using these words!

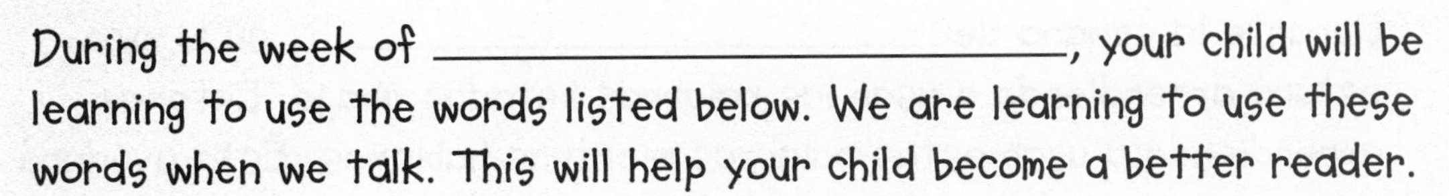

Teacher ______________________

tremendous

If something is tremendous, it is very large or in a very large amount.

Invite your child to show you how he or she would pet a tremendous animal.

sliver

A sliver of something is a small, thin piece of it.

Get a block of cheese, a piece of fruit, or some other kind of sliceable food and have your child give you instructions to tell you how to cut a sliver of it.

amazed

If something has amazed you, it has surprised you very much.

Ask your child to tell you something that will amaze you.

palate

Someone's palate is their choice of what foods and drinks they like.

Have your child describe three foods that please his or her palate.

surplus

You have a surplus of something when you have more than you need of it.

Ask your child to tell you the story of what Mama Provi did with her surplus of rice with chicken.

rearrange

If you rearrange things, you change the way in which they are organized or ordered.

Ask your child to describe how they would like to rearrange a room in your home.

Go to http://www.elementsofreading.com/parentplace for fun, educational activities that you can do at home with your child.

Diversión con palabras nuevas

Estimada Familia,

Durante la semana de ______________________________, su hijo/a estará aprendiendo a usar las palabras listadas abajo. Estamos aprendiendo a usar estas palabras mientras hablamos. Ésto ayudará que su hijo/a llegue a ser un lector mejor.

Esta semana, haga el favor de tratar de usar estas palabras tanto como pueda. A lo mejor, desea hacer las actividades también, para que su hijo/a tenga más práctica con las palabras. ¡Diviértase usando estas palabras!

Maestro/a ______________________________

tremendous

Es algo muy grande o algo en una gran cantidad.

Haga que su hijo/a demuestre cómo acariciaría un animal tremendous.

sliver

Es un pedacito delgadito de algo.

Consiga un bloque de queso, un pedazo de fruta, u otra comida que se le puede cortar en lonchas. Luego, haga que su hijo/a le pida a Ud. cortar un sliver *de la comida.*

amazed

Estar muy asombrado.

Pídale a su hijo/a contarle algo a Ud. que le va a amaze.

palate

Es lo que le gusta a una persona comer y beber.

Haga que su hijo/a describa tres comidas a las que le agradecen su palate.

rearrange

Cambiar la orden de algo.

Pídale a su hijo/a describir cómo le gustaría rearrange *una habitación de su casa.*

surplus

Es cuando hay más de lo que se necesita uno.

Pídale a su hijo/a describir qué hizo Mama Provi con su surplus *de arroz con pollo.*

Fun with New Words

Dear Family,

During the week of ______________________, your child will be learning to use the words listed below. We are learning to use these words when we talk. This will help your child become a better reader.

This week please try to use these words as often as you can. You may wish to do the activities, too, so your child can get extra practice with the words. Have fun using these words!

Teacher ______________________

dull

If you say something is dull, you mean that it is rather boring and not very exciting.

Ask your child to describe a kind of activity that he or she thinks is dull.

petrified

If you are petrified, you are so scared that you can hardly move.

Ask your child to describe something that petrifies him or her.

adventurous

Someone who is adventurous is willing to take risks and to try new things.

Ask your child to draw a picture of what an adventurous person might do.

eager

If you are eager for something, you want it so much you can hardly wait.

Ask your child to plan with you to do something that he or she is eager to do.

rely

When you rely on someone, you count on them to do something for you.

Ask your child to describe three things he or she relies on you to do.

alert

If you alert someone, you make them aware of something important or dangerous that might happen.

Have a fire drill in your home in which your child is the one to alert the family of the fire.

Go to http://www.elementsofreading.com/parentplace for fun, educational activities that you can do at home with your child.

Diversión con palabras nuevas

Estimada Familia,

Durante la semana de ______________________, su hijo/a estará aprendiendo a usar las palabras listadas abajo. Estamos aprendiendo a usar estas palabras mientras hablamos. Ésto ayudará que su hijo/a llegue a ser un lector mejor.

Esta semana, haga el favor de tratar de usar estas palabras tanto como pueda. A lo mejor, desea hacer las actividades también, para que su hijo/a tenga más práctica con las palabras. ¡Diviértase usando estas palabras!

Maestro/a ______________________

dull

Se dice para describir algo que aburra y no es tan interesante.

Pídale a su hijo/a que describa una actividad dull.

petrified

Tener tanto miedo que apenas se puede mover.

Pídale a su hijo/a que describa algo que le hace sentir petrified.

eager

Tener tantas ganas de hacer algo o de que algo pase, que resulta difícil esperar.

Pídale a su hijo/a que organice algo que está eager *hacer.*

adventerous

Se dice para describir a una persona dispuesta a tomar riesgos y probar cosas nuevas.

Haga que su hijo/a dibuje algo que haría una persona adventurous.

alert

Avisarle a alguien que algo importante o peligroso está a punto de pasar.

Haga una práctica de salir de la casa en caso de un incendio, y haga que su hijo/a sea la persona que alerts *a los demás.*

rely

Confiar en otra persona.

Pídale a su hijo/a que describa tres cosas en las que tiene que rely *en Ud.*

Fun with New Words

Dear Family,

During the week of ______________________, your child will be learning to use the words listed below. We are learning to use these words when we talk. This will help your child become a better reader.

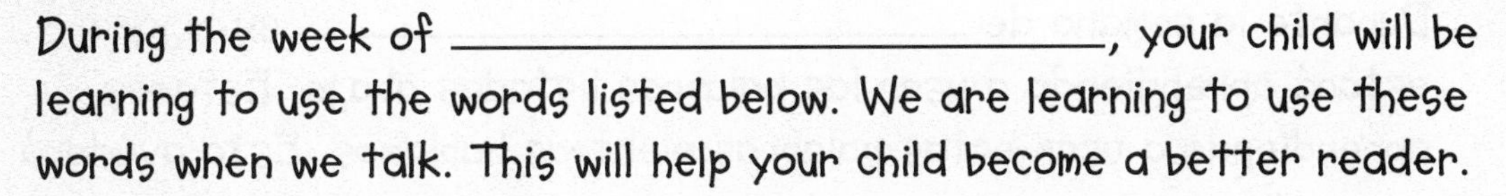

This week please try to use these words as often as you can. You may wish to do the activities, too, so your child can get extra practice with the words. Have fun using these words!

Teacher ______________________

relax

When you relax, you let go of all your worries and you rest.

Pick a comfortable spot in your home to sit and relax with your child.

leisure

Leisure is time you have to just do what you enjoy.

Discuss with your child what activities he or she would like to do with you the next time you both have leisure time.

resourceful

Someone who is resourceful is good at finding ways of solving problems.

Invite your child to explain to you why Penny in the story Flip-Flops *is resourceful.*

appear

When someone or something appears, you are suddenly able to see it.

Ask your child to name a famous person that he or she would like to see appear at your front door.

outgoing

An outgoing person is very friendly and likes to meet people.

Ask your child to explain who he or she thinks the most outgoing person in your family is and explain why.

tumble

When you tumble, you fall head first and roll over into a ball.

Ask your child to demonstrate tumbling across the floor or yard.

Go to http://www.elementsofreading.com/parentplace for fun, educational activities that you can do at home with your child.

Diversión con palabras nuevas

Estimada Familia,

Durante la semana de ______________________, su hijo/a estará aprendiendo a usar las palabras listadas abajo. Estamos aprendiendo a usar estas palabras mientras hablamos. Ésto ayudará que su hijo/a llegue a ser un lector mejor.

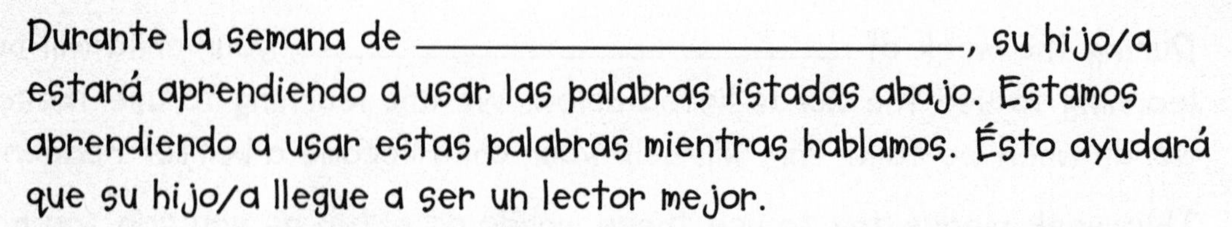

Esta semana, haga el favor de tratar de usar estas palabras tanto como pueda. A lo mejor, desea hacer las actividades también, para que su hijo/a tenga más práctica con las palabras. ¡Diviértase usando estas palabras!

Maestro/a ______________________

relax

Dejarse olvidar de las preocupaciones que tiene uno y descansar.

Escoja un sitio cómodo en su casa para sentarse y relax *junto con su hijo/a.*

leisure

Es lo que se llama a los ratos que pasa uno haciendo las cosas que disfruta.

Hable con su hijo/a sobre las cosas que les gustaría hacer juntos cuando los dos tengan tiempo de leisure.

appear

Es cuando de pronto alguien o algo puede ser visto.

Pídale a su hijo/a nombrar a una persona famosa a quien le gustaría to appear *en la puerta de su casa.*

resourceful

Se dice para describir a una persona inteligente a la hora de resolver problemas.

Anime a su hijo/a explicarle por qué Penny de la historia Flip-Flops *es* resourceful.

tumble

Caerse una persona, primero con la cabeza, y luego ponerse en forma redonda el cuerpo.

Haga que su hijo/a demuestre cómo to tumble *en el suelo o en el jardín.*

outgoing

Se dice de la persona amable que le gusta conocer a otra gente.

Pídale a su hijo/a explicar quién es la persona más outgoing *de la familia y que explique por qué.*

Fun with New Words

Dear Family,

During the week of ______________________, your child will be learning to use the words listed below. We are learning to use these words when we talk. This will help your child become a better reader.

This week please try to use these words as often as you can. You may wish to do the activities, too, so your child can get extra practice with the words. Have fun using these words!

Teacher ______________________

glimpse

To get a glimpse of something means to get a quick look at it.

When you are in a bus or car, ask your child what he or she glimpses out the window.

grand

If you say something is grand, you think it is so wonderful that you almost can't believe it is real.

Ask your child to describe a grand time he or she had with you. Tell your child about a grand time you had with him or her.

pleasant

Something pleasant is very nice and it pleases you.

Ask your child to describe something pleasant that happened today.

skyscraper

A skyscraper is a very tall building in a city.

Ask your child to tell what it would be like to live in a skyscraper.

observant

Someone who is observant pays a lot of attention to things.

Ask your child to be observant and describe all the sounds he or she hears in your home.

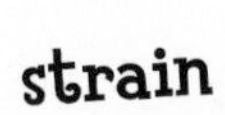

strain

To strain means to push, pull, or stretch something in a way that might hurt it.

Ask your child to act out how people could strain their muscles.

Go to http://www.elementsofreading.com/parentplace for fun, educational activities that you can do at home with your child.

Diversión con palabras nuevas

Estimada Familia,

Durante la semana de ______________________, su hijo/a estará aprendiendo a usar las palabras listadas abajo. Estamos aprendiendo a usar estas palabras mientras hablamos. Ésto ayudará que su hijo/a llegue a ser un lector mejor.

Esta semana, haga el favor de tratar de usar estas palabras tanto como pueda. A lo mejor, desea hacer las actividades también, para que su hijo/a tenga más práctica con las palabras. ¡Diviértase usando estas palabras!

Maestro/a ______________________

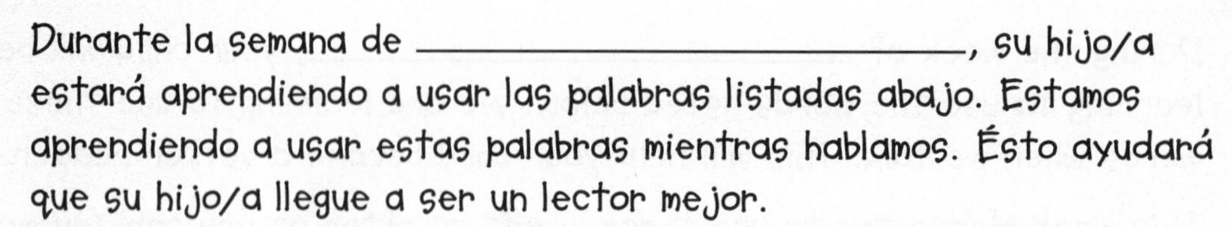

glimpse

Echar un vistazo.

Cuando los dos están en el coche o en el autobús, pregúntele a su hijo/a qué es lo que glimpses *por la ventana.*

grand

Es algo tan maravilloso que casi no puede creer que sea real.

Pídale a su hijo/a que describa una ocasión grand *que han pasado juntos. Describa una ocasión* grand *que Ud. pasó con su hijo/a.*

pleasant

Es algo muy agradable.

Pídale a su hijo/a que describa algo pleasant *que pasó hoy.*

skyscraper

Es un edificio alto en la ciudad, un rascacielos.

Pregúntele a su hijo/a cómo sería vivir en un skyscraper.

strain

Estirar o tender con fuerza de una manera que le puede causar daño a una cosa.

Pídale a su hijo/a que actúe cómo una persona se puede strain *un músculo.*

observant

Se dice de la persona que presta mucha atención a las cosas.

Dígale a su hijo/a que esté observant *y que describa todos los sonidos que escucha en la casa.*

Fun with New Words

Dear Family,

During the week of ______________________, your child will be learning to use the words listed below. We are learning to use these words when we talk. This will help your child become a better reader.

This week please try to use these words as often as you can. You may wish to do the activities, too, so your child can get extra practice with the words. Have fun using these words!

Teacher ________________________

longs

When someone longs for something, they want it very badly, but think they will never have it.

Ask your child to draw a picture of something he or she longs for.

admit

If you admit something, you agree that it is true, even though you may not want to have to say it.

Ask your child to tell about something he or she thinks would be hard to admit.

realize

If you realize something, you begin to understand it or figure it out.

Ask your child to talk about something that school has helped him or her realize is true.

cunning

If you are cunning, you are able to trick people.

Ask your child to describe the cunning character in the story, Rabbit Counts the Crocodiles.

furious

To be furious is to be very, very mad.

Ask your child to tell about something at home that made him or her furious.

gullible

Someone who is gullible is easily tricked because they believe whatever they are told.

Ask your child to tell about a time when he or she was gullible.

Go to http://www.elementsofreading.com/parentplace for fun, educational activities that you can do at home with your child.

Diversión con palabras nuevas

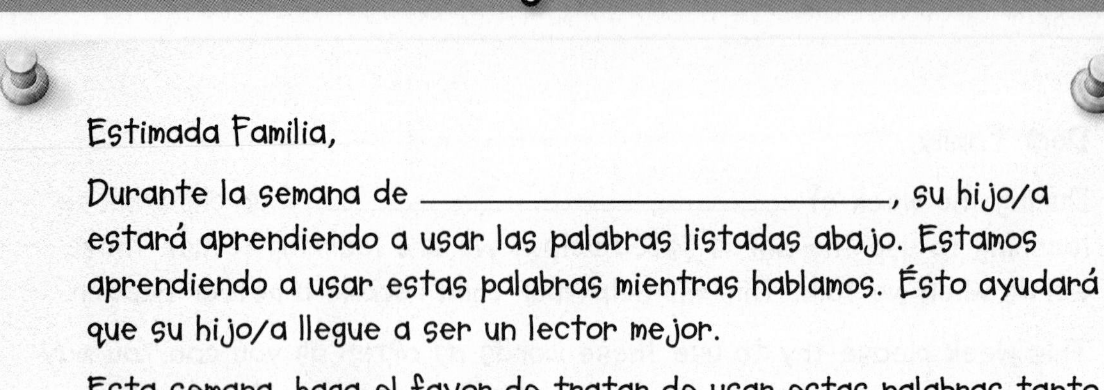

Estimada Familia,

Durante la semana de ______________________, su hijo/a estará aprendiendo a usar las palabras listadas abajo. Estamos aprendiendo a usar estas palabras mientras hablamos. Ésto ayudará que su hijo/a llegue a ser un lector mejor.

Esta semana, haga el favor de tratar de usar estas palabras tanto como pueda. A lo mejor, desea hacer las actividades también, para que su hijo/a tenga más práctica con las palabras. ¡Diviértase usando estas palabras!

Maestro/a ______________________

longs

Anhelar; desear algo con intensidad, sin creer que lo va a conseguir.

Pídale a su hijo/a dibujar algo por que longs *él/ella.*

admit

Ponerse de acuerdo de que algo sea cierto, aunque no quiera decirlo.

Pregúntele a su hijo/a qué es algo que sería difícil to admit.

realize

Empezar a comprender algo.

Pregúntele a su hijo/a qué la escuela le ha ayudado a realize.

cunning

Se dice para describir a una persona con la habilidad de engañar con facilidad.

Pídale a su hijo/a describir al personaje cunning *de la historia* Rabbit Counts the Crocodiles.

furious

Estar muy, muy enojado.

Pregúntele a su hijo/a que diga algo que le ha hecho furious.

gullible

Se dice de una persona fácilmente engañada y que cree todo lo que se le cuenta.

Pídale a su hijo/a que cuente alguna vez que era gullible.

Fun with New Words

Dear Family,

During the week of ______________________, your child will be learning to use the words listed below. We are learning to use these words when we talk. This will help your child become a better reader.

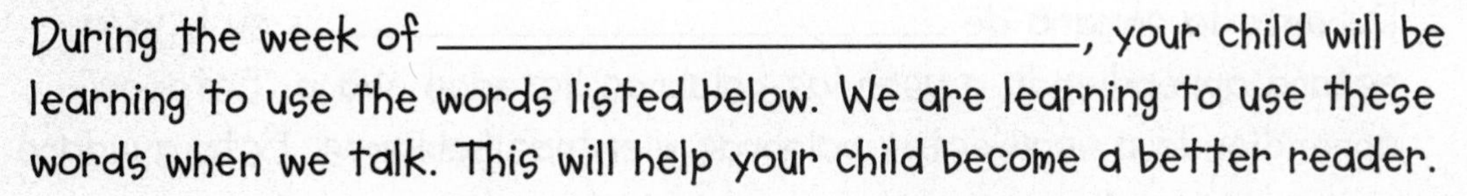

This week please try to use these words as often as you can. You may wish to do the activities, too, so your child can get extra practice with the words. Have fun using these words!

Teacher ______________________

romp

When children or animals romp, they play happily.

Invite your child to romp outside with you.

household

Your household is your house, all of the people who live there, and all of the things that are a part of it.

Draw a floor plan of your household with your child. Write in where each member of your household sleeps.

fad

If something is a fad, it is popular for a very short time.

Ask your child to tell you about any fads he or she is interested in right now. Describe for your child a funny fad that you followed in the past.

entertain

To entertain means to do something like sing, dance, or play an instrument to please an audience.

Sing a song with your child to entertain other members of your family.

creative

A creative person is someone who is always thinking up new and interesting ideas.

Have your child explain to you why Walt Disney was creative when he made Mickey Mouse talk in Steamboat Willie.

gather

When you gather things, you collect them all into a group.

Challenge your child to gather five pairs of shoes from around your home.

Go to http://www.elementsofreading.com/parentplace for fun, educational activities that you can do at home with your child.

Diversión con palabras nuevas

Estimada Familia,

Durante la semana de ______________________, su hijo/a estará aprendiendo a usar las palabras listadas abajo. Estamos aprendiendo a usar estas palabras mientras hablamos. Ésto ayudará que su hijo/a llegue a ser un lector mejor.

Esta semana, haga el favor de tratar de usar estas palabras tanto como pueda. A lo mejor, desea hacer las actividades también, para que su hijo/a tenga más práctica con las palabras. ¡Diviértase usando estas palabras!

Maestro/a ______________________

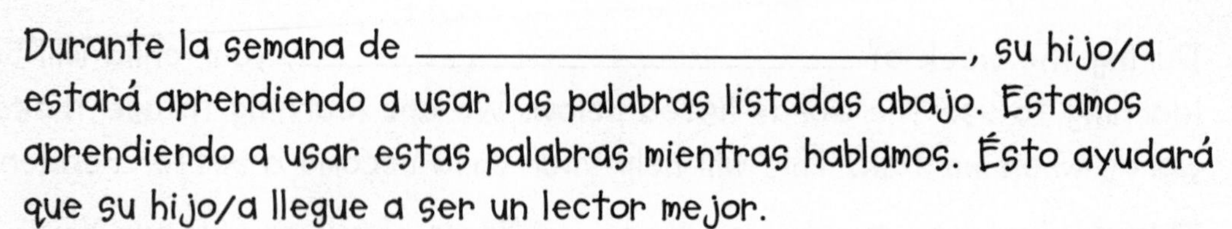

romp

Jugar alegremente.

Invite hacia fuera a su hijo/a to romp *con Ud.*

household

Es lo que se dice de una casa, la gente que vive dentro de ella, y de todos sus contenidos.

Dibuje con su hijo/a un plano del household. *Escriba donde duerme cada miembro de la familia.*

fad

Se dice de algo que está de moda.

Pídale a su hijo/a describir cualquier fad *que actualmente le interesa. Describa a su hijo/a una* fad *graciosa que seguía Ud. en el pasado.*

entertain

Realizar una actividad como cantar, bailar, o tocar un instrumento musical para el gusto de un público.

Cante con su hijo/a una canción para entertain *a otros miembros de la familia.*

gather

Agrupar cosas.

Haga que su hijo/a gather *cinco pares de zapatos que encuentre por la casa.*

creative

Inventar ideas nuevas e interesantes.

Haga que su hijo/a le explique por qué era creative *Walt Disney cuando le hizo hablar Mickey Mouse en* Steamboat Willie.

Fun with New Words

Dear Family,

During the week of ______________________, your child will be learning to use the words listed below. We are learning to use these words when we talk. This will help your child become a better reader.

This week please try to use these words as often as you can. You may wish to do the activities, too, so your child can get extra practice with the words. Have fun using these words!

Teacher ______________________

pasture

A pasture is a field of grass or other plants that animals such as cows and horses like to eat.

If possible, visit a pasture with your child. If not, have your child draw you a picture of a pasture.

mandatory

If something is mandatory, you have to do it.

Discuss with your child some rules that are mandatory in your home.

tempting

If something is tempting, you want it very much, even if you know you should not have it.

Invite your child to tell you about the things that were tempting to Annalisa in Kiss the Cow!

velvet

Velvet is a kind of soft, fuzzy cloth.

Search your home with your child for objects made of velvet.

provide

To provide something, you give it to someone so they can use it.

Have your child point out times when people in your home provide things for one another.

scrap

A scrap is a little piece of something that is left over when you are finished making something.

Ask your child to throw away some scraps of food for you while you are preparing dinner.

Go to http://www.elementsofreading.com/parentplace for fun, educational activities that you can do at home with your child.

Estimada Familia,

Durante la semana de ______________________________, su hijo/a estará aprendiendo a usar las palabras listadas abajo. Estamos aprendiendo a usar estas palabras mientras hablamos. Ésto ayudará que su hijo/a llegue a ser un lector mejor.

Esta semana, haga el favor de tratar de usar estas palabras tanto como pueda. A lo mejor, desea hacer las actividades también, para que su hijo/a tenga más práctica con las palabras. ¡Diviértase usando estas palabras!

Maestro/a ______________________________

pasture

Es un campo que se dedica a la alimentación del ganado.

Si es posible, visite junto con su hijo/a a un pasture. *Si no, haga que su hijo/a dibuje un* pasture.

mandatory

Es algo que se debe hacer.

Hable con su hijo/a de una reglas de su casa que son mandatory.

velvet

Es el nombre de una tela suave y vellosa.

Busque por la casa cosas hechas de velvet.

tempting

Se dice de algo que atrae mucho, aunque sepa que no lo debe tener.

Anime a su hijo/a contarle algunas cosas que le resultó tempting *a Annalisa en* Kiss the Cow!

scrap

Es un pedacito de algo que sobra.

Pídale a su hijo/a tirar unos scraps *de comida mientras Ud. prepare la cena.*

provide

Dar una cosa necesaria para conseguir un fin.

Haga que su hijo/a cite algunas veces en que la gente en su casa provide *cosas el uno para el otro.*

Fun with New Words

Dear Family,

During the week of ______________________, your child will be learning to use the words listed below. We are learning to use these words when we talk. This will help your child become a better reader.

This week please try to use these words as often as you can. You may wish to do the activities, too, so your child can get extra practice with the words. Have fun using these words!

Teacher ______________________

delicate

Something that is delicate is small and light and easily broken.

Have your child demonstrate how to carry something delicate.

variety

A variety is many different kinds of something.

Ask your child to collect and bring to you a variety of socks from around your home.

enhance

When you enhance something, you make it better.

Select a room in your home and discuss some practical things you could do to enhance it (draw a picture for the wall, make new curtains, and so on). Work with your child to enhance the room.

vast

If something is vast, it is so large that it seems like it has no end.

Watch your child act out how he or she would look trying to walk across a vast desert.

accomplish

When you accomplish something, you complete something that was very hard to do.

Ask your child to tell you about something hard that he or she recently accomplished.

investigate

When you investigate something, you try to find out what it is all about.

Ask your child to pick a subject about which he or she is interested and investigate it together.

Go to http://www.elementsofreading.com/parentplace for fun, educational activities that you can do at home with your child.

Diversión con palabras nuevas

Estimada Familia,

Durante la semana de ______________________, su hijo/a estará aprendiendo a usar las palabras listadas abajo. Estamos aprendiendo a usar estas palabras mientras hablamos. Ésto ayudará que su hijo/a llegue a ser un lector mejor.

Esta semana, haga el favor de tratar de usar estas palabras tanto como pueda. A lo mejor, desea hacer las actividades también, para que su hijo/a tenga más práctica con las palabras. ¡Diviértase usando estas palabras!

Maestro/a ______________________

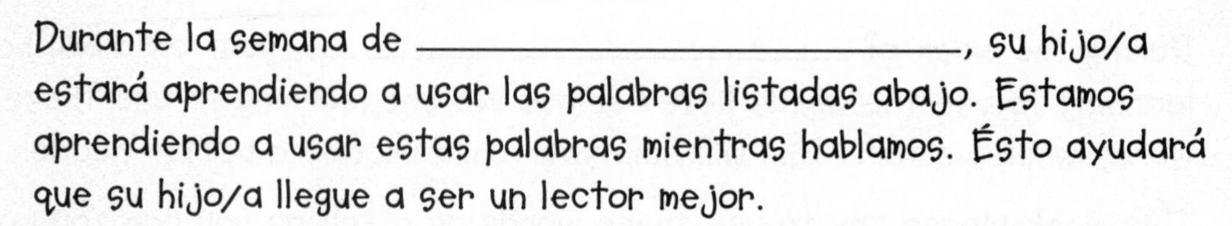

delicate

Es algo pequeño, fino, y que se rompe fácilmente.

Haga que su hijo/a demuestre cómo cargar algo delicate.

variety

Es la combinación de muchas cosas distintas.

Pídale a su hijo/a escoger y traerle a Ud. una variety *de calcetines que encuentre por la casa.*

vast

Se dice para describir algo tan grande que parece no tener fin.

Haga que su hijo/a actúe cómo se vería tratando de cruzar un vast *desierto.*

enhance

Mejorar o añadir algo.

Escoger una habitación de su casa y pregúntele a su hijo/a qué cosas se puede hacer para enhance *la habitación (hacer un dibujo para colgar en la pared, hacer cortinas nuevas, y tal). Colabore con su hijo/a* to enhance *la habitación.*

investigate

Intentar enterarse de algo.

Pídale a su hijo/a escoger un tema que le interese e investigate *el tema con él/ella.*

accomplish

Realizar algo difícil.

Pídale a su hijo/a a contarle a Ud. algo que recientemente ha accomplished.

Fun with New Words

Dear Family,

During the week of ______________________, your child will be learning to use the words listed below. We are learning to use these words when we talk. This will help your child become a better reader.

This week please try to use these words as often as you can. You may wish to do the activities, too, so your child can get extra practice with the words. Have fun using these words!

Teacher ______________________

boast

When you boast about something, you talk about it in a way that is so proud that it is like showing off.

Ask your child to boast about something that he or she does very well.

frighten

To frighten someone is to scare them very badly.

Talk to your child about something that frightens him or her.

enormous

If something is enormous, it is almost larger than you can imagine.

Have your child tell you about any enormous things that he or she has seen during the day.

mighty

When something is mighty, it is very large and strong.

Have your child point out things around your home that he or she could lift if he or she were mighty.

humble

If someone is humble, they do not look for a lot of attention.

Have your child tell you the story of how Zeke the alligator learned to be humble.

flatter

When you flatter someone, you tell them nice things about themselves to make them feel good.

Ask your child to flatter a brother, sister, or other member of the family.

Go to http://www.elementsofreading.com/parentplace for fun, educational activities that you can do at home with your child.

Diversión con palabras nuevas

Estimada Familia,

Durante la semana de ________________________, su hijo/a estará aprendiendo a usar las palabras listadas abajo. Estamos aprendiendo a usar estas palabras mientras hablamos. Ésto ayudará que su hijo/a llegue a ser un lector mejor.

Esta semana, haga el favor de tratar de usar estas palabras tanto como pueda. A lo mejor, desea hacer las actividades también, para que su hijo/a tenga más práctica con las palabras. ¡Diviértase usando estas palabras!

Maestro/a ________________________

boast

Hablar de algo de una manera demasiado orgullosa que parece ser presumida.

Dígale a su hijo/a que boast *de algo que hace bien.*

frighten

Asustarle mucho a una persona.

Hable con su hijo/a acerca de algo que le frightens.

mighty

Es algo muy grande y muy fuerte.

Haga que su hijo/a le indique cosas por la casa que pudiera levantar si fuera mighty.

enormous

Se dice de algo tan grande que casi no se lo puede imaginar.

Pregúntele a su hijo/a qué cosa enormous *vió durante el día.*

flatter

Decirle cosas agradables a una persona para que se sienta bien.

Dígale a su hijo/a que flatter *a su hermano, hermana, u otro miembro de la familia.*

humble

Se dice para describir a una persona que no quiere llamar la atención.

Haga que su hijo/a le cuente cómo Zeke el caimán aprendió ser humble.

Fun with New Words

Dear Family,

During the week of ____________________, your child will be learning to use the words listed below. We are learning to use these words when we talk. This will help your child become a better reader.

This week please try to use these words as often as you can. You may wish to do the activities, too, so your child can get extra practice with the words. Have fun using these words!

Teacher ____________________

determined

If you are determined to do something, you have decided to do it and nothing will stop you.

Ask your child to tell you about something he or she is determined to do this week.

frantic

If someone is frantic, they are behaving in a wild way because they are scared, worried, or in a hurry.

Ask your child to show you how he or she would act if someone were coming to visit and your child was frantic because his or her room was a mess.

savory

Savory food tastes good because it is salty or spicy, not sweet.

Have your child pick a favorite savory dish and help him or her cook it for dinner one night.

stunned

If you are stunned by something, you are so shocked or surprised by it that you can hardly speak or move.

Ask your child to show you how his or her face looks when he or she is stunned.

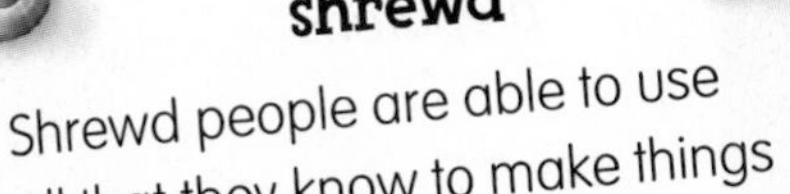

shrewd

Shrewd people are able to use all that they know to make things turn out well for themselves.

Ask your child to describe how Tortoise was shrewd in The Tortoise and the Baboon.

scamper

When people or animals scamper, they move quickly with small, light steps.

Have your child show you how to scamper.

Go to http://www.elementsofreading.com/parentplace for fun, educational activities that you can do at home with your child.

Diversión con palabras nuevas

Estimada Familia,

Durante la semana de ______________________, su hijo/a estará aprendiendo a usar las palabras listadas abajo. Estamos aprendiendo a usar estas palabras mientras hablamos. Ésto ayudará que su hijo/a llegue a ser un lector mejor.

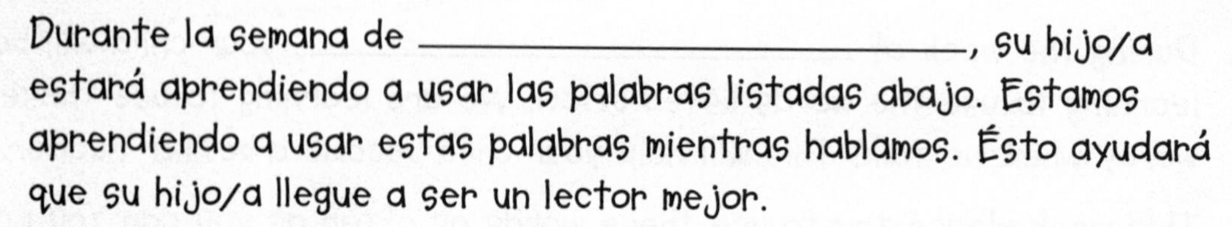

Esta semana, haga el favor de tratar de usar estas palabras tanto como pueda. A lo mejor, desea hacer las actividades también, para que su hijo/a tenga más práctica con las palabras. ¡Diviértase usando estas palabras!

Maestro/a ______________________

determined

Es cuando una persona ha decidido hacer algo y nada le va a parar.

Pídale a su hijo/a que se le cuente a Ud. algo que está determined *hacer esta semana.*

frantic

Es cuando alguien demuestra comportamiento descontrolado o desenfrenado porque tiene miedo, está preocupado, o tiene prisa.

Haga que su hijo/a demuestre cómo se portaría si se sentara frantic *porque viene un invitado a la casa y su habitación está desordenada.*

savory

Es algo con buen sabor porque es salado o picante, pero no dulce.

Haga que su hijo/a escoja un plato savory *para comer y que se le ayude a Ud. a prepararlo.*

stunned

Estar tan sorprendido por algo que apenas se puede hablar.

Haga que su hijo/a le enseñe a Ud. cómo se ve su cara cuando está stunned.

scamper

Moverse una persona o un animal con pasos muy finos y pequeños.

Haga que su hijo/a demuestre cómo to scamper.

shrewd

Es tener la habilidad de utilizar el conocimiento que tiene uno para que se le salga bien una cosa.

Pídale a su hijo/a describir cómo Tortoise estaba shrewd *en* The Tortoise and the Baboon.

Fun with New Words

Dear Family,

During the week of ______________________, your child will be learning to use the words listed below. We are learning to use these words when we talk. This will help your child become a better reader.

This week please try to use these words as often as you can. You may wish to do the activities, too, so your child can get extra practice with the words. Have fun using these words!

Teacher ______________________

injured

A person or animal that is injured has hurt some part of its body.

Have your child list supplies that family members use when they are injured.

elated

To be elated is to feel completely happy about something.

Share a time when you felt elated. Ask your child to provide an example as well.

seasonal

If something is seasonal, it happens every year at the same time.

Ask your child to name a seasonal activity your family does for each part of the year.

bask

To bask in the sunshine is to lie back and enjoy how warm it feels.

Ask your child to name some animals that bask in the sun.

contemplate

When you contemplate something, you think about it very deeply.

Ask your child to tell about some of the things he or she contemplates.

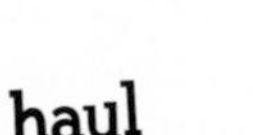

haul

When you haul something, you move something heavy by pulling it.

Ask your child to throw out the trash by asking them to haul it outside.

Go to http://www.elementsofreading.com/parentplace for fun, educational activities that you can do at home with your child.

Diversión con palabras nuevas

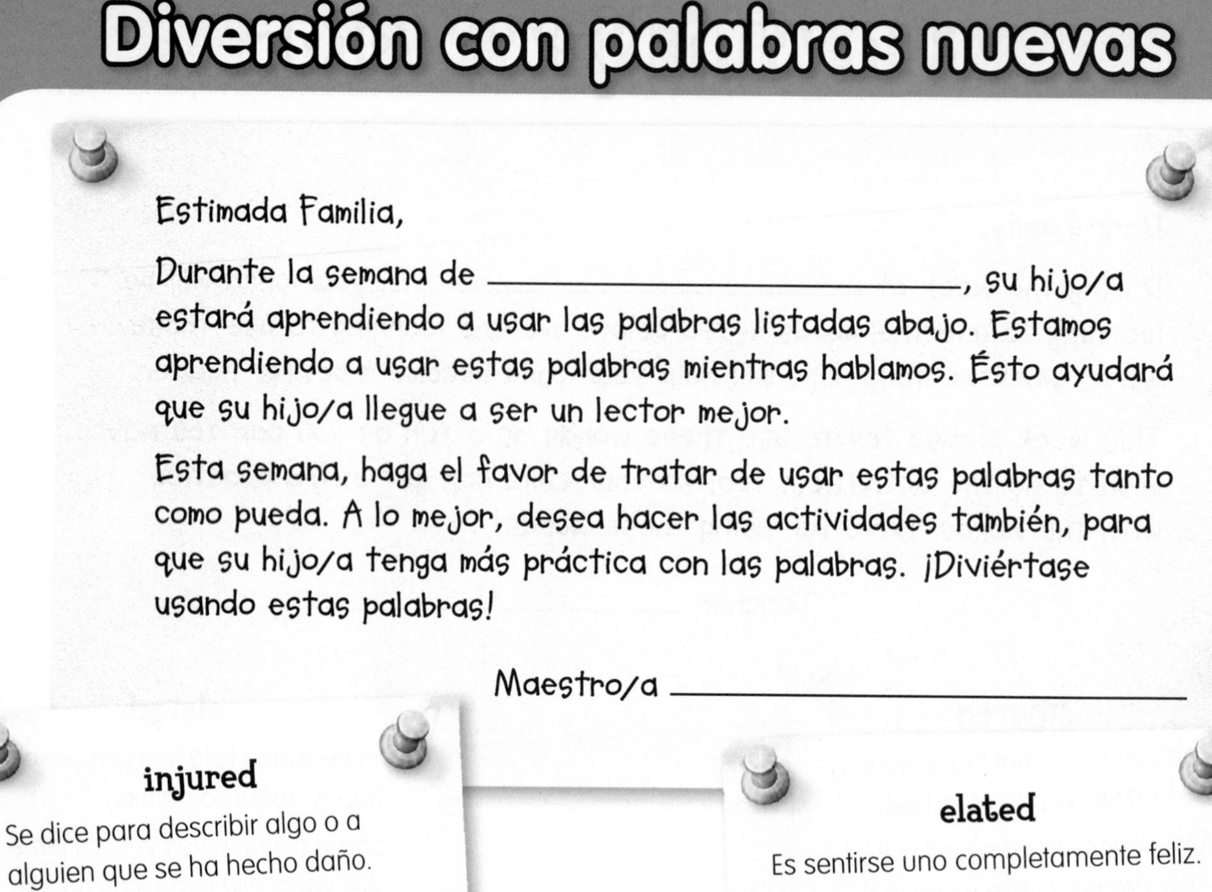

Estimada Familia,

Durante la semana de ______________________, su hijo/a estará aprendiendo a usar las palabras listadas abajo. Estamos aprendiendo a usar estas palabras mientras hablamos. Ésto ayudará que su hijo/a llegue a ser un lector mejor.

Esta semana, haga el favor de tratar de usar estas palabras tanto como pueda. A lo mejor, desea hacer las actividades también, para que su hijo/a tenga más práctica con las palabras. ¡Diviértase usando estas palabras!

Maestro/a ______________________

injured

Se dice para describir algo o a alguien que se ha hecho daño.

Haga que su hijo/a escriba una lista de las cosas que se necesita cuando alguien está injured.

elated

Es sentirse uno completamente feliz.

Comparta con su hijo/a una vez que se sintió elated. *Pídale a su hijo/a compartir una también.*

bask

Bañarse bajo el sol, disfrutando del calor.

Pídale a su hijo/a nombrar unos animales que bask *bajo el sol.*

seasonal

Es cuando algo ocurre al mismo tiempo cada año.

Pregúntele a su hijo/a cuáles son algunas actividades seasonal *que hace su familia durante cada estación del año.*

haul

Llevar una cosa pesada, tirando de ella.

Pídale a su hijo/a sacar la basura por medio de haul *la fuera.*

contemplate

Pensar muy profundamente en algo.

Pregúntele a su hijo/a qué son algunas de las cosas que contemplates.

Fun with New Words

Dear Family,

During the week of ______________________, your child will be learning to use the words listed below. We are learning to use these words when we talk. This will help your child become a better reader.

This week please try to use these words as often as you can. You may wish to do the activities, too, so your child can get extra practice with the words. Have fun using these words!

Teacher ______________________

memorize

When you memorize something, you make sure that you know it without having to look back at it.

Show your child a set of five objects. Tell your child to memorize them. While your child is not looking, take one object away. Have your child tell which object is missing.

relief

Relief is what you feel when you get rid of something that has been bothering you or when you finish something that was difficult.

Have your child share with you something that he or she is relieved is over.

regret

When you regret something, you wish you had not done it.

Ask your child if he or she regrets anything he or she has ever done.

stare

When you stare, you look straight at something for a long time.

Have a contest with your child to see which one of you can stare at each other the longest without blinking.

anxious

If you feel anxious about something, you are worried about what might happen.

Ask your child to describe something that makes them feel anxious. Discuss how you can help your child not feel as anxious about this thing.

exchange

When you exchange something, you give something to someone and they give you something, too.

Ask your child to recall a time he or she exchanged something with a friend or family member.

Go to http://www.elementsofreading.com/parentplace for fun, educational activities that you can do at home with your child.

Diversión con palabras nuevas

Estimada Familia,

Durante la semana de ________________________, su hijo/a estará aprendiendo a usar las palabras listadas abajo. Estamos aprendiendo a usar estas palabras mientras hablamos. Ésto ayudará que su hijo/a llegue a ser un lector mejor.

Esta semana, haga el favor de tratar de usar estas palabras tanto como pueda. A lo mejor, desea hacer las actividades también, para que su hijo/a tenga más práctica con las palabras. ¡Diviértase usando estas palabras!

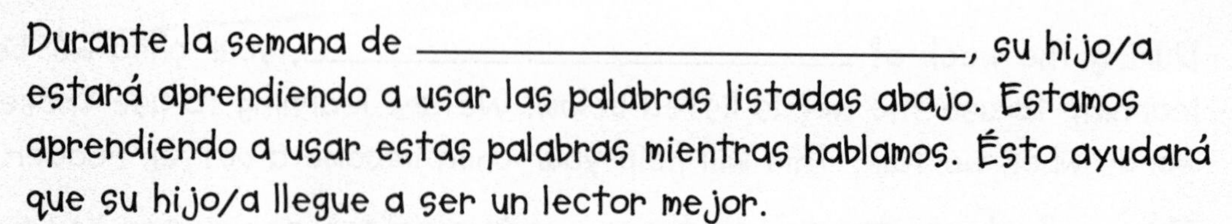

Maestro/a ________________________

memorize

Saber una cosa sin tener que mirarla porque la ha aprendido de memoria.

Enseñe a su hijo/a cinco objetos. Dígale a su hijo/a to memorize *qué son los objetos. Haga que su hijo/a se tape los ojos y quite un objeto. Entonces, haga que su hijo/a le cuente cuál objeto Ud. se quitó.*

relief

La sensación que tiene uno por haber eliminado algo que le estaba molestando o cuando termina algo difícil.

Pídale a su hijo/a recordar alguna vez en que se sentía relief, *o que estaba* relieved *de haber acabado una cosa.*

stare

Mirar algo fijamente durante un rato.

Haga con su hijo/a un concurso para ver quiénes de los dos se puede stare *más tiempo sin pestañear los ojos.*

regret

Sentir pesar por haber cometido una falta.

Pregunte a su hijo/a si se siente regret *por una cosa que ha hecho.*

exchange

Dar una cosa a cambio de otra.

Pídale a su hijo/a recordar alguna vez que él/ella exchanged *algo con un amigo o familiar.*

anxious

Estar nervioso por lo que pueda ocurrir.

Pídale a su hijo/a describir algo que le hace sentir anxious. *Hable con él/ella de cómo no sentirse tan* anxious *por dicha cosa.*

Fun with New Words

Dear Family,

During the week of ______________________, your child will be learning to use the words listed below. We are learning to use these words when we talk. This will help your child become a better reader.

This week please try to use these words as often as you can. You may wish to do the activities, too, so your child can get extra practice with the words. Have fun using these words!

Teacher ______________________

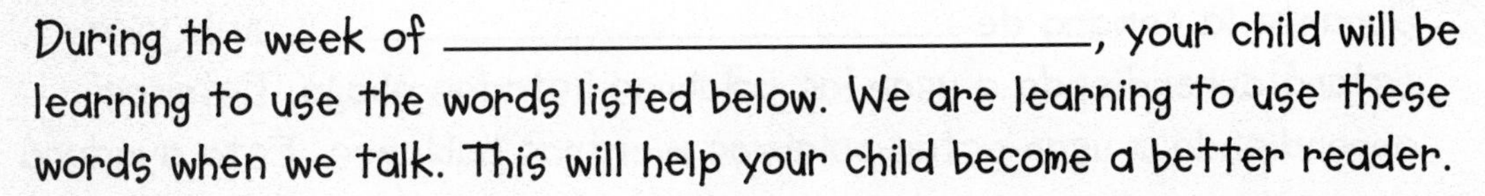

commotion

A commotion is a lot of noise and people moving around.

Ask your child to describe the commotion created by the parade in the story And to Think That We Thought That We'd Never Be Friends.

protest

When you protest something, you make a show of saying that you are against it.

Have your child tell you about something he or she would like to protest. Help your child make a plan for how he or she can protest this thing.

fret

When you fret about something, you look and act as if you are worried about it.

Talk to your child about something that makes him or her fret.

conflict

When two people or two sides have a conflict, they can't agree about something and have a big argument.

Discuss with your child a recent conflict he or she has had with someone else and how they resolved this conflict.

harmony

Harmony is created when different sounds come together to create beautiful music.

Point out the harmony in a song you and your child are listening to together.

soothe

When you soothe someone who is angry or upset, you calm them down.

Invite your child to tell you about a time when he or she soothed someone else.

Go to http://www.elementsofreading.com/parentplace for fun, educational activities that you can do at home with your child.

Diversión con palabras nuevas

Estimada Familia,

Durante la semana de ______________________, su hijo/a estará aprendiendo a usar las palabras listadas abajo. Estamos aprendiendo a usar estas palabras mientras hablamos. Ésto ayudará que su hijo/a llegue a ser un lector mejor.

Esta semana, haga el favor de tratar de usar estas palabras tanto como pueda. A lo mejor, desea hacer las actividades también, para que su hijo/a tenga más práctica con las palabras. ¡Diviértase usando estas palabras!

Maestro/a ______________________

commotion

Se dice para describir mucho ruido y movimiento de personas.

Pídale a su hijo/a describir la commotion *creada por el desfile en la historia* And to Think That We Thought That We'd Never Be Friends.

protest

Demostrar que está uno en contra de algo.

Haga que su hijo/a le cuente algo que le gustaría to protest. *Ayúdele a hacer un plan de cómo se puede* protest *esta cosa.*

fret

Preocuparse por algo.

Hable con su hijo/a sobre algo que le hace fret.

conflict

Es cuando no se pone de acuerdo la gente y surge una discusión.

Hable con su hijo/a de un conflict *que recientemente tuvo y cómo resolvió este* conflict.

soothe

Tranquilizarle a una persona que está enojada o agitada.

Anime a su hijo/a contarle alguna vez que soothed *a otra persona.*

harmony

Es la unión de varios sonidos que resulta agradable.

Señale la harmony *en una canción que está escuchando con su hijo/a.*

Review

Listen. Circle yes or no.

1. Yes No

2. Yes No

3. Yes No

4. Yes No

5. Yes No

6. Yes No

Name ______________________

Word Wheel

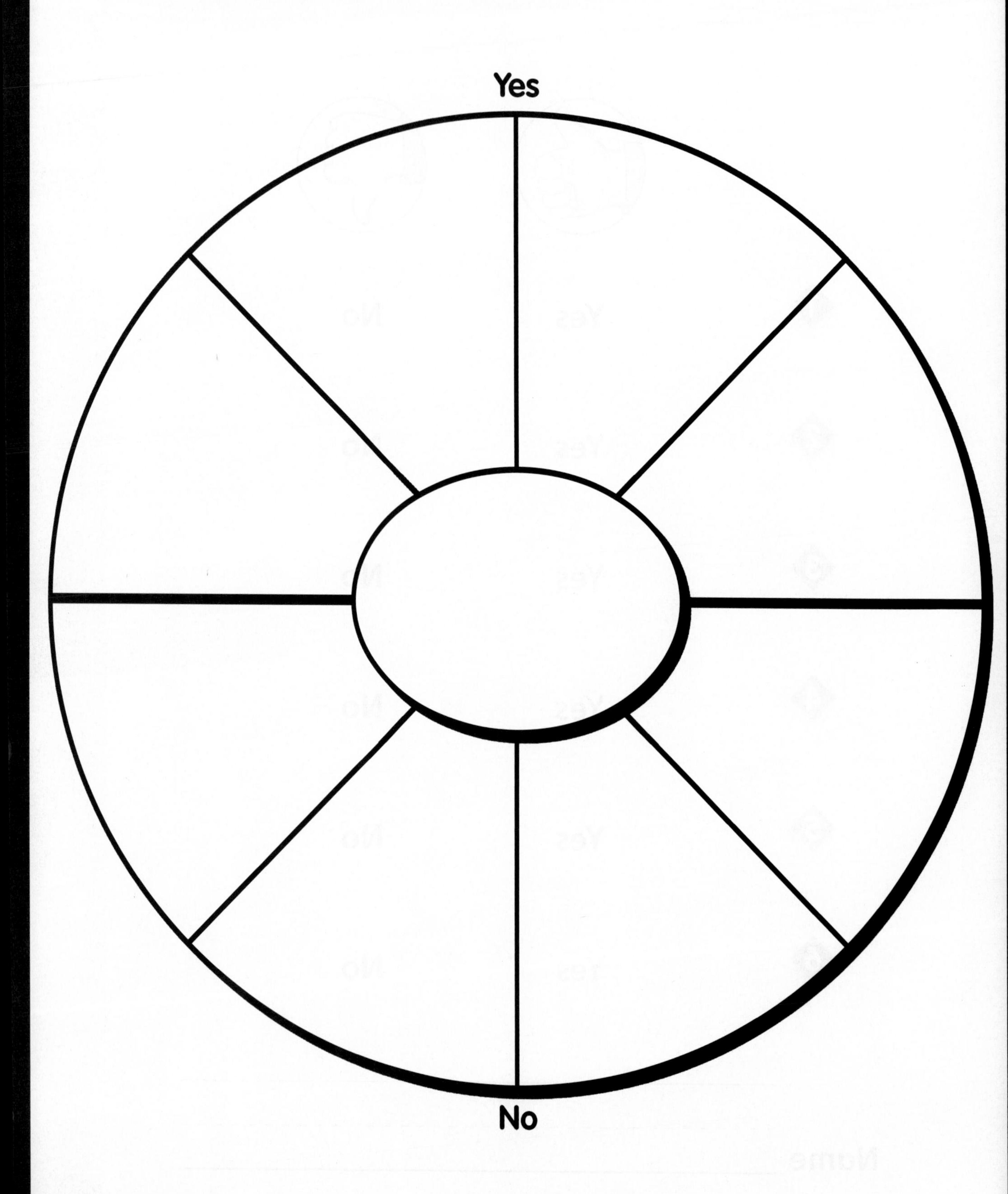

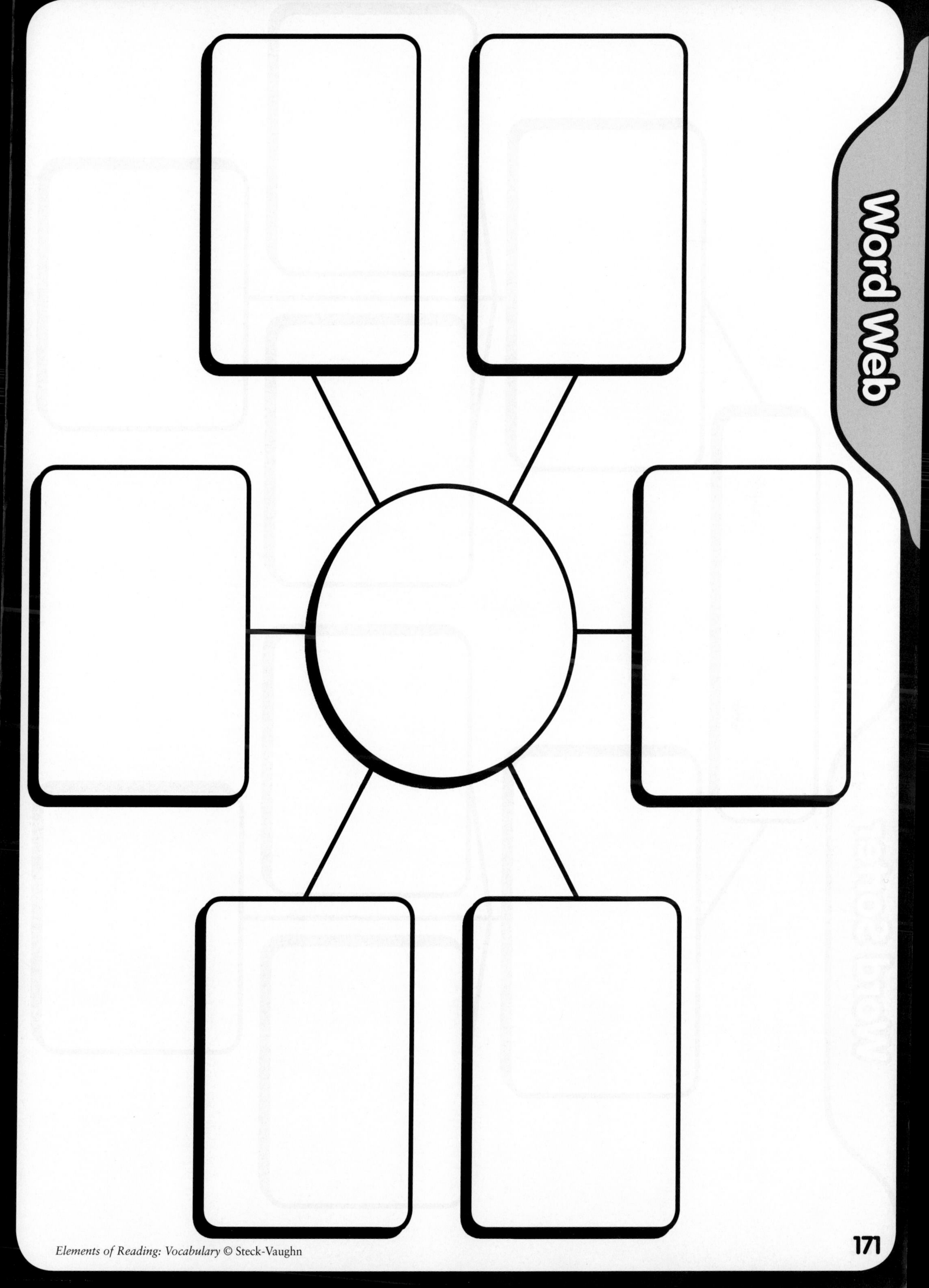
Word Web

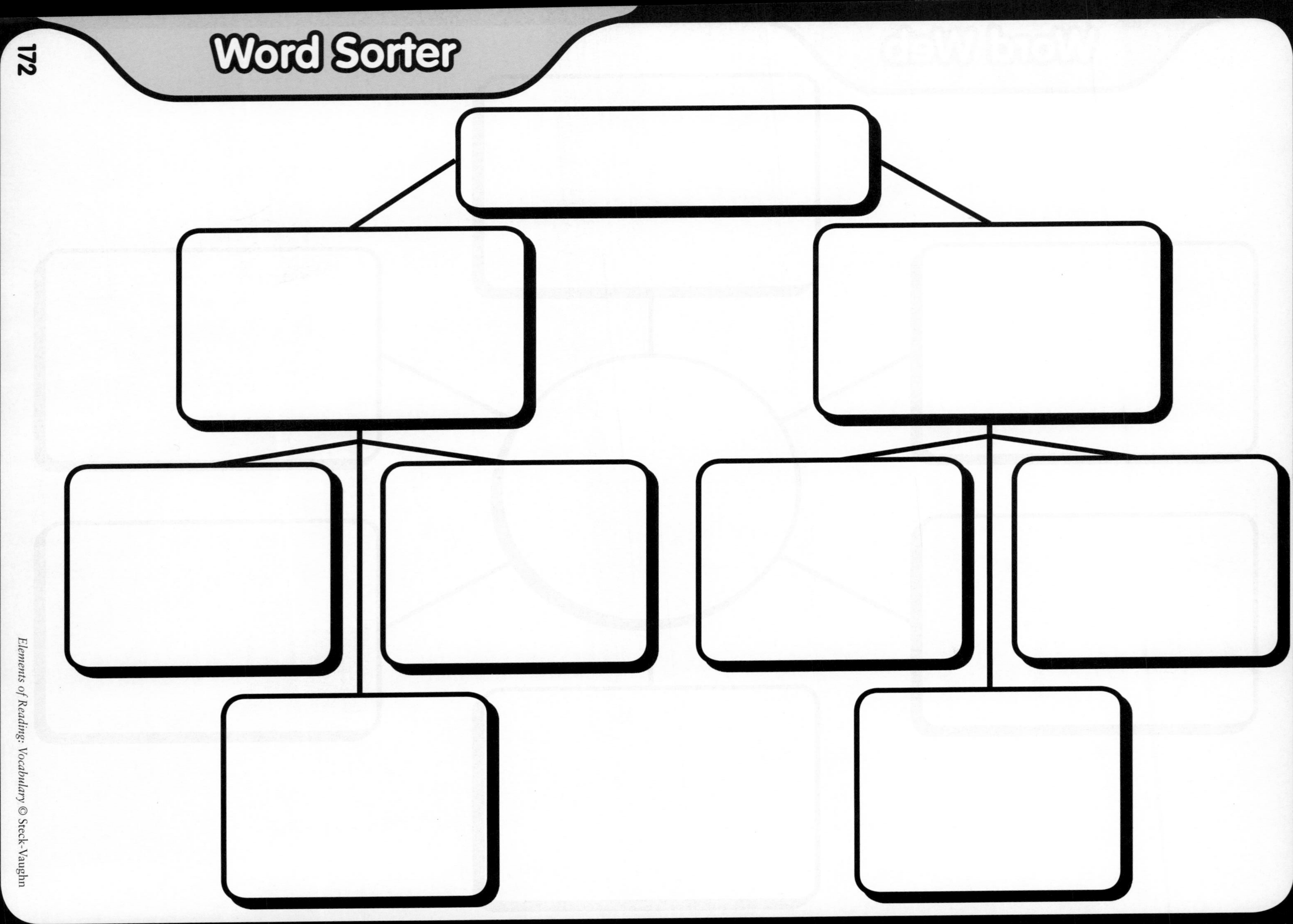
Word Sorter

Word-O-Meter

Word Map

Describe it!

Give examples!

1.

2.

3.

WOW!
is a
Word Watcher!
WORD
WATCHER